Humane Warfare

D0221654

'Christopher Coker has written a masterful analysis . . . a book of deep understanding and real insight. Literate, witty and subversive, this book is a pleasure to read the first time, and a discomfiture thereafter. Liberating and disturbing in equal measure, it is difficult to read this book without being changed by it.'

Michael Clarke
Director, Centre for Defence Studies, King's College London

'In this challenging work, Chris Coker tackles directly one of the fundamental dilemmas facing the West today: how to reconcile the inhumanity of war with the desire to fight a humane war. The result is both fascinating and provocative. Essential reading.'

Colin McInnes
University of Wales, Aberystwyth

The decision to fight 'humanitarian wars' – such as Kosovo – and the development of technology to make war more humane, illustrates the trend in the West to try to humanise war, and thereby humanise modernity. This highly controversial and cutting-edge book asks whether the attempt to make war 'virtual' or 'virtuous' can succeed and whether the West is deluding itself (not its enemies) in thinking that war can *ever* be made more humane.

Christopher Coker's radical conclusion is that western humanitarian warfare is in fact an endgame as other non-western societies will make sure it does not succeed. Eminently readable, this book combines theory with accounts by politicians and serving military personnel, alongside illuminating literary insights. It will be vital reading for all those interested in international relations and strategic studies and defence issues, including journalists, students and politicians.

Christopher Coker is Reader in International Relations at the London School of Economics. He is the author of a number of books including *War and Illiberal Conscience, Twilight of the West,* and *War and the Twentieth Century: A Study of War and Modern Consciousness.*

Humane Warfare

Christopher Coker

London and New York

First published 2001 by Routledge
11 New Fetter Lane, London EC4P 4EE

Simultaneously published in the USA and Canada
by Routledge
29 West 35th Street, New York, NY 10001

Routledge is an imprint of the Taylor & Francis Group

Typeset in Baskerville by Florence Production Ltd, Stoodleigh, Devon
Printed and bound in Great Britain by Biddles Ltd, Guildford and King's Lynn

British Library Cataloguing in Publication Data
A catalogue record for this book is available from the British Library

Library of Congress Cataloging in Publication Data
Coker, Christopher.
  Humane warfare/Christopher Coker.
    p. cm.
  ISBN 0–415–25575–9 – ISBN 0–415–25576–7 (pbk)
  1. War. 2. World politics – 1989. 3. War–Moral and ethical aspects. I. Title.

U21.2.C64. 2001
355.02–dc21   2001019136

ISBN 0–415–25576–7 (pbk)
       0–415–25575–9 (hbk)

Contents

Introduction

On 16 July 1945, the full destructive potential of modern military technology was realised in the New Mexico desert with the detonation of the first atomic bomb. Upon viewing the awe-inspiring aesthetic beauty of unprecedented destruction, Robert Oppenheimer, the bomb's creator, waxed religious. He is said to have quoted a passage from a Hindu spiritual text known as the *Bhagavad Gita* or Song of the Lord. The passage was, 'I am become death, the destroyer of worlds.' A lesser known quotation from that historic moment came from Oppenheimer's low-ranking military escort who, in reaction to the scientist's hubris, uttered, 'Now we're all sons of bitches.'

Oppenheimer's choice of a Hindu text was significant because Hindu theology is particularly concerned with the paradox of creation and destruction embodied in the deity, Shiva. That Oppenheimer had given birth to the most awesome agent of death the world has ever known, paradox aside, seemed profound enough for him to delve into a religious text to mark the occasion. There are other important religious invocations in the atom bomb project worth noting. The fact that the site of the first atom bomb explosion was called 'trinity' and that scientists were intent on calling the initial shock wave of the blast a 'halo' of destruction point to a peculiar religious fixation that marks a tension between technology and religion. But weeks after the event the scientists began to recognise that in dehumanising war they were displacing not only God from the imagination but also Man.

The inhumanity of the war against Japan had already become marked in the final five months of the Second World War. Even before the atomic attacks on Hiroshima and Nagasaki, US bombing raids claimed the lives of more than 900,000 Japanese civilians. On the night of 9–10 March 1945 234 Super Fortresses dropped more than 1500 incendiary bombs over downtown Tokyo. Nearly 84,000 Japanese bodies were found the next day in the charred remains of the city. The first foreign journalist to enter the city after the US occupation recorded that: 'Everything had been flattened . . . Only thumbs stood up from the flat lands – the chimneys of bathhouses, heavy house safes and an occasional stout building with heavy iron shutters.'[1] The first newsreel footage stunned cinema audiences in America who had never really grasped one of the realities of modern warfare: what it meant to incinerate a great city.

And this was the 'good' side fighting for the principles of liberty and liberalism that had been affirmed by the allied powers in the Atlantic Charter a few years before. In the Cold War that followed when the liberal world found itself engaged against another enemy, its former ally in the war against fascism, the inhumanity of war remained one of its principal features. In Korea the USAF killed just under one-ninth of the North Korean population in air raids that were even more savage than those of the Second World War. A decade later in Vietnam the Americans dropped almost three times as much explosive tonnage as they had used in the war against Germany and Japan.[2]

Looking back from our more peaceful vantage point, these figures are striking, but with the exception of the United States most other industrial powers never really recovered from the Second World War. They no longer felt able to play by the old rules or employ the old methods. Something was lost in the mayhem – that inner belief in war (even though western societies still believed in the justice of their cause). Dresden and Hiroshima ensured that modern warfare reached a dead-end: not so much an endgame as a point beyond which it was impossible to play the game by the old rules any longer.

Fifty years later we live in another era – or at least, it would appear so. Opening the new Reichstag building during the Kosovo War, Chancellor Schroeder quoted the Albanian writer Ismail Kadare as saying that 'Atlantic Europe . . . [was] becoming a *humane* Europe'.[3] The conflict which was then unfolding was Europe's first 'humanitarian war', as well as its first experience of what I have called in this book 'humane warfare'. Two hundred and fifty thousand people died in the Bosnian civil war (1993–95); 15,000 Hungarians in the uprising of 1956. The Kosovo War was not without human bloodshed, but the air campaign against Serbia involved far fewer casualties than any similar conflict in history, and a ground war was avoided. Humanitarianism, it would seem, is not just an objective. Western societies can now only fight wars which minimise human suffering, that of their enemies' as well as their own.[4]

In this respect, as in many others, Kosovo marked a decisive break with the past. According to the German sociologist Ulrich Beck, it marked the birth of a 'new military humanism'.[5] What distinguishes warfare today is its purported 'humanity'. Western societies (we are told) not only fight humanitarian wars; they do so in a 'humane' fashion. The simple truth, wrote Sir Charles Guthrie, Chief of the British Defence Staff, who was responsible for directing the British role in the campaign, is that western society is not very well adjusted to the prospect of fighting. It involves risks to people's lives when they have become used to the idea of not having to die for their beliefs. It involves uncertainty when people have got used to the idea that there is a clear answer to every question. It involves killing and being killed when our television screens encourage western citizens to view warfare as a kind of grown-up arcade game.

> Perhaps, most difficult of all for the West it involves fighting by the Queensberry Rules when by the very nature of the conflict we are likely to be involved in we will be fighting against thugs who know little and care less about civilised behaviour.[6]

Guthrie went on to add that the West was no longer able to do precisely what it wished: the 'rules' were there to define its own behaviour. Public opinion would not allow the targeting of Serbia's cities or civilian population on the scale it had in 1941 when Belgrade was last bombed.

For the moment, the West is still in the war business but it is attempting to change its nature by fighting wars more humanely. Post-material societies fight post-material wars – they try to avoid the material (human and environmental) damage which was essential to warfare for two millennia. They are intent on sanitising war, on purging it of those elements which, though once familiar and accepted without question, now cast it in a light that is offensive to the liberal conscience.

Of course, there are many who find the very concept of 'humane warfare' unconvincing, if not cynical or even meretricious. In his book *The Warrior's Honour* Michael Ignatieff quotes a Red Cross official who was all too aware of the charge that his organisation should be seeking to end war, not humanise it. In modern ethics, he remarked, war is inhuman and therefore increasingly indefensible. 'The driving ideologies of this world are ecology, human rights and humanitarian ethics. War is increasingly banned from modern culture.'[7] Some western soldiers too are less than happy with the concept of 'humanitarian war'. One pilot flying missions into Kosovo from the aircraft carrier *USS Kearsarge* found the term doubly distasteful: first, because it made the bombing missions sound like philanthropy; second, because it fed the illusion that in today's wars people do not or should not get killed.[8]

Whether the change in the way war is fought strikes one as ironical or not, the western world seems intent on re-marketing war or *revaluing* it (it all depends on one's point of view). Whatever one's perspective, what is happening marks a much more significant break with the past than is often acknowledged and it is for this reason that I have chosen to write this book.

The book is divided into eight chapters. We start with history. One of the definitive features of modern warfare was its inhumanity. Twentieth-century Europe, as Ismail Kadare observes, was not particularly 'humane'. Even the liberal democracies tended to treat humanity in the abstract, to reduce men and women to abstractions, such as nations, classes or civilisations. Industrialised warfare, in turn, produced the mass anonymity of the modern battlefield on which so many died anonymous deaths. Finally, the tendency to put themselves at the centre of human life encouraged some societies to dehumanise their enemies or at least render them 'history-less'. All this has changed, or at least, so it appears. Western societies are trying to humanise war, and are likely to continue doing so for some time to come. It is the great project for the twenty-first century.

Chapter 2 takes the reader on to new ground by looking at the most important feature that made war inhumane: its cruelty. The First World War challenged this most directly by revealing what Nietzsche called 'war's true ugliness' which had been concealed before then by the poets who had celebrated the heroic virtues of the warrior. With the arrival of industrialised warfare the common soldier and the civilian victim whose fate had been glossed over in the past replaced the prince and the commander as central figures in the interpretation of war in western art. Midway through the twentieth century the common soldier had not only become the central figure in images and photographs of war; increasingly the images were painted or photographed from perspectives that sought to be his.

Reviewing a book on Second World War art, J.G. Ballard who experienced the war as a child in a civilian detention camp in Shanghai was struck most by the war depicted by the Soviet artists. Their work was by far the most memorable, for it evoked an overwhelming national crisis that had summoned up the will of every Soviet citizen from the peasant to the factory worker. The Homeric scale of their stand against German barbarism emerged through these paintings more strikingly than in any other, but what it also suggested was that the idea of the will to power had died in the West. Here were no pronounced heroic themes. Indeed, what was most noteworthy about the war depicted by British painters was the absence of any sense of triumphalism. Anyone surveying them and knowing nothing about the war would find it hard to decide who had won and who had lost.[9]

Once the individual was re-centred in the picture it became impossible to justify war as an assertion of the 'will to power'. The phrase, of course, is one of the key terms in the modern philosophical lexicon. Employing Schopenhauer's terminology, Nietzsche used it to describe a cruel world at the heart of which lay the 'will' and the wish to assert it. It took the Second World War to force a change of consciousness in attitudes to the enemy, in respect of cruelty to others, and it took the Vietnam War to force a change of perspective in the United States, the last great power that still conscripted its citizens to fight wars in the name of its own 'will to power'.

Chapters 3 and 4 look at two related features of war which Clausewitz, its greatest phenomenologist, took to be part of its 'essence'. Courage and hatred made war a human activity even when the battlefield became heavily mechanised in the early twentieth century (the century which, more than his own, took Clausewitz's writings to heart). Today, western societies appear to be intent on factoring out both emotions. Our citizens have been demobilised; they are no longer required to serve in the military or to endure the passive stoicism in the face of great danger which was expected of their forefathers for much of the last century. Nor are they expected to hate even the regimes with which they engage in war, still less demand their unconditional surrender. Social changes including greater individualism and the discovery of the uncivil nature of our civil societies has focused attention on the need to avoid incivility in warfare too.

Chapter 5 looks at the emergence of what I have called 'the humane soldier' – a 'warrior' type new to the western world. The ethos of the military profession has changed significantly in recent years. The military has become a 'post-traditional' force, a term I borrow from the work of the British sociologist Anthony Giddens. Society too has become 'post-military' and demands that the traditional distinctions between the civilian and military worlds be transcended. An emphasis on civility obscures the traditional divide between the two worlds, a point I shall illustrate with reference to the greatest break with tradition of all: what is often referred to pejoratively as the 'feminisation of the military'.

In Chapter 6 I will discuss the limits of humanitarian warfare. For the West's attempts to humanise war, to rob it of those features such as cruelty, hatred and courage runs against the grain of much of what is happening in the non-western world. For one of the disturbing trends in contemporary conflict is that inhumanity and incivility seems to be on the rise. In some cases both may even be a response to the way the western world is trying to re-market war. Even if they are not, the growing *inhumanity* of war across the globe is making it increasingly difficult to maintain public support in the West for military intervention of any kind, humanitarian or not.

This brings me to the last two chapters which may be said to constitute the second half of the book. 'Everything is post these days,' writes Margaret Atwood in her novel *Cat's Eye*, 'as if we are all just a footnote to something earlier that was real enough to have a name of its own.'[10] Well, the post-modern condition is certainly more than a footnote. And one thing that it is 'post', upon which philosophers as different as Jürgen Habermas and Richard Rorty agree, is that it is 'post-metaphysical'. Metaphysics has been abandoned along with the invocation of God as a justification for war or legitimisation of its practise. Instead, we have re-grounded war on humanism, we have put humanity back at the centre of our philosophical and ethical systems of thought – hence the interest in humanitarian warfare, and the importance attached to 'humanity' in the wars we now fight.

This is important because it removes any philosophical or moral defence of cruelty. To be just, wars have to be humane. In our eyes this represents a revaluation of war. Unfortunately, in the eyes of others, it devalues both war and the warrior.

It only remains to add that writing at length about a contemporary phenomenon has its obvious disadvantages: lack of perspective, ignorance of the future, the temptation to mistake vogue for value. Nevertheless, the exercise can be rewarding for it requires an author to pose the right questions but not necessarily provide the right answers. Such works call for explorations more than explanations. They remind us of the exploratory nature of much of social science and encourage a degree of personal commitment on the part of the author. My own understanding of 'humane warfare' is not necessarily the reader's. All I offer in this study is a more or less ordered gathering of the reflections, impressions and objections that the phenomenon has provoked in me. I can only hope that it will stimulate further discussion.

Christopher Coker

1 Humanising war

Surfing the Zeitgeist

The unsuspecting reader of David Ogg's classic account of the history of seventeenth-century Europe would come across an arresting passage. He was writing about what was quite unique to the century: the first serious attempt in an age in which Europe was almost constantly at war to mitigate its worst horrors. Some contemporary writers, like the French politician Sully, had advocated a pan-European union of Christian powers committed to a general peace. Others were more practical in their thinking and, of these, none was more important than Grotius.

Grotius was a Christian rationalist and, if not exactly a pacifist, he was a pacific man. It was a mark of his humanity that he believed it possible to mitigate some of the worst horrors of war by sparing infants, women and the aged. The great jurist wanted to exclude from military service not only agricultural workers (the main economic resource of the time), but also men of letters, indeed anyone who contributed to the life or illumination of the state. He wanted wars to be fought by small bands of professional soldiers. If Grotius had had his way, war would have been waged only by men whose lives the state could easily dispense with. Peaceful occupations would have been interfered with as little as possible. War would hardly have impacted on civilian life. While out campaigning, the welfare of non-combatants would have been uppermost in a commander's mind.

Grotius was prompted to propose rewriting the rules of war by the evils of the Thirty Years' War (1618–48) whose cruelty was captured graphically in Jacques Callot's *The Large Miseries of War*, a series of etchings published in 1633. If Callot himself did not witness the worst excesses, the etchings are the work of an informed eye. No one at the time could have harboured any illusions about war. The scenes he depicts – rape, looting, the burning of villages and the destruction of a convent – show the part played in war by criminality and senseless violence. The emphasis placed on this dimension of conflict has led some critics to speculate that Callot equated war with crime. It is more likely both of the man and his times that its message is no less universal but more complex: war, whatever its motivation, nourishes crime, murder and cruelty – the very features Grotius wanted to eliminate.[1]

Writing as he did in 1925, only seven years after the end of the First World War, the bloodiest in Europe's history, Ogg was not much impressed by Grotius' scheme. While conceding that many of these proposals had been embodied in the Hague conventions, he criticised him for being both impractical and idealistic, for failing to acknowledge the true nature of war. 'For while he allows war, he purports to rob it of its *essential elements* – its misery, waste and cruelty.'[2] He faulted Grotius above all for thinking that war could be made *humane*.

In arriving at this conclusion Ogg may well have been struck by the similarities between the century about which he was writing and his own. For the religious wars of the seventeenth century had involved the leading European powers of the day in a protracted and murderous engagement which another twentieth-century historian, C.V. Wedgwood, thought the unhappiest period in Europe's history until the onset of her own. It was 'a time (like our's) in which man's activities outran his power of control.'[3] Indeed the damage to Germany in the 1630s was even more catastrophic than the damage it suffered in the twentieth century, for it lost up to a third of its population. For at least a decade after 1650 the city fathers of Nuremberg allowed men to be married to two wives at the same time in an attempt to repopulate the city.

The Thirty Years' War was as close to a 'total war' as wars come, in its impact on Germany and the lives of its people, but it gave way to a period of limited war. The momentous change from total to limited war took place 'insensibly' insofar as no one intended the change, or was even aware of it at the time. For the change took place not in individuals who followed their own purposes, and who were not alive to the historical significance of their own acts, but in society, and it involved a transformation of the reason why people went to war. As symbolic of that change in attitude, Wedgwood took the respective battle-cries shouted by the Spanish soldiers at the White Hill in 1620 (the first battle of the Thirty Years' War) and Nordlingen (the last great Catholic victory fourteen years later). At the first they shouted: 'Sancta Maria'; at the second, 'Viva Espana'. Anyone who might have witnessed the two battles would almost certainly not have appreciated their historical significance which lay in the contrast between them, a contrast accessible only to a historian like Wedgwood who saw in it a sign that 'insensibly and rapidly the Cross gave way to the flag'.[4]

In drawing this contrast, Wedgwood was describing the cycles of limited and total war which distinguished European history in terms of war's inhumanity. The American strategist Hermann Kahn once drew up a chart of the long cycle of limited and total wars which had distinguished western history since the eleventh century, and his chart repays a visit (see Table 1.1).

Table 1.1 Cycles of wars

1000–1500	*Limited*
	• feudal
	• dynastic
1500–1648	*Total*
	• religious
1648–1789	*Limited*
	• dynastic
	• colonial
1789–1815	*Total*
	• national
	• revolutionary
1815–1914	*Limited*
	• colonial
	• commercial
1914–1989	*Total*
	• ideological
	• national
1989–	*Limited*
	• commercial
	• humanitarian

Source: Hermann Kahn 1989.

Kahn, who used to boast that he had the highest IQ in American history, was the model for Dr Strangelove in Stanley Kubrick's film of the same name. He was one of the trio of nuclear thinkers who formulated America's doctrine of nuclear deterrence in the early years of the Cold War (the others being Bernard Brodie and Thomas Schelling). We should not be discouraged by the fact that his interest in history notwithstanding, he was by training a physicist and was confident in his ability to predict the future. He was one of the first futurologists, and the Hudson Institute which he founded was commissioned by governments and corporations to engage in what is now called 'future history'.

Neither Kahn's lack of modesty nor his preoccupation with the future may recommend him to us as an analyst but his chart is interesting, especially in the revised form that I have presented it. The fact that he died in 1983 has required me to add to it a new period of humanitarian wars. In replacing religion with politics, the Europeans were able to return to an era of limited war. In a world that was now 'unpatrolled by God' the cruelty of war was much reduced, in scale at least.[5]

Unfortunately, the era which opened with the French Revolution and ended in Napoleon's defeat saw a return to total war, or something like it. For what was truly revolutionary was not the revolution so much as the revolutionary wars which followed in its wake, for they exported the ideas of the republican government in Paris. As Edmund Burke complained, the revolutionaries were engaged in expounding 'the catechism of the Rights of Man'. Killing for a collective purpose in the name of man (for an idea) was even more potent than killing in the name of God (for religion).

The result was devastation on an extensive scale. Perhaps as many as three million soldiers lost their lives, and another million civilians; 800,000 soldiers died in one campaign (that of 1812) alone. The memory of the wars is still pervasive in more isolated communities, even if it has been largely forgotten in the cities. One historian was told in the early 1990s by the pastor of a small Thuringian village that his community had lost more dead in the period 1803–14 than it had in any other war in which the Germans had fought since the seventeenth century.[6]

The nineteenth century saw a return to sanity. Fearful of revolutionary sentiment, governments were much more cautious in going to war, and when they did they limited their ambitions. Even the defeat of France in 1871 was followed by forty years of peace. The First World War which brought the curtain down on that halcyon era changed the pattern once again. If that was horrendously destructive the level of savagery in the Second World War exceeded anything known to history. The main explanation for this, namely that more civilians died than soldiers, was true, of course, of the Thirty Years' War too – described so memorably by Grotius as: 'a riot of fury in which authorisation was given to every crime'.[7]

The Swiss playwright Max Frisch saw the extent of the inhumanity of war at first hand when he travelled through Frankfurt in 1946:

> At the railroad station. Refugees lying on all the steps . . . their life is unreal, awaiting without expectation, and they no longer cling to life; their life clings to them, ghostlike . . . It breathes on the sleeping children as they lie in the rubble, their heads between bony arms, curled up like embryos in the womb, as if longing to return there.[8]

The fate of the Soviet Union was even more poignant. It lost up to twenty-seven million people in the war in four years of fighting that can probably claim to be the most barbaric of any conflict in any century. The novelist John Steinbeck saw the destruction for himself when he visited Stalingrad – or what was left of the city – in the summer of 1947, a year after Frisch's tour of a Germany that also lay in ruins. One day, Steinbeck saw a girl emerge from the rubble in which she lived outside his hotel and feed on what scraps of food she could forage. Clearly she had been traumatised by the battle that had waged a few years before. How many more might there be like her, he wondered, 'minds that could not tolerate living in the twentieth century'?[9]

The twentieth century was unique, in fact, for producing the 'death event' – the mass murder of a million or more men and women.[10] The characteristic of war was no longer the defeat of an army in the field but its total destruction; it was no longer forcing a society to surrender but eliminating the society itself. Mass destruction became the only aim. Whether the 'death event' was a battle like Verdun (1916) in which nearly a million soldiers perished on a battlefield no larger than the area occupied by the London parks; or a political act like the Holocaust which claimed the lives of seven million people, death became anonymous. For the victims – whether soldier or Jew – the event itself appeared to be autonomous of human action; it had a logic of its own. When Primo Levi asked a guard in Auschwitz why he was there he was told, 'Hier is kein Warum – there is no why here.' Worse still would have been the ultimate holocaust – a nuclear war between the Superpowers which strategists like Kahn expected would produce 100 million victims. It was an event that need not have had a 'cause' at all. In *Dr Strangelove* the enemy is a colonel who goes mad and sends an air wing into Russia. War could now be accidental; it no longer needed a cause.

Irony and war

Clearly the face of war has changed significantly. Let me quote a contemporary voice, a retired USAF officer commenting on the battle sequences of what is commonly held to be the most realistic Hollywood war movie, Steven Spielberg's *Saving Private Ryan*:

> As a career Air Force aviator I have no experience with the kind of intense ground combat depicted in this film. When it comes to the titanic clash of mighty land armies where thousands of young men are thrown into each other's line of fire, I have to rely on the reviews of the experts who say it's pretty realistic.[11]

Looking back on the Normandy campaign, which is the subject of Spielberg's film, the conditions which the allied soldiers (the great majority conscripts at that) were expected to endure are unimaginable today. Although we stand only half a century from it, we have great difficulty envisaging both the conflict and its cost. One British soldier on the road to Caen saw a landscape that reminded him of the war he had read about when young: 'a country fought over and destroyed like the Somme and Passchendale battlefields of the Great War . . . pocked with shell holes . . . scarred with slit trenches . . . sullied by the stench of unburied dead.' With a casualty rate of 2354 soldiers per day, the Normandy campaign was one of the bloodiest the British Army has ever fought.[12]

In today's military profession, our airforce pilot adds, there is no place for 'the bloody boots on the ground realists' who insist that victory cannot be bought without wading through the blood of one's comrades – a reference to those still left in the western military establishments who are appalled that the pain and dislocation of mortal combat is being reduced to a 'stand-off' conflict in which aircraft and missiles deliver their weapons of death over hundreds of miles. We have entered a new era of limited war which will be more humane not only for the soldiers who fight it but

our enemies as well. We are told that the *incivility* of war which Ogg took
to be its principal feature can be significantly reduced. As a thoroughly
modern man Ogg would be sceptical of our attempts to do precisely that
– to revalue it by making it humane. He would probably find unconvincing our attempts to divest it of its cruelty; to eliminate its waste – both
material and human; to reduce its misery to soldiers and non-combatants
alike. He would no doubt criticise us for being as 'disingenuous' as Grotius
but he would be wrong to doubt our intentions. For the western powers
have engaged in a real, if possibly unrealistic, attempt to transform not
only the character of war, but also its nature.

We have not, of course, gone out of the business of war. Instead, we
have been forced to re-market it, to fight it in a different fashion. We now
fight humanitarian wars, and we try to fight them more humanely. This
is why we find war *ironic*. We are struck by how different it is from fifty
years ago. Irony has many definitions but one is the difference between
what we are told something is and what we find its true nature to be.
The principal difference today is war's real or purported 'humanity'.

- What struck many observers as ironic about the Gulf War was the
  low number of casualties incurred by the allied forces. The Americans
  expected to lose up to 10,000 men. They lost 270 (some of them in
  accidents). So low was the eventual death-toll that questions began to
  be asked which had never been asked in war before. Was it not safer
  to serve in a war zone than be billeted back home? In *Life* magazine's
  fourth and final special issue on the war two sociologists calculated
  that as of 6 March 1991 the death-toll on the US side represented
  only 40 per cent of those who might have died had they stayed in
  the United States – the casualties of traffic accidents, muggings,
  domestic incidents or other distinctly unheroic forms of death.[13]
- Another ironic note was sounded by a Pentagon official who insisted
  that 'the battlefield is no place for a soldier'.[14] On the penultimate
  day of the war a group of Iraqi soldiers tried to surrender to a remote
  controlled machine called 'Pioneer', the first occasion in the history
  of warfare in which human beings tried to capitulate to an inanimate
  enemy. Tomorrow, soldiers may be removed from the battlefield
  altogether – we call it 'disengaged conflict'.
- The Gulf War was 'unmanned' in another respect. It was the first
  major conflict in which women were more integrated into a combat
  support role than ever before. Although they represented only 6 per
  cent of the Coalition's forces, the novelty of their deployment in a
  combat zone received a disproportionate amount of media attention
  because it was taken to be indicative of the new spirit of the times.
  Indeed the recruitment of women marks the most radical social break
  with tradition in the past 3000 years – for it involves the recruitment
  of 50 per cent of humanity that by tradition has been excluded from

military service. Women, we are also told, are more 'humane' than men or at least more compassionate. In the aftermath of the war a former consultant to the US Secretary of the Army suggested that the problem of gender integration might be solved in future if the military agreed to eliminate such 'masculinist' attitudes as 'dominance, assertiveness, independence, self-sufficiency and the willingness to take risks' – in a word, all the traditional soldierly qualities which have made war, however just the cause, innately 'uncivil'.[15]

The Gulf War was not a humanitarian war; but it was a humane one for the allied forces. And it was humane for the American public back home who were spared the scenes which had shaken their self-confidence during the later stages of the Vietnam War. Nearly everyone watched the Gulf War on television. Disengaged from direct experience, what they knew of war they knew from television. The war was the first to be seen in real time: it was played out on television screens night after night as it was happening. It is estimated that 600 million people throughout the world watched the nightly TV news reports as the conflict unfolded.

Yet the war that was shown to the public was not the war behind the lines. It was a sanitised war for the United States, but what of the death-toll on the other side? The CIA estimated between 100,000 and 250,000 Iraqis were killed; Greenpeace estimated that the war left 150,000 dead (15,000 of them civilians). The Allied Commander Norman Schwartzkopf did not think the number really mattered. In an interview he admitted '50,000, or 100,000 or whatever' – the fact is, the right side won.[16] Given the disparity in the death-toll and the sanitising role of television it is not surprising that the Gulf War has its critics. Some commentators were aghast at the media determined reality which the American people tended to take at face value. They were critical of a world so constructed by television images that no one knew what to believe any longer.

It is possible, however, to argue that in an age which can live without metaphysics, humanism has centred man back as the subject of history. Indeed, in the Kosovo War (1999) eight years later, the United States and its allies went to great lengths to reduce the risks to soldiers and enemies alike:

• It was striking that not one allied pilot was killed in the seventy-eight-day air campaign over Kosovo and Serbia. When two American pilots were shot down over enemy territory enormous resources were utilised to rescue them including an AWACS aircraft, Special Forces helicopters and dozens of helicopter gunships. Fifty years earlier it had taken only a small squad of men to rescue Private Ryan, and even then Ryan had insisted on staying to defend an important bridge against German attack. The pilots shot down in the Balkans were flown home to a hero's welcome.

- The media paid much attention to three American soldiers who fell into Serb hands. For their troubles all three were awarded six medals apiece including the Purple Heart. Even for a country that suffers medal inflation, the army found itself subsequently criticised for awarding so many decorations to soldiers who had done so little to merit them – but the public was happy enough that the soldiers had been captured not killed, and had been repatriated to the United States even before the end of the conflict.

- During the bombing of Belgrade it was rumoured that the Allies refused to target one of Milosevic's residences because it contained a Rembrandt painting. Instead, they designated it a historic cultural site. 'That is one measure of our madness,' wrote the Canadian writer Michael Ignatieff, 'that we allow a Rembrandt to save a criminal – but to us it is a necessary madness, since the truth is that we are more anxious to save our souls than to save Kosovo.'[17] As it turned out the story was apocryphal, but it was also plausible – it rang true.

- The truth is that war in the past has often been soulless – it has involved the destruction of much of the cultural heritage of the societies that have been involved. The Second World War saw the destruction of some of the great architectural treasures of old Europe: the old city of Warsaw; the monastery at Monte Casino (the mother of European monasticism); as well as museums and art galleries which stored the glory of European art. In one fire in Berlin, 434 old masters were destroyed including works by Caravaggio, Titian and Veronese. Two years later the American writer Edmund Wilson wrote a book called *Europe without a Baedekker* in which he charted the cultural fall of a continent that had been reduced to rubble, and which was now dispossessed not only of its power, but its soul.[18]

If the lives of its own men came first in Kosovo, the allies also went to great lengths to limit war-related deaths on the other side:

- Every war, writes Paul Fussell in *The Great War and Modern Memory*, is worse than expected. 'Every war constitutes an irony of situation because its means are so melodramatically disproportionate to its presumed ends.'[19] One example he gives is the Second World War in which the allies who went to war against fascism ended up by engaging in the cruellest anti-civilian air bombardment in history. It was supposed to shorten the war; instead it prolonged it by inviting those who were its targets to cast themselves in the role of victims. The air campaign merely stiffened their resolve. In Kosovo the Allies also conducted a ferocious bombing campaign on the scale of the London Blitz, but for the Serbs it was much less worse than expected. The Allies, it is true, killed more civilians than soldiers (1400 compared to 400 Serb soldiers), but considering that this was the largest air barrage since the Second World War it is striking how few civilians and soldiers were killed. The increasing accuracy of precision-guided weapons has made war much more discriminating than in the past.

• By contrast, the war on the ground claimed the lives of thousands of Kosovars and saw 800,000 more displaced from their homes; but then, as the German writer Hans Magnus Enzensberger remarked at the time, this was a disynchronic conflict. Two wars were fought in different time zones. Over the skies of Belgrade and Kosovo the Allies fought a 'space invader's' game with laser-guided weapons and graphite bombs which knocked out the electricity supply to Belgrade. On the ground in Kosovo people were ethnically cleansed. The latter conflict reminded Enzensberger of the Thirty Years' War (1618–48).[20] There are many specialists who believe that the *asymmetrical* nature of contemporary conflict will be a definitive feature of the future.

Humanising modernity

'One of the foremost objectives in the development of new weaponry should be the reduction or total elimination of human risk.' So argue Alvin and Heidi Toffler whose book *War and Anti-War* has become a revered text in the US military since its publication in 1991. 'Put simply, weapons or equipment in harm's way should – to the extent possible – be unmanned.'[21] It is a telling word in its double-meaning: that of making war no longer an exclusive activity of men, but more to the point taking courage or the need for it out of conflict. The question this raises in turn is a disturbing one. In making war more 'humane' do we make it less human?

We can look at this issue in the long-term historical perspective, or what historians used to call the *longue durée*. In one of the seminal books of the past few years, *Cosmopolis*, Stephen Toulmin contends that since 1914 we have been attempting to humanise modernity, to redeem philosophy and science by reconnecting them to humanism. We cannot cling to modernity as we once did without question, and we cannot reject it totally as many post-modernists assume. What we can do is *humanise* it.[22]

As Toulmin contends, it was the inhumanity of modernity that, looking back, is what is most striking. In architecture, to take one example, the historian Charles Jencks tells us the exact date (and even hour) when we endeavoured to humanise it – 3.32 p.m. on 15 July 1972 when the Pruitt Igoe housing estate in St Louis was dynamited as an uninhabitable environment for the low-income people it had housed. The act was of symbolic importance, for it coincided with the 'collapse' of 'high modernism' and its tendencies towards standardisation.[23]

At the time it was built, the Pruitt Igoe estate was hailed by architects as 'a perfect machine for living'. One of the most distinguished of the modernists, Le Corbusier, wanted to transform the city into a 'perfect machine', a term he coined for a city without the labyrinth of narrow streets which characterised the urban centres of the past. What disting-uished modern urban planning was the effort of local authorities to corral the population, to divide the city into residential areas distinguished by their separate and distinctive functions. Abolishing the street meant abolishing the crowds who gave the cities their distinctive character.

In other words, the masters of modernist architecture were more interested in aestheticism than they were in individual lives. One of the most celebrated, Mies van der Rohe, once remarked, 'the individual is losing significance. His destiny is no longer what interests us.'[24] Modern architecture put very little emphasis on whether people wanted to live in the great tower blocks that sprouted up in the major cities. The buildings they designed were, in that sense, dehumanising. Commenting on his own design for the building L'Unité in Marseilles, Le Corbusier claimed he had drawn upon the ideal of the Acropolis. The Greeks, he argued, had 'drawn the desolate landscape around them into a single thought'. It was a stirring vision, but the thought of Periclean Athens was numinal and spiritual, while the Acropolis captures the style and purpose of a people united in their beliefs. L'Unité, by comparison, achieved a unique desolation of its own in the purely phenomenal (not numinal) world of Corbusier's 'modular man'.

Toulmin also shows how in the natural sciences we have come a long way from the mechanistic physics of high modernity as it took shape in the seventy-five years after Descartes' manifesto *The Discourse on Method* which reduced man to a bit part in a larger cosmological play. Nils Bohr puts it very well in Michael Frayn's play *Copenhagen* (1998). Throughout history man was displaced. We kept exiling him to the periphery. First, he was turned into a mere adjunct of God's unknowable purpose. Then he was dwarfed by the laws of classical mechanics that were supposed to survive until the end of eternity. Science took very little account of whether or not man existed.

With quantum physics a new form of measurement was introduced in which the whole possibility of science depended on man, no longer on impersonal events. There is no precise determinable universe, we are told. The universe exists only as a series of approximations within the limits deter-mined by our relationship with it.[25] This is particularly true of Heisenberg's Uncertainty Principle, one of the foundation stones of quantum physics which called into question the old Newtonian vision of reality from the middle distance. It asserts instead that an object observed changes in the act of observation, and that it is impossible to establish what is 'objectively' real. 'What we observe is not nature itself, but nature exposed to our method of questioning.' The Uncertainty Principle brings into question the very conception of an objective reality that runs its course regardless of our interest in it. Such an understanding of the world is inherently humane because it puts humanity back into the picture.

We can see the impact which humanising modernity has had in many other fields. One is medicine where doctors are involved not only in the technical but moral features of their profession, and now acknowledge that they have to take the patient's wishes into account. Case ethics too is important, the need to avoid concentrating on abstract universal issues and to regard the particular or local as all-important. Toulmin also cites the new understanding in politics. The attempt to essentialise the nation at the expense of minorities has been replaced by a commitment to multi-culturalism. The old idea of political stability that emphasised an unchanging order has been replaced by the belief that states only survive if they are willing and able to change.

What Toulmin is describing is the extent to which we have repudiated not modernity itself but what it produced: alienation. Modernity was alienating: it was alienating for the worker tied to the soulless existence of assembly line production; to the citizen housed in the stifling tenement buildings of cities in an age of rapid urbanisation; and to soldiers who became anonymous victims on the industrialised battlefields of the European world. And the question he raises implicitly (without addressing it directly) is whether we can humanise war.

Humanising war

It is clear, at least, that the West is trying to re-invent it. When looking back at the Kosovo War in particular we can see that something profound was at work. One British historian, Eric Hobsbawm, called it the first 'consumer war': the 'first war fought under the conditions of consumer sovereignty'.[26] It was the first war to be fought in which the life of the individual, in the allied ranks at least, was given absolute priority. Unwilling to risk the lives of their own men in battle, the allies wanted to secure a 'permissive environment' before launching a ground offensive.

The American strategist, Edward Luttwak, called Kosovo the first 'post-heroic war' because states are no longer in the business of heroism. Instead of the drama and theatre of war we are interested only in its traumatised victims. Air power, it was claimed, won the war, and that is what we like to believe even if it is not true. We like to think that technology can be put totally into the service of man, that soldiers are no longer central. Instead of soldier pitted against soldier, machine will be pitted against machine.[27]

Kosovo, claimed the writer and historian Timothy Garton Ash, was also the first 'post-Westphalian' war, the first in nearly three hundred years in which neither the nation nor the state played a major role. Instead it was fought without a specific state or national concern. It was conducted on behalf of a foreign ethnic group – it was the first 'humanitarian conflict' in history.[28]

What all three views share in common is the importance attached to humanity in war. We value life more highly, our own as well as that of our enemies. As Hobsbawm remarks, we have returned to a Hobbesian world in which the social contract between the state and citizen has been decisively revised in favour of the latter. In Hobbes' contractual society the commitment to obey the state was not considered either arbitrary or unconditional. It was entered into for the security of the citizen. Its binding force was conditional on the effectiveness of the state in securing that end. The state did not enjoy unconditional authority. 'The obligations of subjects to the sovereign is understood to last as long and no longer than the power lasteth by which he is able to protect them.'[29] Even in *The Leviathan* there are two things which the sovereign cannot do: he cannot conscript the subject and he cannot require him to risk his life in battle. The subject may owe the state absolute loyalty but he does so in the performance of a contract, in return for a service: protection. Hobbes' Commonwealth, unlike the twentieth-century state, could not send its citizens off to die in battle.

In turn, Luttwak argues that we have taken heroism out of war. We can no longer justify or legitimise death in terms of a sacrifice for the many myths that once sustained warriors in the past. It is the duty of generals to keep their soldiers alive for as long as possible. It is a responsibility of commanders to use technology in place of men. The modern battlefield has no place for the 'bloody boots on the ground realists who insist you cannot win without planting the flag on enemy turf while wading in the blood of your comrades'.[30]

Finally, it seems clear that the responsibility to conserve life is not one that should be confined to one's own side. The Kosovo conflict was 'post-Westphalian' for that reason. Western societies now purport to go to war on behalf of others. NATO considered itself to be morally mandated to intervene to save citizens from the iniquities of their own, undemocratic and unaccountable, government.

What all three writers argue is that the individual has been placed at the centre of the moral imagination: the individual as citizen (Hobsbawm), as soldier (Luttwak) and as the reason for going to war (Ash). What all three contend with varying degrees of scepticism is that the West is trying to *humanise* war. It is a claim that prompts us to think of the Kosovo War which it is claimed was the first humanitarian war in history. But the attempt long pre-dates Kosovo and encompasses more than just humanitarianism. It encompasses three distinct but related themes – humanism, humanity and humanitarianism.

Humanism

One of the distinguishing features of the modern age was the embattled condition of humanism. The death of individualism on the western front had been anticipated long before in the industrial workplace. As Marx told us, modernity was alienating: it condemned assembly line workers to the monotony of factory life, and later the tyranny of time schedules associated with the American capitalists Ford and Taylor. It also condemned soldiers to an anonymous death on the battlefield – to being killed long distance by an enemy they never set eyes on. It reduced war to butchery, robbing it of its romance.

In the course of the twentieth century, society went beyond the anthropocentric, as individuals were seen as cogs in a wheel or system in which all human subjectivity was denied. In many of the century's great works such as Sartre's *Nausea* and Kafka's *Trial*, the individual is reduced to a condition. Many of the characters of the twentieth-century novel were not important in themselves but as representatives of mass society, a society distinguished not by its people but by its problems.

Governments also customarily measured the costs of war in terms of money, lost production or the number of soldiers killed or wounded. Rarely did they attempt to measure the costs of war in terms of individual human suffering. Enemies were stripped of their humanity. Little thought was given to individuated death. The democracies had no more compunction than totalitarian regimes in raining down death and destruction on the heads of citizens, even children. 'Two years ago we would all have been aghast at the idea of killing civilians', complained George Orwell in 1942. 'I remember saying to someone during the Blitz. . . "in a year's time you will see headlines in *The Daily Express*: Successful raid on Berlin orphanage. Babies set on fire." '[31]

Today, by contrast, we are inclined to individualise both death and human suffering more than ever before. We could write the history of central Europe, writes Garton Ash, 'over the forty years from 1949 to 1989 as the story of attempts by European peoples to become once again the subjects rather than the objects of history'.[32] With the fall of the Berlin Wall the peoples of the East once again won back their subjectivity. No longer were they passive spectators or their countries historical no-man's land in which competing historical forces fought it out – Catholicism against Protestantism; Liberalism against Communism.

Our humanism also rests not as it did in the past on the redemption of humanity over time (the purported 'end of history'). It rests on 'real time'. Our age is intensely self-referential. Increasingly we experience events without the need for historical perspective that characterised the past. We are not products of a grand narrative; instead, we have become our own source or object of reflection. Accordingly, our achievements are no longer directed at the future. Few of us are much interested in the opinion of the next generation. Few if any look to posterity for their reward. Instead, we demand immediate recognition. Most of our popular heroes are disinclined to postpone the results of their efforts beyond their own personal existence. Humane wars are likewise predicated on the belief that martyrdom is illegitimate unless freely chosen; that the martyr should no longer be expected to bear witness to the future. The victims of history should be avenged at the time.

Even the ethics of war – and for war to remain both legal and legitimate in the eyes of its practitioners it must be ethical – is no longer
determined through abstract concepts as in the past. We consider it to be
an integral part of human conduct and interaction dependent on and
involving responsibility for others. Our ethical codes are crafted not by
abstract philosophy but by practical action. Ethics, in a word, is a human
endeavour, and humanism is reflected in the wish of civil society to reduce
the incivility of warfare, both for the soldiers who serve in society's name
and the enemies with which our societies find themselves at war.

Humanity

In attempting to make war more humane we are not breaking new ground.
The St Petersburg Declaration (1863) and the better known Hague
Conventions of 1899 and 1907 to which Ogg referred attempted to mitigate
slaughter by banning certain weapons whose use was considered particularly inhumane. Even some of the nineteenth century's greatest inventors
of weapons assumed that as their products became more deadly, responsible governments would shy away from using them indiscriminately against
each other. Gattling hoped his prototype machine-gun would supersede
the necessity of large armies. Alfred Nobel, the inventor of dynamite,
hoped that he had invented a means of destruction so deadly that no
civilised society would ever use it against another.[33] All that resulted, alas,
in that disingenuous hope was the Nobel Peace Prize which in certain
years is not awarded.

In retrospect, we can see that Nobel's dream ran against the grain of
history. After 1870 the West invested all its hopes in technological advances.
Advances there certainly were – in automatic weapon fire, massed artillery
bombardment, aerial bombing and unpiloted missiles, but all they resulted
in was greater inhumanity still: wars of bloody attrition.

Today, we see little value in 'area killing' or the targeting of civilians.
The experience of aerial bombing in the Second World War showed it
to be surprisingly counter-productive. What history (and modern history
in particular) tends to show is that civilians and soldiers can withstand the
actuality of fear, death and destruction during artillery and aerial bombardment without losing their will to fight. Pioneers of the new American
school of battle – the war of manoeuvre – such as Robert Leonhard and
William Lind, have focused their writing on how the will to fight can be
destroyed without the attritional warfare that was characteristic of the
modern era.[34]

In the future we will continue to become more discriminating. In the Gulf
War, precision-guided weapons accounted for only 8 per cent of ordnance
dropped by air on Iraq; in Kosovo, the figure rose to 35 per cent and we
can expect it to rise even higher as the years pass. A corollary of this is that
we are also increasingly interested in reducing the material and human

destructiveness of the battlefield, in limiting damage to the environment and human habitat. What experts began calling 'non-lethal violence' in the 1960s exploits a technology that was not available at the time: non-lethal weapons. We may not yet be on the frontier of an age of 'immaculate coercion' (the term the USAF used in Kosovo) but we seem intent on getting there if we can. The reason for this is as much to reduce the incidents in which our own soldiers are traumatised or maimed or in danger of being killed, as it is to mitigate our own inhumanity to our enemies.

Humanitarianism

The fact that we fight humanitarian wars – or at least claim to – is a final indication of our attempt to humanise modern warfare. There was little humanitarianism, of course, in the previous century. Marxists and non-Marxists alike were usually dismissive of the claims of small people to nationhood, not to mention 'unhistorical peoples' who got in the way of progress. Many states still saw history as a form of historical selection, the spoils going to the fittest. The South Slavs, colonial peoples and classes like the Kulaks were all dispossessed of their future in the name of history.

In the past we did not fight for individuals and certainly not the bulk of common humanity, and for an explanation of why this was the case we need look no further than Adam Ferguson's *Essay on the History of Civil Society* which introduced the term into political discourse for the first time. We might think that the author, good Scottish Enlightenment thinker that he was, would have endorsed the principle of civility even in war. But Ferguson was not a twenty-first-century thinker; he was very modern in his thinking and he would have little sympathy for or even understanding of our post-Westphalian world – the concept of an international civil society with its rules and norms of behaviour that are enforced against regimes who engage in ethnic cleansing.

As a historical activity Ferguson divided warfare into three types: wars fought to defend honour (that of the prince); to defend an interest (commerce); and to defend virtue. As a model Enlightenment thinker he found the last to be most fitting. Quoting Xenophon's description of the Spartan people – 'the Spartans should excel every nation being the only state in which virtue is studied as the object of government' – Ferguson called them a singular people in that 'they alone in the language of Xenophon made virtue an object of the state'.[35]

From our perspective all three types of war were distinctly devoid of humanitarianism. In a princely society courage was deemed to be the virtue of a class, and the respect a warrior was expected to show his enemy derived from a code of conduct from which the majority of combatants and non-combatants alike were excluded. Medieval chivalry, for example, was the code of a guild rather than a society. Knights might be courteous enough to each other, but no such chivalry was shown in the ranks.

In societies such as eighteenth-century Britain which were preoccupied with commerce, the common man tended to be devalued too. Utilitarianism was everything. Little thought was given to the contingent victims of those wars: the natives or even one's own soldiers (in the British case many were mercenaries or Irish). Even those societies which fought for principles rather than profit, the 'virtuous' tended to devalue human beings in their own particular fashion. In mediating humanity through the 'nation in arms', or the revolutionary state, or the racial state locked in a historic struggle against ancient adversaries, they put principle first and individual human life second. In making the world safe for democracy, few Americans asked themselves whether democracy could be made safe for the world.

Today we fight for 'others' as well as ourselves. We call it 'human security', a new concept which brings into question all our assumptions regarding 'security', and challenges the distinction between the national and public interest, between 'high' and 'low' politics and the bias towards the former at the expense of the latter especially in the context of the prevailing national security paradigm.[36] We have extended our concept of humanity from the local community to the 'imagined community' of the nation state and further afield still to the 'global village' which encompasses Rwanda and East Timor. 'We are all internationalists now', claimed Britain's Prime Minister twenty-two days into the Kosovo War.[37] Acts against commoners, such as ethnic cleansing, genocide or political oppression in its many forms are now deemed grounds for going to war. In that sense, humanitarian warfare is unprecedented. It puts the individual at the heart of the political discourse. In holding governments accountable for the treatment of their own citizens, the western world has redefined sovereignty for the first time since the Westphalia Conference (1648) at which it had been redefined too – in the hope that Europe would never again experience what Grotius called 'the riot of fury' that had been the Thirty Years' War.

One thing is certain: there is no going back on this agenda. Kosovo may indeed be the first and last humanitarian war, as some writers maintain,[38] but even if we find ourselves engaged in other wars which involve old-fashioned conflicts between states rather than peoples, we will try to mitigate war's inhumanity as best we can. Even if we cannot fight humanitarian wars we will try to be humane to others. Even if we accept that selective targeting cannot work – that air power and cruise missiles do not always allow ethical choices, that we cannot target the evils of the world with the blunt instruments in our possession – we will insist on being more humane than we have in the past.

A second paradox is that humane warfare is a largely western phenomenon (though some societies, including Russia, are spending money on non-lethal weapons). Elsewhere in the world war is becoming more inhumane, not less. In some wars children now account for the great majority of casualties: 300,000 child soldiers, some of them as young as nine years old, are fighting in some part of the world today. Weapons of mass destruction with biological and chemical agents are being manufactured, and one day may be used. War is becoming more dirty. The experts call it 'asymmetric warfare'. Whatever we wish to call it, whether we prefer to label it 'nihilistic' or 'irrational' or 'perverse', it has a logic and the logic runs counter to what the West is trying to do – to make war less cruel.

2 War and the renunciation of cruelty

Religious canon, civil law are cruel? Then what should war be?
(Shakespeare, *Timon of Athens*)

Cruelty has always been the essence of war, but we will not understand this if we restrict its meaning simply to its incidental nature – the fact that in war all restraints on human action are usually lifted, or control breaks down. This is true – but it is also something of a truism. And it has not held men back from going to war – indeed, quite the reverse.

It was Nietzsche, the most penetrating philosopher of the late modern age, who as a modern man confronted the truth – war is ugly. The Greeks were able to disguise this fact by giving it artistic expression. Homer's *Iliad* is replete with horrifying scenes, but the genius of Homer was through 'an artistic deception' to deify or glorify its 'unspeakable ugliness'. The Greeks captured not only the reality of war but its spirit in tragedy and epic poetry, and they philosophised it into a human art: those 'distended human bodies, their sinews tense with hatred or with the arrogance of triumph, writhing bodies, the wounded [and] the dying.' They 'spiritualised' cruelty, they ennobled it by making war the ultimate expression of human achievement: the will to create by dominating others.[1]

'Cruelty is part of greatness', Nietzsche wrote in his notebooks.[2] What still makes him such an attractive thinker is his honesty – which is also one reason, of course, why he still has many detractors. Humanity cannot stand too much reality. Nietzsche had no time for those who sanctioned sacrifice in the name of the truth or God or morality or any of the other abstract concepts in which society has traded to justify war's cruelty. But he was also rooted to the modern world, and in particular the late nineteenth century in his claim that in abandoning the search for the truth, in seeking what is true for us, we would have to 'reconsider cruelty and open our eyes, [as] almost everything we call "higher culture" is based on the spiritualisation of cruelty, on it becoming more profound.'[3] As a thoroughly modern man Nietzsche wanted to treat the cruelty of war honestly by acknowledging not so much that cruelty is the essence of war, but that it is the essence of what makes us human.

Like so much of his work Nietzsche's view is based on his own ontological construction of a man 'who seeks above all to discharge [his] strength . . . for life itself is the will to power'.[4] To make war more profound in the modern era he tried to connect the private and public spheres – private self-realisation through 'willing one's destiny' and thus empowering one-self with membership of a community (though not necessarily a nation state, for Nietzsche abominated nationalism) that willed its collective future as well. This was the true expression of the will to power, as well as for him the ground on which freedom had to be defended in order to be made real. That is why he approved of war in principle, for it pro-vided society and the individual with the experience of being an effect-ive agent in the world, one who is able to transform what 'is' into what 'will be'.

The American Century and the will to power

This point comes out particularly vividly in the ruminations of General Cummings, the most vivid character in Norman Mailer's novel *The Naked and the Dead* (1948). Mailer's novel was and remains the most important novel to come out of the Second World War, and describes the innate ruthlessness of America's attempt to impress its will on the rest of the world, on its allies and enemies alike. No other book succeeds quite so well in dramatising the psychology of the 'will to power' – and revealing its historical culmination in the twentieth-century conflict between the world's principal ideologies – all of them contesting the right to speak not only for their own followers but for History (in the upper case).

Indeed, if we seek a definition of the American will to power there is no better one than Cummings' concept of historical energy:

> There are countries which have latent powers, latent resources,
>   they are
> full of potential energy so to speak. And there are great concepts
>   which
> can unlock that, express it. As kinetic energy a country is
>   organisation,
> co-ordinated effort: your epithet, fascism.[5]

The last remark is a reference to Cummings' interlocutor Robert Hearn, who believed that there was a process of osmosis in war: that at the end the victors always tend to look like the vanquished looked at the beginning. The United States had fought a war against fascism and become a fascist state. This was the claim of many in the anti-war movement in the 1960s, and the view of many on the Left during the Cold War. I will return to this later not only because it is wrong, but also because it shows a grave misunderstanding of the American 'will to power' which is what Cummings means by 'fascism'.

Let us deconstruct Cummings' definition of America's will and its willingness to exercise it.

1   Not for nothing does he invoke the latent power and resources of America. The United States was quite simply the most powerful country in history – certainly the most powerful in the twentieth century, a fact grasped very early by writers such as Joseph Conrad in his novel *Nostromo* (1904). The novel's most interesting character is the Yankee businessman Holroyd who has 'the temperament of a Puritan and an insatiable imagination of conquest'. Holroyd looks at the world through globalising eyes and is contemptuous of the aspirations of lesser powers.

> We shall be giving the word for everything: industry, trade, law, journalism, art, politics and religion, from Cape Horn clear over to Smith's Sound and beyond too, if anything worth taking hold of turns up at the North Pole. And then we shall take in hand the outlying continents and islands of the earth. We shall run the world's business whether the world likes it or not. The world can't help it – and neither can we.'[6]

2   Great concepts were needed to unlock that power. The twentieth century was an intensely ideological age and liberalism was the most persuasive ideology. Its institutions, if not its message, were aped by all the other ideologies who paid lip-service to parliaments, elections and even references to the Rights of Man (differently construed, of course, in the fascist case: not the brotherhood of man so much as the community of blood: the brotherhood of one's fellow countrymen).

3   A country is kinetic energy. The resources of the nation state harnessed to the ideas of the twentieth century created a formidable force. America, claimed Gary Wills, became an 'ism' in the course of the twentieth century. This combination of forces was made possible by nationalism which was the real force of the twentieth century which all the principal ideologies – liberalism, communism and fascism – harnessed for their own ends.[7]

America's principal rivals in the twentieth century were Nazi Germany and the USSR. As a nation state the Third Reich was indeed formidable; so was the Soviet State at the height of the Great Patriotic War. But it was the United States that was the most formidable of the three in imposing its will on others through war. As General Cummings observes, 'Historically the purpose of war is to translate America's potential into kinetic energy.'[8]

His was an authentic twentieth-century voice. For he recognised that the world had become a laboratory for releasing reserves of energy and that a powerful state, provided it had the courage of its convictions, could sweep aside all the old conventions that had inhibited the release of human energy in the past, including all the old religious taboos and social constraints. Conflict was the instrument by which energy moved from its promise to its realisation. To this end individuals and individual people were merely tools of their destiny.

Let me cite two voices from the two world wars. The first, is the Jesuit priest Teilhard du Chardin who served as an ambulance stretcher bearer on the Western Front. The Front he saw not as a 'flaming line where the accumulated energies of hostile masses are released and mutually neutralised'. He saw it not as a line of fire, an interface of people attacking each other but 'the crest of a wave' bearing the nations towards their collective destiny.[9] Writing twenty years later, Ann Morrow Lindberg described the Second World War as a conflict of historical forces:

> I cannot see this war . . . simply and purely as a struggle between the forces of good and the forces of evil. If I could simplify into a phrase at all it would seem truer to say that the forces of the past are fighting the forces of the future.[10]

Significantly, this quotation is taken from her book *The Wave of the Future* (1941). It was a title that Kennedy borrowed in 1961 when he warned the American people that unless capitalism was seen to prevail the world would conclude that communism was the future, and the West would be swamped in its wake.

That was the cruelty of history as the will to power. The subject of history was not the individual but the representatives of humanity who could take many forms: the nation, a class, even a civilisation. History was the place in which humanity became many: slaves and masters, workers and the bourgeoisie, peasants and the state. History was a discourse between them, a dialectic that could only be resolved in a final struggle between two opposing social forces.

I find Mailer's novel intriguing because it captures this theme so well, especially when we remember that it was written so early, in 1948. 'We are out of the backwaters of history', remarks Cummings, to which Hearn remarks ironically, 'We have become destiny, eh?'[11] What was the American Century if not the belief that America represented mankind's destiny? In Mailer's novel Hearn may refer to a process of osmosis: claiming that having defeated fascism the United States would itself become a fascist state. And Cummings' philosophy can be interpreted in fascist terms, although to do so would be to misread not only the book but America as a nation. For Cummings is really a follower not so much of Nietzsche as the idea of 'the will to power', and that will included not only power over others but also power over oneself. Morality, Nietzsche tells us, is the self-overcoming of a people: a herd turns its desire for power against itself; it learns to obey its own self-imposed commands, and in obeying becomes 'a people' and learns the need for sacrifice.

In compensation the citizen is offered transcendence through identification with the myth of national supremacy. It is compensation for the cruelty of war in two respects: for the alienation of the soldier on the modern battlefield, for becoming a cog in the anonymous and hideous 'machine' that war had become; and for the cruel acts that soldiers are asked to visit on an enemy which frequently they never see, as in the case of the technologically inferior Japanese.

But ultimately what makes Cummings such an authentic figure of the times is that his vision of the world can be found in the philosophy of the century's three great American philosophers: Charles Peirce, John Dewey and William James who 'Americanised' the will to power. James' book *The Will to Believe* was in a tradition of Schopenhauer's *The World as Will and Idea* and Nietzsche's *The Will to Power*. All were declarations of a will against pessimism and nihilism. All were moral reconstruction efforts. The shared idea behind the will to power was the slowly germinating conviction that there was no such thing as a factual, objective meaning of the world and that it was necessary to use a nation or people's strength to create such a meaning within a realm accessible to human reason. History thus became the will to power and war became history.

The American version of this idea, nevertheless, was distinctively different from Nietzsche's. That is why it is worth looking at James' philosophy more closely, for his voice and speech and even turn of phrase were all authentically American. He deliberately employed such characteristic expressions as 'cash value' and 'results' and even 'profits' in order to bring his ideas within reach of the 'man in the street'. He spoke with a force and directness which made his philosophy of pragmatism second nature to his fellow citizens.

In James' philosophy of action, the first principle is 'purpose'. If our experience, he argued, discloses an unfinished world, a world with a future, with aspects which are still in the making, we must ask what part we have in shaping that process. We cannot decide what is morally good or bad until we have a moral order. But if we do not want such an order in the first place we cannot be made to believe in what is good or bad by rational argument. That we make moral distinctions and take them seriously is decided by our will, not our intellect.

When Woodrow Wilson declared war on Germany in 1917 he confidently asserted that 'our object is to vindicate the principles of peace . . . we are glad to fight for the ultimate peace of the world'.[12] The idea that war was being fought for peace was the ultimate conclusion of America's historic mission to rid the world of tyrants whether they took the form of eighteenth-century kings or twentieth-century German gauleiters. It was only inevitable that Soviet commissars would later be added to the list. In that sense the Cold War was indeed a war, rather than an armed peace, for it could end in only one outcome: the unconditional victory of one side, and the unconditional surrender of the other.

James' second principle is 'effort'. Effort tells us that we are free, that our will (or free-thinking) is capable of bringing about change. We are not passive spectators but actors in our own history. It is not enough, however, to await evidence that will confirm us in this opinion. It we resolutely refuse to consider the possibility of God's existence, for example, until we have proof of it, we will fail to put ourselves in a place where we may find proof, or where we may experience the reality if it is there to be found. The 'cash value' of abstract ideas, James declared, is such that they can only be known when lived through. Only by wishing to believe in them (in the possibility of their existence from the outset) will we be willing to act in ways that will put us in the presence of them (if they are there to be found). And that may require that at some point we fight our way into history.

Effort, of course, was endless in the twentieth century. 'It will be our business,' declared Woodrow Wilson when he took the United States into the First World War, 'to fight for a new era.' 'All our lives,' Dean Acheson told the American people in 1946, after the Wilsonian order had collapsed and another war had been fought to punish those held responsible for its failure, 'the need for effort will always be with us.'[13] There appeared to be no end to America's labours, only a constant striving.

The final element in James' philosophy of action is 'will' itself. For effort would be of little avail if it were no more than a blind will to power. Our efforts must be governed by our purposes, and our purposes, in turn, must be framed in the light of our beliefs. A belief which has nothing to do with conduct is not a proper belief. Our conduct, however, must be informed by ideas. In the end, we hold our beliefs through our will to believe.[14] If German thinkers can be said to have subscribed to the will to power, Americans like Cummings believed with equal force in the will to truth. Few liberal writers of importance ever doubted the veracity of their convictions even in the darkest moments of their history. The need to believe was all the greater, of course, in the conflict with twentieth-century totalitarianism, for in such a conflict neither side took hostages.

It is in that sense this Cummings may be considered a Nietzschean thinker. 'The only morality of the future,' he tells Hearn, 'is a power morality and a man who cannot find his adjustment to it is doomed.'[15] Cruelty was for Nietzsche too the essence of war which, in turn, was the ultimate expression of life, the wish to live it on terms of one's own choosing. War was merely 'an application of the original will to become stronger'. It was 'the primordial fact of history', and as such was intrinsically cruel, for cruelty provides 'the highest gratification of the feeling of power'.[16]

Cruelty for Nietzsche could be considered neither good nor bad; it could only be judged good or bad with respect to the ends it served, and in particular the attainment of human excellence. As a thoroughly modern man, he did not shrink from endorsing cruelty to others: that, after all, is the inevitable result when one country or people tries to impress its will on another.

Vietnam: the end of America's will to power

The United States was the last great power to embrace the will to power in 1917, and the last to renounce it. It was the last great power that showed a willingness to resort to war to forge a new world order and to send its own citizens into battle. Its efforts foundered, however, in Vietnam. In his novel *Libra*, DeLillo calls Kennedy's assassination 'the seven seconds that broke the back of the American Century'.[17] But it could be claimed that the Vietnam War also subverted America's 'will to power', perhaps more so. For it exposed the cruelty of war in three respects, and in so doing prompted a national re-examination of History (in the upper case) – in the name of which cruelty was 'spiritualised' in the late modern era.

Irony

The first and most subversive theme was irony, which Monroe Engel called 'the normative mentality' of modern art. It soon became the expected tone of war writing too.[18] For the First World War made a mockery of the heroic stories people had learned at school. It made a nonsense of the epic poetry of the past and discredited the history of war as a tale of heroes and heroism.

In the most popular American Great War novel, Ernest Hemingway's *A Farewell To Arms*, one of the characters enigmatically comments: 'Many people have realised the war this summer. Officers whom I thought could never realise it, realise it now.' To 'realise' the war is to understand what it really meant, to jettison faith in a world one once thought was real – to find reality deeply ironic. Hemingway's novel is a farewell to 'arms' as the fathers have defined war – as 'a glorious sacrifice'. It is precisely war as an *abstraction* which can no longer be tolerated. To fight it in good faith one's notions must be real. 'Abstract words such as glory, honour, courage or hallow [had become] obscene beside the concrete names of villages, the numbers of roads; the numbers of rivers; the numbers of regiments.'[19] The movement from the belief in slogans to an encounter with the realities of war is the main theme of the book. The move from an unquestioning belief in the idea of war to the ironical encounter with reality (to a person's own experience of war, his authentic experience) leads directly to Lt. Henry's feeling of betrayal. Irony demanded that men should experience war for themselves, that they should live in the present, not the imperfect, tense.

It also demanded that the ugliness of war be concealed by euphemism. As Paul Fussell maintains, while it would be incorrect to trace the impulse of all euphemism to the First World War it was perhaps the first time in history that the horror produced by a unique event made public euphemism 'the special rhetorical sound of life'.[20]

When commanders are no longer happy to call things by their proper name, when they distance themselves from their own actions through the use of language, they are no longer content with the reality of what war has become. Nor are we: that is what makes us find it ironic. In Vietnam the US Army chose to hide the cruelty of the conflict; it chose to disguise its true nature even from the soldiers who had to fight it. Battlefields were called 'free fire zones' in which anything that moved could be shot at. It was easier to treat peasants as potential 'hostiles' rather than non-belligerents or refugees. Bombing became 'aerial support' or more inaccessible still, 'limited duration protective reaction air strikes'.

Euphemism even extended to the maiming of American soldiers both in the psychological and physical sense. Men were no longer killed; they were 'degraded' or 'attrited'. Even the accidental death of civilians was written off as 'collateral damage'. In his account of his own war experience Michael Herr tells the story of a friend who was sent home suffering from what the army called 'acute environmental reaction'. Vietnam spawned a host of such delicate circumlocutions. 'Most Americans would rather be told that their son is undergoing acute environmental reaction,' he complained, 'than to hear that he is suffering from shell shock because they could no more cope with the fact of shell shock than they could with the reality of what happened to this boy during his five months at Khe Sahn.'[21]

The military's embarrassment about calling war by its true name continued into the final years of the Cold War. War even ceased to be 'war'. The invasion of Grenada in 1983 was described memorably by a Pentagon spokesman as 'a pre-dawn vertical insertion'.[22] Today when armies are sent into battle, they are despatched in the name of 'peace enforcement'. In Iraq a seventy-two-hour Anglo-American air strike called Desert Fox (1998) was called an 'against a threat to peace action'.[23] Neither Britain nor America declared war on Iraq: they merely bombed its capital city. Nowadays countries do not even go to war; they enforce the peace. In Kosovo, NATO's air campaign was called 'a risk management strategy with missiles'.[24] History it would appear is no longer made; it is managed.

Relativism

In the course of the twentieth century reality also became a matter of individual perception. In this regard the individual point of view was greatly aided and abetted by photography which invited people to see the truth for *themselves*. Unlike the great pictorial battle panoramas of the past, the photographs that came out of the front line did not show the big picture, or illustrate a single theme. Instead of showing stirring landscapes of battle, they showed war in its most brutal form. Photographic technique helped in that transformation. Diagonal angles, suppressed horizons, bird's-eye and worm's-eye views, serial portraits and close-ups were relatively commonplace by the 1930s. Low camera angles, out of focus foregrounds, subjects caught unawares mid-gesture; juxtapositions of two unrelated images that drew the viewer into complicity with the photographer and editor against the subjects depicted – an ironic understanding shared by all but the subjects themselves – made life even more relative than ever.

Americans were at the forefront of these developments. During the Spanish Civil War (1936–39) Robert Capa was the first photographer to apply these techniques widely to war. In doing so he made the photographer for ever a participant in the game. His insistence upon personalising war through close-ups of individual faces, his use of juxtapositions to create a sense of war's' irony, his low-angle, line-of-fire battle pictures all stress the photojournalist's essentially priestly role (later taken over by the television cameraman): both witness all for us, and in so doing enable us to make our own judgements about the cruelty of war.

But the main impact of photography was that it devalued the future in the name of the present. The chief reference point of modern societies was either the past or the future. The point of reference for our societies today is the present. The young in particular live in the present tense and the revolt of youth against the Vietnam War marked a historic caesura in the history of the United States. Of the two million young men who were called up to serve, an unprecedented 139,000 refused to be drafted. The main reason for this was that historical metaphors such as manifest destiny which had mobilised the nation in the past had begun to lose their imaginative appeal. Instead, the war saw the emergence of what the sociologist Ulrich Beck calls 'a social surge of individualisation'.[25] Faced with the disintegration of some of the certainties of industrial society, individuals tend to invent new certainties for themselves. Biographies are self – not socially – produced. People are compelled to put themselves, not society, at the centre of life.

In Vietnam they were encouraged to put the present first because they found the Vietnam War to be *historically* incoherent. They could not locate themselves within history. The war offered no single theme or story; it was incoherent and even meaningless. This was a war without direction, a story without a plot. The fighting itself was not shaped by specific events. Even the set-piece battles like the siege of Khe Sahn, the centre piece of Michael Herr's account *Dispatches*, did not fit into the wider campaign; they did not signal final victory or defeat. There was no *momentum* to the war.[26] Because they were unable to locate the war in the past, or project it into the future, the soldiers located it in the present, in their own 'time'.

It was doubly important that they went to Indo-China at a time when the present tense was becoming the most important in the grammar of western life. It was important that the young were in the process of developing a new culture of experience and experiment. One of the most vivid metaphors which holds together Herr's classic account of the war is that war is like taking drugs: it is like being 'stoned'. Most Vietnam narratives, in fact, do not have much to say about drugs at all, but it was from books like *Dispatches* that the drugged-up vision of the war took the form it did in its Hollywood version.[27] What was important about the drug culture was its preoccupation with the present. In *The Doors of Perception* (1954) Aldous Huxley had suggested that mescaline and LSD were drugs of unique distinction which offered a visionary feast for the young, for those with an open mind. His book was a bewitching account of the inner world of the mescaline taker where there is only a 'perpetual present made up of a continually changing apocalypse'.[28] Not surprisingly the book became a set text for the beat generation and later the hippies in the psychedelic 1960s. The Doors, whose lead singer Jim Morrison became one of the defining icons of the age (rendered more iconic still by his drug-induced early death), named themselves after it. Huxley even secured a place on the Beatles' *Sergeant Pepper* album. Back from the war, Michael Herr could not tell the war veterans from the rock and roll veterans. For the 1960s generation 'its war and its music had run off the same circuit for so long they didn't even have to fuse'.[29]

But the present was enhanced not only by psychedelic experience but also by the musical idiom of the day. The popular taste in music was in favour of the new. Revolutionary styles, revolutionary fashions and new sounds were each replaced by the next at a dizzying rate. Rock grew from a form of musical expression into a social phenomenon: giving music itself a new significance, a particular form of energy. The appeal of popular music was that it offered experience rather than an argument. It was not cerebral or rational. It was expressly experiential because it was rhythmic, and rhythm was concerned with extending the boundaries of the present. It expanded the time in which the young could live in the present tense.

The music of the hour was the music of youth protest: it was subversive and seductive at the same time. It subverted the traditional resignation the young had shown to war throughout history. Most, of course, did not desert, or evade the draft, or go into exile in Canada. Most went to Vietnam but they did so sullenly and reluctantly and under protest, and the music they listened to helped frame the revolt in these terms. It was a rock and roll war, writes Samuel Hynes. The music of Bob Dylan, the Rolling Stones and Jimmi Hendrix gave the young a voice as well as a message that was explicitly critical not only of war but its cruelty: it denied the promise of youth.[30]

Heroism

Heroism too died a death in Vietnam. As the western Europeans had found in 1914, the heroic virtues tended to serve abstractions such as humanity, or the nation state or even the ideal of heroism itself. Heroism involved courage and self-abnegation, of course, and to that extent was admirable, but for the heroes of the past it was the cause that counted, not one's fellow human beings. Many heroes sacrificed themselves for an abstraction and thus can be said to have embraced death readily. Love of an abstraction tended to take precedence over the interests of individual human beings.

Both acts of heroism were worthy of praise but the hero wants to be remembered even after death. Individual heroic acts on the battlefield (saving a comrade, defending a line) are different from the myths which call for acts of heroism (death) for something as abstract as a nation. Dying for an idea is different from dying for other people. Heroism of the second kind is not abstract but concrete and it relates more to the private than to the public realm.

Industrial warfare, of course, put an end to that ideal, for heroism involves above all death freely chosen. For the hero the choice is between a noble death and an ignoble life. He chooses death not because he is in love with it but because death is his destiny, the natural completion of his life. It is also his guarantee of immortality (or death transcended), the act by which he is remembered by the community. It is the supreme act which sets him apart from ordinary men. But in modern warfare he is not set apart. His death is not individualised; it is anonymous. The soldier who was remembered after the Great War was 'unknown'.

In the mid-twentieth century this was not always recognised in its strictly military sense for it was bound up in the protest against the cruelty of modern life. Industrial society with its assembly line uniformity and alienating bureaucratic values so transformed the former concept of the hero that it became hard not to agree with Lionel Trilling's 'test' for whether a novel or play was 'modern': 'Do you want to be a hero? If you do, the work is bad.'[31]

In contrast to the hero who gives his life for his country, Vietnam transformed the notion of the hero into a man whose appetite for courage is not transitive: it does not lead to anything beyond itself. Indeed, the modern hero is the soldier whose ingenuity, toughness, competitiveness and efficiency help him survive. In surviving he becomes a hero.

Nothing illustrates this better than Joseph Heller's novel *Catch 22* (1961). When it first appeared it attracted little critical comment. Within a few years, however, it had become a 'Vietnam War' book and was taken to be a critical commentary not on the Second World War but the unfolding conflict in Indo-China. As a work of fiction it was merely the first of a slow trickle of books including Vonnegut's *Mother Night* and Thomas Pynchon's *V*, which, with their surreal exaggeration, satirical punch and blend of fantasy and history, were soon acknowledged to be the fore-runners of post-modern fiction. Heller's novel was the most popular of them all, for it was the most accessible intellectually and it soon became associated with the Vietnam War.

What it captured was a feeling of the times that there is no role for heroes in modern warfare. War had become too mechanised and mechan-ical in direction for individuals to see either war or their own actions in heroic terms. In *Catch 22* the focus is directed towards the air force, the most mechanised branch of the US military. For the book's main character, Capt. John Yossarian, the death of most of his colleagues is pointless. Yossarian is frankly terrified of his own fate, and is always fleeing to the hospital to escape being sent on dangerous combat missions. But he is not a coward. He is afraid because he has correctly perceived that side by side with the men who fight it, there seems to exist a barely human machine concerned only with war as an end in itself. That is the cruelty of war for those who are called upon to fight it.

In Heller's novel the machinery of war is most graphically represented in the famous 'catch'.

> There was only one catch and that was Catch 22 which specified that a concern for one's safety in the face of dangers that were real and immediate was the process of a rational mind. Orr was crazy and could not be grounded. All he had to do was ask; and as soon as he did, he would no longer be crazy and would have to fly more missions. Orr would be crazy to fly more missions and sane if he didn't, but if he was sane he had to fly them. If he flew them he was crazy and didn't have to; but if he didn't want to he was sane and had to. Yossarian was moved very deeply by the absolute simplicity of this clause of Catch 22 and let out a respectful whistle.
> 'That's some catch, that Catch 22', he observed.
> 'It's the best there is', Doc Daneeka agreed.[32]

The doctor can ground flyers if they are crazy, but they have to ask him first. If they ask him, of course, they are not really crazy at all, since it is no mark of madness to avoid suicide missions. That *is* the catch. What is the punishment for cowardice? Death. What is cowardice? The fear of death. Wherever he turns, Yossarian is confronted by the cruel logic of mod-ern warfare.

But *Catch 22* is not a traditional twentieth-century anti-war novel. The important point is that Yossarian is not a victim like Hemingway's Lt. Henry who sums up his experience in the famous lines: 'You did not know what it was about . . . you never had time to learn. They threw you in and told you the rules and the first time they caught you off base they killed you.'[33] Yossarian is neither an innocent nor a victim. He is a survivor. He chooses free will and thus escapes his fate. In the modern war novel the tragedy of the anti-hero is that he never escapes or never makes it to the other side. Yossarian does and thus secretly triumphs.

In a critique of the novel when it first came out, Norman Mailer (true to his mid-twentieth-century understanding of the will to power and cruelty of war) condemned the author for allowing Yossarian to live, and accused him of sentimentality and romanticism.[34] Heller could have killed off Yossarian, of course, or got him to accept the catch. He could have allowed him to compromise with the enemy: his own side. Instead, he allows him to opt out, to desert. Yossarian refuses to accept defeat. But he is not victorious either. He fights on knowing that there is no absolute victory, that free will is its own reward. The struggle will always continue. But 'though victory is questionable defeat is not final'. So wrote Albert Camus in a statement that could be taken as the humanist's credo.[35] In surviving, Yossarian rejects heroism and chooses to individualise his own life.

Into the slaughterhouse

The United States also came out of the conflict with a transformed view of the cruelty of war to others. The 'will to power' like so many other nineteenth-century ideas such as progress, History and, in the American case, manifest destiny, barely took into account other people or nations, let alone individuals, and when it did it subsumed the latter into larger categories to be redeemed or rescued as the power that willed their fate saw fit. The ontology of the 'will to power' was ethical, but it was self-referential. It referred everything back to the source of that will. In that respect it was self-absorbed and self-regarding and in the end – in Vietnam – self-reproaching as well.

The war was America's first 'post-modern' war if we can use the term as Paul Fussell defines it: it was the first conflict in which the American people were unwilling to subject their own soldiers to the cruelty of war. The Vietnam War film, like the novel, centred largely on the fate of the Americans themselves – especially their alienation from their own humanity. But the principal explanation for the latter was the way the war was fought against the enemy: the 'body counts' – the number of enemy soldiers killed, which was taken to be an actuarial indication of success and failure; and massacres like My Lai (the worst) which became a defining symbol of the soldier's individual and collective cynicism as well as the deterioration of morale. The soldiers returned home to be vilified for the first time for the cruelty they had visited upon the civilian population, though long before their return they had read about America's disenchantment with the war in the pages of *Time* and *Newsweek* which had cast them in a particularly unflattering light. As a result they felt doubly betrayed, first by their own commanders and then by the war protesters at home. There were no victory parades in this war, no national acts of expiation and little forgiveness. The veterans carried their psychological scars with them into civilian life.

This was a *victim's* war. The psychological scar tissue which the draftees carried with them into civilian life ensured that victimhood would become the war's main language. Acts of cruelty of which they were considered guilty if only by association etched themselves on the national conscious- ness (and still do): children running down a road after their village had been hit by napalm; a South Vietnamese police chief shooting a suspected terrorist in the head. The soldier's tale had been extended to the limits of war's cruelty, its human and material waste.

In that sense, Vietnam was the first war in which the American people were forced to confront as perhaps never before the cruelty of war in its full implications for the enemy as well. The war against civilians was exposed for what it was, indeed what all such wars are: cowardly, and therefore nakedly cruel, or cruel without mitigation. Traditionally, the death of civilians has offended moral sensibilities, not because they were considered more innocent or helpless but because no courage was involved on the warrior's part. Civilians are usually helpless victims. The ugliness of war cannot be veiled by invoking the heroism of the combatants. Cruelty against non-combatants is nearly always contemptible because it is so cowardly. And cruelty without extenuation reinforces the cult of victim- hood, and robs war of any moral charge.

Civilians, of course, have often been the principal casualties of war. What mattered was that their fate in Vietnam was shown on television. History, reflects one of the characters in DeLillo's novel *Libra*, 'is the sum total of all the things they aren't telling us'.[36] But by the end of the twentieth century it was becoming increasingly difficult not to know what was going on. Beginning with Vietnam, television made both the war correspondent and cameraman participants of war in a way that was not true of the two world wars. Television management is now part of war management, and what television does is implicate all of us in what is going on or is being accom- plished in our names. When we see the plight of peoples which involve us we do not always feel guilt if we think the cause 'just', but we often feel shame. We do not always feel implicated in their death but we are frequently shamed into a response. The victims are no longer anonymous.

By the time the war ended the American attitude towards war itself had come to be situated in an ethical discourse which was distinctly 'humane'. Western communities no longer embrace an ontology which was concerned only with the language of self; they tend to derive their identity from the conditions that make social life possible for others as well as themselves, or rather they no longer recognise a difference. In other words, 'we' are always ethically situated for our sense of self is derived from a prior ethical relationship with others. We have a duty to think of others when we act, not only to think of ourselves. What is important is not that states should act in the world but that they should engage in the world, and in the process, forge a world in which it is possible to live in peace with others.

Television contributed to this development by forging a common language of experience. As a medium it tends to create empathy rather than sympathy between the viewer and victim and this distinction is important. We can often feel sympathy for someone's plight, including the plight of the enemy. When we see images of suffering on our screens, however, we tend to project ourselves into a different dimension. We understand something more about the human condition and, in enlarging our knowledge, come to understand more about ourselves.

The art critic Herbert Read thought photography important for that reason. Photography is therapeutic, cathartic and liberating. On seeing images we often experience a release of anger, not only a release of feeling but a heightening of feeling or, in his words, a 'sublimation'. When we read of someone's plight we may be moved, but we are rarely changed. A visual image, by contrast, can offer a release of emotion. It can shake us out of our complacency.

Read spelled out another important distinction: he saw the visual image as an extension of the psychological point of view. The point is that it is a view. In the past, ideas of humanity had held centre ground and for that the proper medium had been language. Visual images do not deal in ideas. They deal in emotional responses to the world around us. What they show us is ourselves reflected back, the universal in the single and the single in the universal. In portraying others they show us ourselves, at the same time denying us an alibi for indifference.[37]

This became a theme of a series of novels, the most widely read of which was Kurt Vonnegut's *Slaughterhouse 5* (1969). Like Joseph Heller, Vonnegut found himself caught up in the Second World War. He was taken prisoner at the Battle of the Bulge (1944) and afterwards transferred to Dresden. He was present the following year (holed up in Slaughterhouse 5, one of the abattoirs which serviced the city) when the city was bombed in the last large-scale air raid of the war. What he offers his readers is a graphic account of the inhumanity of a raid in which 60,000 people were killed in a single night.

What is important is that Vonnegut only came to write about his experiences twenty years later. He offers an eye-witness account to an event that was barely known in the West until it became the subject of a historical study in the 1960s. The cruelty of the event is made manifest by Vonnegut as a witness; but the gap in time between seeing and recalling was significant too. 'I would hate to tell you what this lousy little book cost me in money and anxiety and time', he tells us.[38] But time is the point. It took him twenty-three years to record his experiences. By the time he came to write the book the world had moved on and he with it. *Slaughterhouse 5* is not a conventional anti-war novel (any more than is *Catch 22*) because its author refuses to provide an explanation for why the tragedy happened. What he offers instead is an implicit critique of the will to power.

'You have to balance history with science fiction,' declares a character in another of DeLillo's novels. 'It is the only way to keep sane.'[39] Vonnegut's response to the absurdity of contemporary warfare is to use the language of science fiction. His hero, Billy Pilgrim, traumatised by the bombing of Dresden, thinks he has been abducted to an alien planet where the inhabitants can move in the fourth dimension – time. Like Pilgrim himself, however, they are condemned to impotence. There is only one universe, however many dimensions of time they may travel. Nothing they can do can change history even if they have a vision of a better future.

That is why for Vonnegut war is ironic. For all our power, and despite our technological inventions, we too are condemned to impotence. We cannot always change things for the better, for we cannot always anticipate the consequences of our deeds. At the end of the novel Pilgrim clings to a motto that is meant to bring consolation:

> God grant me
> The serenity to accept
> The things I cannot change
>   Courage
> To change the things I can
>   And wisdom always
> To tell the
>   Difference.

But as Vonnegut is the first to tell us, 'among the things Billy Pilgrim could not change were the past, the present and the future.'[40] Consequently, he has no need of courage.

In the novel that followed, *Mother Night*, he admonished his readers: 'we are what we pretend to be, so we must be careful about what we pretend to be.'[41] We must pretend (that is what human beings do), but in acknowledging this we must scale down our ambitions and quest for truth. We must act more carefully and for others, not just for ourselves. Otherwise our firm beliefs will become the predicament itself, not the solution. While 'the will to believe' helps make sense of tragedy, it also encourages us to repeat the same tragedies. It offers no way out, no transcendence of our condition. That is why we should think about the fate of others – even our enemies: in this case, the victims of Dresden.

The post-modern ethics of responsibility requires what Hans Jonas calls 'an ethics of self-limitation'.[42] Before we embark on something, we have a duty to think through and visualise the consequences of our actions. It is no longer possible to follow orders without question, or see the people we are asked to bomb in abstract terms. Each individual has to rely on his own sense of responsibility and behave accordingly. It is the attempt to do that, of course, which makes Vonnegut's book ironical because he is applying a post-modern (or humane) ethic to the last major war of the modern era.

In the end, however, it is important to recognise that irony is not cynicism. If he had written the novel in the 1950s, Vonnegut would doubtless have penned a satirical account to highlight the gap between the high principles for which the allies claimed to be fighting and the methods employed to realise their aims. By the 1960s even satirists had begun to lack the moral certainties of old. Contemporary irony is not satirical. The satirist knows, the ironist doubts. The satirist uses humour to change the world, the ironist uses it as the only sane response to a world which cannot be changed without changing human nature. The satirist uses irony as a device, the ironist as an end. Satire seeks to make certain people or practices seem ridiculous in order to free people to change. The defining trait of the satirist is that he knows better.

Like other post-modern writers including Samuel Beckett, John Barth and Thomas Pynchon, Vonnegut is sceptical that a collective national will can achieve anything without damaging life as it should be lived. Instead, he offers his readers a distinctively humane theme, that there is only this life, and how we choose to live it will have unintended consequences for others as well as for ourselves. Consequently, we have an obligation to think of others if we are to avoid the fate of Billy Pilgrim, the hapless spectator of political events who escapes across time and disintegrates in the present.

What makes *Slaughterhouse 5* important as a novel (its literary merit apart) is that it offers the reader no metaphysical argument against war. All it asks its readers is to see war for what it is: cruel. In other words, if metaphysics was a pre-condition of inhumane warfare, the abandonment of metaphysics is a pre-condition of humane warfare. In the words of Richard Rorty, America's most influential contemporary philosopher, without metaphysics we can dedicate ourselves to save other people from pain and humiliation.[43] Our first obligation must not be to seek the 'truth' but to eliminate pain. Humane warfare challenges the claim that any other aim can take precedence. It allows civil society to assume its dominant ethical stance: a contempt for cruelty.

Judith Shklar and cruelty

> Anaximander discovered the contradictory nature of the world:
> it perishes from its own qualities.
>
> (Nietzsche, *Unpublished Writings*, 1872–73)

Between the seventeenth century with which I began this book and our own time we have been trying with varying degrees of success to engender a little humanity in warfare. Our treatment of prisoners of war; our rules of battle; our legal conventions to ban the use of weapons which were considered especially inhumane, all testify to the limited success of that endeavour. Now the West has attempted to go further: it is trying to humanise war.

We are trying to put man first, above the claims of scientific rationality, historical necessity or metaphysics. In advancing the claims of humanism we are putting others (including our enemies) into the picture; we are revising or revaluing our relationship with them. And to do that we have to think seriously about eliminating cruelty which Nietzsche considered to be the underlying principle of life.

Nietzsche tried to steer western thinking away from metaphysics – or what he called metaphysics – the principle from Plato's day to his own of discovering the ground which will allow us to speak in accordance with the truth and to act in accordance with what is just. The central theme of his writing is that there is no concordance with truth because there is no 'truth' or ground as the idea of the good was for Plato. Every discourse including philosophy is a perspective or point of view. But at just that point he introduced his own perspective, his own ground of history and called it the 'will to power'. The metaphysics of the will, and with it inevitably cruelty, is itself in accordance with the western metaphysical tradition. Like the will to power itself Nietzsche's defence of cruelty is metaphysical.

Now as Judith Shklar reminds us, to be truly humane a society must put cruelty first on the list of vices to be addressed, before pride and betrayal, hypocrisy and misanthropy. And as she recognises, putting it first is very different from 'mere humaneness'.[44] The reasons for this are many, but two stand out from the rest. A post-Christian culture is poorly placed to condemn cruelty, for it is not one of the seven deadly sins and traditionally works of piety and ethics did not usually discuss it. But what is more difficult still is what also explains why to hate cruelty more than any other evil in the world has rarely been attempted or recommended even by moralists. The problem is that it would involve a radical rejection both of religious and political conventions. To put cruelty first would be to disregard the idea of sin as understood by revealed religion, a world in which the ultimate sin is directed not against man but man's creator. To put cruelty first (rather than pride – the worst sin against God) would be to judge morality not in terms of God or a higher norm but to make a judgement within this world and thus close off any appeal to any order other than that of actuality.

Above all, it would also require us to put scepticism first as did Montaigne (which is why Shklar takes him as a model of the humane life), and to be sceptical about even our own first principles is to find the world ironic. That is at odds with absolute political belief. It requires a politics without ideology. The question we must ask today is not only whether we can fight wars without a metaphysical system, but also whether we can do so ironically too.

What Shklar calls 'humaneness' in war is not the problem. War has always brought out humanity even in the victors. Inhumanity has never been extolled in the epic poems and narratives celebrating the soldier's valour. Nobility, charity and mercy have all been part of a warrior's code of honour But these have all been invoked to hide what Nietzsche called 'war's ugliness', to veil its cruelty. And they have all been required of the higher principles which have sanctioned the killing of our fellow human beings. In sparing the lives of civilians we did so as not to dishonour ourselves (blood-lust has rarely been considered a fitting subject for epic poetry).

War has always been cruel but its cruelty has been mitigated, when at all, by both the invocation of religious or metaphysical orders within which warriors locate themselves, as well as the absolute certainty that allows us to kill with a good conscience. To find war ironical, as Hasek did for the First World War in *The Good Soldier Svejk* and Evelyn Waugh did for its sequel in his *Sword of Honour* trilogy, was either to condemn the folly of the generals or the hypocrisy of a political leadership which fought evil with evil, and which honoured Stalin as one of the good fighting the bad. To find war 'ironic' demands much more of us than that.

One definition of irony is the difference between what we say and what we do. But what we say has in the past always carried with it the absolute belief in the good against the bad, not the scepticism of the world that is necessary if we are not to be cruel. The problem today is that the irony with which we survey the world when we do fight appears like moral relativism to others. Many consider it the product of a failure of faith: many suspect that it shows that the western world no longer has the courage of its convictions. As Stephen Toulmin reminds us, the Second World War was the last time when the people of Europe could endorse and act out the ideals and ambitions of the modern age in a quite *unselfconscious manner*.[45] The same can be said of the United States in Vietnam. Today even Americans find war ironic because they are deeply self-conscious. Our age is marked by a pervasive inability to take our own presuppositions seriously, and thus to be always at some ironic distance from ourselves. Nothing is more characteristic of the present mood then the ironic, detached self-consciousness that not only the public but many soldiers too now have of contemporary warfare and their own profession.

We live in an age which is highly suspicious not only of history and heroism; it is also sceptical of absolutes and unambiguous outcomes. It is aware that the world is a constructed reality, a projection of our own cultural norms. All human understanding, Nietzsche taught us, is an interpretation of reality, and no interpretation can be final. The post-modern mind is not grounded in a 'weltenschaung' or world view. For that reason the West does not like behaving badly.

Instead, it is haunted by bad conscience: by the memory of what it did in the past in the name of its former unquestioning belief in reason, civilisation or progress. That was the point of Ignatieff's apocryphal story of the allies' refusal to target one of Milosevic's residences because of the fear of destroying a Rembrandt painting inside. Apocryphal or not, the moral of the story was that the West was more concerned to save its soul than to save the Kosovars. As an anecdote it has the ring of truth for that reason. For the West is determined to avoid acting badly again. Its underlying ethos is deconstructing texts; deflating pretensions; exploding beliefs; and unmasking appearances. Paul Ricouer calls it 'the hermeneutics of suspicion'.[46] In a later chapter of this book we will have to ask whether such a hermeneutic underpinning of war can ever sanction or legitimise war.

3 The redundancy of courage

One of the principal reasons that war became increasingly inhumane in the modern era was the extent to which it was deemed to test the viability of entire societies and their way of life. That was the terrible imperative of 'a people's war'. The technology of mass destruction was mobilised by entire communities which had an inexhaustible will to carry on to unconditional victory at the risk, of course, of unconditional defeat. Every society (democratic or totalitarian) expected greater courage from its citizens than perhaps ever before.

The experience of the twentieth century prompts one to enquire whether courage changes over time. In one sense it clearly does. Social courage was prized more highly in the modern era once people became the subject of history for the first time, but some form of social courage existed long before the twentieth century. In the Middle Ages the philosopher Aquinas located courage midway between despair and presumption. The medieval world believed it had seven potential characteristics: magnanimity, confidence, freedom from anxiety, magnificence, constancy, steadfastness and perseverance.

The historian Phillipe Contamine cautions us not to think that the Middle Ages saw courage entirely in terms of individual bravery, despite many accounts of warfare which often refer to it as a duel between the major participants. The medieval world knew that it could be communal, that it could derive from lineages, races and peoples. The religious order of the Templars was renowned for its valour during the Crusades. In fourteenth-century Florence two months' wages were granted collectively to victorious units. In other words, *esprit de corps* was recognised long before the modern era.[1]

Machiavelli and the virtuous state

Two centuries later one of the greatest Florentines of all, Nicolo Machiavelli, became the first major writer since the Roman Empire to devote his attention to civic *esprit*, to the collective courage of a city state including his own. Mindful of the decline of parental, religious and civic authority in the fifteenth century he believed that the restoration of civic virtue was the only sure way to arrest the process of internal disintegration, and to once again instil in the city states themselves a sense of 'heroic achievement' in place of a predisposition for the easy life.

For in the course of the late fourteenth century Italy's citizens had become reluctant to shoulder arms. Too proud to fight themselves, they preferred hiring mercenaries, mainly Swiss or Italian *condottieri* who were recruited each campaigning season and paid off every winter. Unfortunately, some of the mercenaries were 'ravening, deceitful and violent'; they did not hesitate to blackmail or betray the states that hired them. Some even seized power themselves and established their own dynasties.[2]

The *condottieri*, of course, were in the business of fighting. They were not a warrior class. They did not go to war for glory but for profit. Getting killed made nonsense of their profession. Accordingly, they took good care to ensure the rules of war operated in their favour. Machiavelli recounts one battle in which no one was killed. He describes another, Zagonara (1424), 'a defeat renowned throughout all Italy [in which] there died only Lodovico degli Obizzi with two of his own men-at-arms who, falling from horseback, were smothered in the mire'. Given such stories (however exaggerated in the telling), it is not surprising that the Florentine Commissioner of War proposed in 1479 that the mercenary commanders should be given viva-voce examinations to ascertain whether they knew anything about war. His suggestion did not meet with favour, not least because, if they had been found wanting, no one else could have taken their place.[3]

It was in an attempt to deal with the problem that Machiavelli drafted a militia law, the *Ordinanza* of 1505, which was intended to liberate the city from the mercenary scourge. To meet the challenge, he advocated schooling the citizens in civic discipline by enrolling them once again in local militias. It proved to be an imperfect instrument for securing Florence's independence. In 1512 the militia incurred a crippling defeat at Prato. In fairness it had received little or no training. Its members had never faced a competent or well-trained army in the field as had the Spanish veterans who eventually defeated it.

Within eighty years, however, Machiavelli's *Art of War* became almost compulsory reading for military commanders until it was displaced by a new series of military commentaries in the eighteenth century. It was read not because of what Machiavelli had achieved, or failed to, in the field. It was read for what he had to say about the role of courage, and especially for the fact that he had refused to draw a distinction between civic and military courage. On the contrary, he insisted that an army reflects the society from which its soldiers are recruited. A society lacking in civic courage could not be expected to put a competent army in the field.

The virtuous citizen who had shown discipline in civic life would make an excellent soldier; and an ex-soldier who returned to civilian life would honour the republic no less than he had honoured the army he had once served. Machiavelli put *virtu* at the heart of the political life of his ideal republic. *Virtu* in his writings means strong will and conduct in a crisis. It denotes force of will, inner strength and resolution, above all the courage to commit forces to war and see it through to a successful conclusion.[4]

Machiavelli never used the term 'civil society' but that is what he meant when he defined civic humanism as republican rather than monarchical in nature. For the 'democratic' element in a republican constitution made available resources of manpower and morale which allowed the state to expand its borders and engage its neighbours in battle. His belief in the democratic element was important, for it suggested that military success was based on institutional rather than moral forces, contrary to the view of most writers in the ancient world. A disciplined society at home (a society in which the state and citizen recognised obligations to each other) was one that could put a formidable fighting force into the field.

Hegel and war as a vocation

By the time Clausewitz superseded Machiavelli as required reading in the military academies and staff colleges of Europe, another writer had stolen upon the scene as the most perceptive commentator of civic discipline. Hegel was one of the few philosophers to write about war as a social activity and he took Machiavelli's endorsement of social courage much further because he was writing about the modern, not pre-modern state.

Heroism was no longer the virtue of a feudal class, or the prerogative of the warrior at arms. With the birth of the nation state, courage had become a social phenomenon. 'The true courage of civilised states,' Hegel wrote in *The Philosophy of Right*, 'is the readiness to sacrifice in the service of the state so that the individual counts as only one amongst many.'[5]

War exists, Hegel contended, not because of man's inability to conceive the principles of a peaceful society but because the warrior is a man who has adopted a particular strategy in experiencing the external world. The warrior, in other words, is a specific human type who realises the nature of his own freedom through courage. War was the way by which the warrior apprehended himself as a free agent.[6] Courage, however, has a social as well as an individual value. War confronts the individual with death, it is true, but in teaching him the contingency of life it also teaches him the importance of the social in life. Social life does not come to an end when an individual dies. Society continues. Sacrifice is never in vain if it is made for, or on behalf of, one's fellow citizens.

What had changed by the nineteenth century was that a personal vocation had turned into a professional one. The warrior's courage was manifest in his willingness to sacrifice himself for the greater good of all. In the professional ethos of the nineteenth-century army Hegel saw something specifically modern. War was now waged, not by feudal retainers of the king or rapacious mercenaries who hired themselves out to the highest bidder, but by professional soldiers who saw themselves for the first time as public servants. The warrior no longer pursued his own financial interests, or served the particularist interests of a feudal master often in conflict with the state (the Crown); he now served society. War forced the citizen to recognise that his private world of family, marriage and property existed only because they were guaranteed by civil society. War forced the soldier to experience the responsibilities of citizenship for the first time – indeed, that was one of the decisive factors which made nineteenth-century warfare 'modern'.[7]

Looked at another way, and to use a language with which we are more familiar today, we might say that professional armies had moved from having a contract with a feudal master or the Crown to a covenant with society. Social contracts produce governments, nations and centralised power: they are the basis of all political society. A covenant, by comparison, produces families, communities and traditions. It is the basis of civil society. The two forms of association are maintained in different ways: a contract by external threat if it is broken and a covenant by internalised identity, loyalty, obligation and responsibility. What makes a covenant more 'virtuous' than a contract is that it is *unconditional*. Contracts are bilateral and are based on terms. They are enforced by penalties. Their conditions precede agreement. Covenants, by contrast, tend to be open-ended. What Hegel saw in the modern soldier was a man with a vocation, not a job. If one speaks of soldiering as a profession, then the soldier is a profess-or, someone who professes a vocation.[8]

Nietzsche and the masses as a military caste

Much of Hegel's writing is obscure and obscured by the persistence with which his Anglo-American critics, in particular, have misinterpreted his writings, claiming that they sanctioned nationalism, or militarism, or both. Hegel approved of neither. He was honest enough, however, to recognise that wars would only come to an end when society had no need of them. War would only be discredited in a *post-heroic* age.

It was Nietzsche's personal misfortune to believe that he lived at just such a time. He quite often wrote about war in his writings and he did so specifically in protest at a phenomenon of which Hegel himself would not have approved: the rise of mass conscript armies in the late nineteenth century.

In the modern European polity the military became an important force in the life of the citizen. The armed forces were one of the central features of the political communities described by the theorists of the modern state such as Hegel, Max Weber and Carl Schmitt. The extent of the militarisation of western societies at the turn of the century is still difficult to grasp or even convey. With industrialisation the tactical formations and tactics of war also changed. It is still disputed which was more influential: the development of the modern industrial state or the modern conscript army. But the impact of military discipline was all-pervasive. It was the ideal model for schools when education became compulsory in the late nineteenth century. Schools were compared to factories. This analogy came in two versions. One, less soul-destroying, was that schools were factories and children workers; the other was that schools were factories and that children were the raw material to be transformed into finished products as their industrial masters saw fit.

But it could also be argued that industrialisation made conscription possible. The assembly line demanded uniformity. The conditions of factory life legislated against unsynchronised individuality. The regimentation of industrial life led the workers naturally into the regiments which were sent into battle twice in the two world wars.

Nietzsche recognised these developments very clearly. He disapproved of conscription for three reasons. First, he was deeply sceptical about the value of taking citizens out of their natural trades or professions and turning them into soldiers. 'Year in and year out the ablest, strongest and most industrious men are taken in extraordinary numbers from their own occupations and professions in order to become soldiers.'[9] The result was not only to diminish them as individuals (to brutalise them during their compulsory service in the ranks), but also to sap the moral vigour of the society from which they were requisitioned. For the process not only devalued the life of the soldier; it also militarised civilian life.

Second, it was the devaluation of military life that concerned him even more. War could only be a life-enhancing activity if the warrior remained true to a military code. That code could not survive the state's increasing inclination to apply civilian values to a largely civilian force – especially its tendency to draw up a balance sheet of profit and loss, to quantify military performance, to weigh up the list of casualties, to make war a matter of calculation. Nor could it survive an age in which soldiers became technicians. Even the German Army, he lamented, the best in Europe, was no longer representative 'of the kind of people who alone matter: I mean those who are heroic'.[10] Long before the First World War confirmed his prognosis that there would be no place for the warrior ethos on the industrialised battlefield of the future, Nietzsche's prophet Zarathustra complained, 'I see many soldiers, would that I saw many warriors'.[11]

Third, in making the whole of society into an army conscription redefined heroism itself. For it was now increasingly judged by whether entire societies could stand up to attritional blows – like the allied naval blockade of Germany in the First World War and the aerial bombing campaign of the Second. Ultimately, the problem with conscription was that it tended to debase courage as a virtue once it was no longer *freely* chosen. In industrialised warfare courage was often devoid of purpose. It was unwilled.

Acts of heroism, displays of courage, even martyrdom – all essential to war as an experience – frequently went unnoticed. Courage also became passive rather than active and increasingly associated with victimhood. From a quality attributed to those who courted danger it became associated with individuals who passively exhibited stoic endurance in face of extreme circumstances. Inevitably, the soldier and citizens both became passive victims rather than active heroes.

Courage was still important in war: the narratives of both world wars are full of heroic acts. But increasingly the courage which is extolled is not that incurred in acts against the enemy – in hand-to-hand fighting, or assaults on heavily defended lines; the courage is the stoicism of men under fire, of bravery shown in rescuing comrades in the field, or of pockets of men fighting on when all is lost. Courage was still possible, but the *ideal* of courage was not.

In the Platonic state death in battle was honoured when it helped preserve a polity in which virtue was cultivated. But death was not loved for its own sake. As the allied armies closed in on Berlin in 1944 to 1945 the Third Reich made war life-denying not life-affirming, and thus trivialised war itself. Virtue was nothing; sacrifice everything. What is so remarkable, of course, looking back, is the extent of the German people's capacity for self-sacrifice. In the last eighteen months of the war when it must have been clear to most that the war was lost, they still fought on to the very end. Their nerve did not crack until the Red Army finally hoisted the red flag over the Reichstag building in Berlin. After the July plot in 1944 (when some of the generals tried belatedly to remove Hitler from the scene and arrive at a compromise peace) the statistics tell their own story: 2.8 million German soldiers died before July 1944; 4.8 million million died after it. The figures are even more dramatic if we add the civilian population. Before the coup, 1588 German citizens were killed every day. After the coup, the death-toll ran to 16,641, nearly ten times as many. And, of course, some of the greatest German cities, especially Berlin and Dresden, were destroyed after the coup, not before.

Germany's war effort was a remarkable example of civil courage but it was also the last time the German people were able to fight a war on such terms. The July plot itself led to the eradication of the Prussian military caste at Hitler's hands, and he did a far more thorough job of destroying it than the allied powers would have done. The post-war German state devoted itself to winning back the world's respect on the assembly line not the battlefield, and much though its young radicals in the 1960s might complain that it had become an *Ersatz Vaterland*, a society devoted to material consumption, even they had little interest in living history on more 'heroic' terms. The same was true of the Japanese, another martial people who embraced the path to economic regeneration of the nation after the war as the focus of a national will to power.

The end of the virtuous state

To understand why social courage of the kind we are discussing had been devalued we must turn once again to Hegel. We find an explanation in one of the most disputed phrases in the Hegelian lexicon: 'What is real is rational and what is rational is real.' The phrase appears in the Preface to Hegel's textbook on politics *The Philosophy of Right*. The term 'real' in his logic plays on the implicit meaning he attached to the word. What is real is also that which is often thought 'necessary', and what is necessary in his work is whatever promotes freedom. His very conception of history and its long development over the centuries was about human freedom or self-realisation and the increase in human self-worth.

In terms of language we often say the chance to realise our true potential, or to improve our position in life, presents us with a 'real opportunity', meaning that it offers us a chance for self-fulfilment. For Hegel the very 'real' aspects of war were those which contributed to human freedom. War became 'unreal' when it undermined human self-worth. Writing when he did, he believed that war could be creative; that it could reinforce civil society by uniting the citizens in a common purpose; that it could fashion a nation state as the Germans succeeded in doing in the mid-nineteenth century and so many others in the century that followed. Ultimately, he believed that war could also promote human rights and values.

The nuclear age made a nonsense of all this, of course, at which point war became 'unreal'. Increasingly it threatened human existence. It locked societies into a nuclear trap from which they could not escape. It also made a nonsense of history: that things did *not* happen after all was the logic of nuclear deterrence.

This brings me to another Hegelian concept: 'the cunning of reason'. When nations or historical epochs are born they are free of contradictions. The contradiction between the freedom of mankind (World Spirit) and a particular social structure (such as the nation state, or in this case modern war) is not in evidence. Spirit and 'the spirit of the age' (*Zeitgeist*) are at one. But when the 'objective' world that exists and persists in a particular custom or law, or way of conducting war, grows old, it ceases to represent the full potential for reason that has developed among its citizens. Within society people begin to question whether their own social formations are rational or merely accidental, contingent or irrational. This is what happened to modern warfare. Social courage had become irrational and self-defeating. By 1945 it had ceased to be rational or, in Hegel's word, 'real'.[12]

At the same time Hegel tells us that while the more far-sighted citizens look to the future for an alternative way of organising life, others through selfishness, unbounded passion or egotistic interest tear the old order to pieces. They do so, however, as the unconscious agents of History. This is an example of the 'cunning of reason' which not only uses the positive search for a new rationality to destroy the old order but also makes use of the more base materials that lie to hand.

The two atom bombs that were dropped on Hiroshima and Nagasaki, writes David MacGregor, are an excellent example of the cunning of reason at work. The scientists who built them did so to pre-empt Germany from developing the bomb. When it became clear that the war in Europe would end before the first bomb could be tested, the government decided to use it instead against Japan (to the dismay of most of the scientists themselves). After Hiroshima a second bomb was dropped on Nagasaki. There is a long historical debate about whether the United States needed to drop a second bomb at all, or whether Japan was already near to surrendering. Some historians have long argued that Truman dropped the bomb on Nagasaki to signal to the Russians – the emerging enemy in the wings – that America was the more powerful of the two countries.

Whatever the reason, the Superpowers soon found themselves in a nuclear stand-off which preserved the world from catastrophe while history moved on. The bombing of Japan, writes E.L. Doctorow:

> can be seen in this light as a kind of *inoculation*, and while this hypo-thetical benefit of the bombings cannot acquit those who ordered them of their moral responsibility for sufferings that were all too real, it does at best suggest those sufferings were not in vain.[13]

Hegel might well have read into the bombing of Hiroshima an example of the cunning of reason: the atomic scientists effectively discredited modern warfare at the very moment of the allies' greatest success. 'Hiroshima opened the age of nuclear war,' writes MacGregor; 'hopefully Nagasaki sealed it?'[14] Perhaps, perhaps not. But we know one thing. As one of the characters in Don DeLillo's novel *End Zone* remarks: 'Nagasaki was an embarrassment to the art of war ... I think what'll happen in the not-too-distant future is that we will have humane wars.'[15]

At Nagasaki the West was forced to stand back from the way of warfare it had perfected. It was forced, as Hegel would have put it, to look the negative in the face and tarry with it. It was forced to put man back into the picture as the subject not object of history. In so doing it devalued war as a social experience by rendering courage redundant or 'unreal'. Well before the end of the Cold War the western world set out to revalue war, by making it more humane for its own citizens. Not only did it demo-bilise them as citizen soldiers, in effect standing them down; it also set out to remove the need for social courage.

The risk society

> The natural role of twentieth century man is anxiety.
> (Gen. Cummings in Norman Mailer, *The Naked and the Dead*)

Traditionally, social courage has been defined in two ways. One is passive endurance in the face of adversity, the willingness to continue fighting despite setbacks and defeats. Perhaps one of the best definitions of courage of this kind was given by Artur Schopenhauer in an essay on the subject of ethics:

> Courage . . . implies that one is willing to face a present evil so as to prevent a greater evil in the future, while cowardice does the reverse. Now the nature of *endurance* is similar to that ascribed to courage, for endurance consists precisely in the clear consciousness that there exist greater evils than those present at the moment but that in seeking to escape or prevent the latter one might call down the former. Courage would consequently be a kind of *endurance*; and since it is endurance which gives us the capacity for self-denial and self-overcoming of any kind, courage too is, through it, at any rate related to virtue.[16]

The virtuous state knew endurance; indeed, its ability to endure was remarkable in the first half of the twentieth century as one war seemed to be followed by the next, often against the same enemy in different forms: Imperial Germany and the Third Reich, the Russian Empire and the USSR. The citizen was told he would have to endure long-term sacrifice if the next generation was to escape a worse fate in the future. That is what Churchill meant in 1940 when he told the British people that, even if their empire were to survive another thousand years, the struggle in which they were engaged would be their 'finest hour'. This is what Hitler meant when he told General von Paulus that the future of the Thousand Year Reich depended on the successful defence of Stalingrad. The present was the moment in which the future was being secured.

A second definition of courage is an active determination to go to war because of one's first principles; we call this the courage of one's convictions. One of the ironies of modern warfare was that despite its inhumanity societies displayed both kinds of courage. One of the ironies of humane warfare is that our societies seem deficient in both cases. Today, the West is becoming increasingly risk averse and less willing than ever to court the risks war entails. Yet in every field of life – including war – we are becoming more *anxious*.

One of the first writers to address this phenomenon back in the 1970s was the chemist and Holocaust survivor, Primo Levi. What he described was the rise of what sociologists have come to describe as the 'risk' society. What he identified in his own country (Italy) was a society afflicted by a general 'malaise'. The very word, he added, seemed at first glance to be a curious, even ironic term to use of a country which was one of the most materially prosperous societies in history. Yet though ironic it seemed particularly apt.

For by the late twentieth century most western European societies no longer feared war, interstate or civil. Their citizens did not even fear illness or infant mortality. They were more prosperous than they had ever been before. Yet they appeared to be more anxious, even if their anxiety was often shapeless. What made it shapeless (and for that reason all the more pervasive) was that they were more anxious about risks they had never experienced before. Their fears were 'mathematical': the product of expected damage multiplied by the probability that it would take place. What distinguished their anxiety most was that they lacked the only instrument which would help them estimate the probability of a future event: the count of how many times and under which circumstances it had taken place in the past.

> If we are logical we would resign ourselves to the evidence that our fate is beyond human knowledge, that every conjecture is arbitrary and demonstrably devoid of foundation. But men are rarely logical when their own fate is at stake; on every occasion they prefer the extreme position.

To Levi, his fellow citizens seemed more credulous than ever when it came to assessing the risks of contemporary life. Free from material need, they were not free from fear about the extreme unknowability of the future.[17]

Since Levi's own death in 1987 western societies have become even more risk averse than ever. Risk assessment and risk management when they first appeared in the 1970s were prompted by public disquiet about hazardous technologies. The risk calculus now used in every walk of life has become part of political culture too. The prevention of risk is becoming the chief principle of administration. The precautionary principle which emerged in the sphere of environmental management has gradually extended to other areas of social life.

We live, writes the sociologist Ulrich Beck, in 'risk societies'. Perceived and actual threats are challenging the version of 'the good life' around which modernity's vision of the future was constructed. What distinguishes post-modern society (as Levi recognised) is our success: our *material security*. We have turned our back on the scarcity societies of the past. The problem of overweight now takes the place of hunger. We expect to live twenty years longer but our anxieties about health have increased enormously. We may be living in what sociologists call a post-materialist age but we have witnessed an exponential rise in the number of material hazards we face.[18]

The same is true of our material success in industry which has created problems in the environment. Ecological disaster threatens everyone. What happens when extensive areas of the rain forests of the Amazon burn-down threatens the ozone layer on which we all depend. The small amounts of ultraviolet light that get through the atmosphere are the main cause of skin cancers which have been fast increasing. The incidence of melanoma, the most dangerous, increased by 80 per cent in the United States during the 1980s. Ultraviolet light also suppresses the immune system, helping cancers to become established and increasing our susceptibility to other diseases. And ultraviolet light is most dangerous for people with light skin.[19]

In addition, one of the problems of contemporary life is that those hazards have become more unpredictable than ever. In the past they were largely perceptible: we could see insanitary conditions for ourselves, and localised areas where we were at risk. Today, the risks are global, implicit in industrialisation and largely unseen. The hazard may not even take effect in our lifetime. One of the most poignant covers of *Time* was of the children of Gulf War veterans who had suffered genetic defects as a result of their fathers' exposure to chemical agents on the battlefield. The article which accompanied the photographs was called 'The tiny victims of Desert Storm'. That is the problem. In future, soldiers may survive a campaign; their children may not.[20]

As a result of the latency of contamination or certain illnesses we are also increasingly reliant on experts. We are made aware of risks from non-cognitive sources such as expert reports, commissions set up by governments, or even newspaper articles. We do not see the risks we run, we read about them. We are becoming dependent on external knowledge. In the process we are losing part of our cognitive sovereignty: we can no longer judge for ourselves the risks we run. In the language of the hour, we feel increasingly disempowered.

Many of these themes were captured by the novelist Don Delillo in his prize-winning novel *White Noise*. Published in 1984, the book is a critical analysis of our risk-aversive times. 'White noise' is a scientific term that refers to a band of wavelengths of sound that mask all other wavelengths within a specific range. To the human ear, white noise sounds like a monotone hum, and is often used to drown out unwanted external noise. Delillo employs the title to establish a correlation between the masking function of white noise and the way technology shapes our lives, threatening us with increased vulnerability.

The larger purpose of the novel is to raise the reader's awareness of the dangers posed by technological take-over. As we become more and more dependent on technology so we have to face the incalculable consequences or side effects of the world we find ourselves inhabiting. If something goes wrong, ascertaining the source of the breakdown can prove difficult. DeLillo demonstrates this threat with one of the novel's most compelling scenes: the evacuation of an elementary school attended by the son of the novel's chief protagonist:

> They had to evacuate the grade school on Tuesday. Kids were getting headaches and eye irritations, tasting metal in their mouths. A teacher rolled on the floor and spoke foreign languages. No one knew what was wrong. Investigators said it could be the ventilating system, the paint or varnish, the foam insulation, the electrical insulation, the cafeteria food, the rays emitted by microcomputers, the asbestos fireproofing, the adhesive on shipping containers, the fumes from the chlorinated pool, or perhaps something deeper, finer-grained, more closely woven into the basic state of things.

Denise and Steffi stayed home that week as men in Mylex suits and respirator masks made systematic sweeps of the building with infra-red detecting and measuring equipment. Because Mylex is itself a suspect material, the results tended to be ambiguous and a second round of more rigorous detection had to be scheduled.[21]

DeLillo graphically captures the defining anxiety of the age: what makes us even more anxious than ever is the fact that the risk is all the greater because it has not yet occurred. Our anxiety stems from calculating damage into the future and multiplying the risks we face in our own imagination.

> The men in Mylex suits moved with a lunar caution. Each step was the exercise of some anxiety not provided for by instinct. Fire and explosion were not the inherent dangers here. This death would penetrate, seep into the genes, show itself in bodies not yet born. They moved as in a swale of moon dust . . . trapped in the idea of the nature of time.[22]

As Levi tells us, the concept of risk involves anticipating a catastrophe that has yet to happen. Risk management signifies a future to be prevented, if we can. We are all the more anxious for predicting hazards which, should they occur, could mean destruction on such a scale that any remedial action would be just that: remedial.

In short, the centre of risk consciousness lies not in the present but in the future. In the process, the past loses the power to determine the present. Instead, we are always looking forward. We are always speculating about something that is fictive, non-existent, even invented, but none the less very real. We become active today in order to prevent a future we would not wish to experience, particularly in old age. We are obsessed with projecting the consequences of our present actions. 'Consequence management' is becoming an important factor in the thinking of the US military. The relevance, and even importance of these variables, of course, is directly proportional to their unpredictability.

Yet what is most astonishing about our risk societies is that we are deeply schizophrenic. On the one hand, we project our fears into the future; on the other we seem at times to be wantonly indifferent to the consequences of our own actions. We live for the moment. No one knows the effects on the environment of the plutonium we will leave the next generation to clean up. No one knows the full impact on the ozone layer of the production of carbon chlorofluoride. At the same time, we may be exaggerating the threats of both because of the ahistoricity of our thinking. We tend to assume that what is true for us must also be true for the next generation, and even the generation after that. We have lost our sense of perspective because we are not really interested in the past which can be the only guide to the future.

This is not a new phenomenon. Back in the 1930s Huxley painted a particularly graphic picture of a neo-Pavlovian society whose members are incapable of feeling unhappy because they live entirely for the present. Children can take the drug 'soma' to make them forget the past and to discharge them from having to think about the future. 'Was and will make me ill; take a gram [of soma] and only am.' In our brave post-modern world we have no past to refer back to for the new technologies have no precursors. We no longer commune with the past; we live only for ourselves. But we still fear the future, and in real life there is no magic drug to block it out.[23]

Risk-aversive war

Our civilian societies are in the business of managing risks – a factor not unrelated to the information societies western states have become. For risks are a consequence of late modernisation; they can be managed but not eliminated. Distributional conflicts over 'goods' such as income, jobs and social security (the traditional agenda of modern politics) have given way to distributional conflicts over 'bads'; that is, the risks created by advances in technology (chemical and nuclear), genetic research, the threat to the environment. Politics is about the control and prevention of such risks. Society is risk aversive, and the same is true of how our politicians conduct war. War is no longer used to advance 'goods' (constructing a new world order, putting a new regional security system in place) but managing 'bads' (nuclear proliferation, terrorism). Generals are no longer asked to produce security, but to manage insecurity. War too has become *risk averse*.

The risks that are dealt with are selective, of course, but they apply to larger groups of people. The risk of nuclear proliferation or ethnic cleansing is not restricted to the Middle East or eastern Europe; it extends across the globe. Dangerous countries are now designated members of 'risk groups', and these are under constant surveillance by satellite. As a result war is fought not to remove regimes from power, or defeat their armies in a decisive battle, but to reduce the opportunities for bad behaviour, to prevent them from posing an even greater risk in the future.

A similar strategy is applied to criminals in the United States. It is called 'situational crime prevention'. The management of crime is focused on dealing with individual criminals, not the causes of crime. Criminal behaviour is controlled by altering the environment of crime and reducing opportunities for it in the future. The focus is the prevention of crime, not the punishment and rehabilitation of offenders.[24] These strategies are also intended to reduce the risks to the law enforcers. It is called 'the new prudentialism'. The strategies are pursued to reduce the risks for the police.

The management style of risk-aversive warfare is dictated by the profile of the risk societies that now make up the western community. Humanity requires distance to be put between the soldiers and pilots and their targets.

The style is one of containment and confinement and dissuasion. As battle is 'unprudential' it is best avoided not because the outcome is necessarily in doubt but because in all battles the costs of success are unpredictable for the individual soldier.

It is not the future, however, but the past which offers us the best insight into risk-aversive war. In the eighteenth century campaigns were designed to manage risks – not so much to defeat as to outmanoeuvre the enemy, to exhaust him or wear him down. An emphasis was put on minimising bloodshed, the reason being that society had no other alternative. There were many explanations for this excessive caution. I intend to look at three which have some relevance to our own risk-aversive age.

Desertion

Eighteenth-century armies were small and plagued by desertions. Both made decisive wars difficult to fight. Frederick the Great began his book *The General Principles of War* (1748) with fourteen different rules to prevent desertion. Unless they were strictly adhered to, he warned his readers, a commander could expect his army to slowly haemorrhage away as men sought to return to their farms to harvest the crops on which their families depended. Frederick knew all about desertion. At the battle of Molwicz a few years before, his first baptism of fire, he fled from the battlefield in a moment of panic. Encountering a group of officers in the rear he asked defiantly, 'Have you seen any deserters?', to which one of them replied (safe in the knowledge that Frederick was an enlightened King, not a tyrant), 'No, sire. You are the first.'

Western armies, of course, do not face that problem but they still have to husband their human resources. Public support for a campaign cannot be taken for granted even if it meets – at the beginning – with broad public support. When it does not, even a single incident can have devastating consequences. Public opinion will not tolerate large casualties, a problem compounded by the fact that the demographic core from which western armies recruit their volunteers is getting smaller: the citizens will not fight. It is the public today that tends to desert, to insist that forces be pulled out when eighteen soldiers are killed in a fire fight in Mogadishu, or 241 marines are destroyed by a car bomb in a single evening in Beirut.

That is one reason why long-range, stand-off missiles utilising advanced information-processing systems are the weapons of first resort. In Kosovo 14,006 of the 37,465 sorties flown were intended to strike and suppress enemy air defences, to deny Serbian radar stations the information on the whereabouts and number of allied aircraft. Even then the extreme political sensitivity of post-heroic, risk-averse societies to casualties dictated that NATO pilots had to fly at 15,000 feet to minimise the chances of being shot down. Inevitably this led to errors (such as mistaking a refugee column for a Serb armour on the Djakovica road). More important still from the perspective not of 'perception management' but actually winning the war, the Serbs were able to fool NATO planes most of the time and ensure the survival of all but twenty-six of their tanks.

During the war, commentators frequently contrasted NATO's overwhelming strength with its apparently underwhelming commitment to victory, a fact that led to divided councils within the military themselves. Win it, NATO eventually did, but the balance of informed opinion concludes that the outcome was due more to diplomacy than the air war and the threat of a land campaign which might indeed have involved substantial casualties on the ground which the allies were desperately anxious to avoid.

Saving money

Eighteenth-century governments also recognised that the threat of desertion was not the only explanation for why war tended to be limited. The governments of the day were also anxious to save money. They could not afford to spend much or to tax their citizens unduly, still less to borrow and thereby run up unsustainable public debts.

The important principle was to conserve the lives of their men, not risk them in battle, in order that the same army (or one substantially the same) could be fielded the following year. One of the main reasons why the English government refused to countenance the Duke of Marlborough's plans for invading France was that his final battle – Malplaquet (1709) – was the bloodiest of the century: the allies lost a quarter of the army. The loss persuaded the English to negotiate a compromise peace rather than seek to dictate peace terms from Paris.

The object of going to war was not to engage the enemy in a decisive battle; that is, weakening or destroying the armed forces of the enemy to such an extent that organised military resistance was no longer possible. This could be achieved only if one side committed the bulk of its forces and if the military on the other side had the resources and will to follow up and take full advantage of the enemy's temporary weakness. Since eighteenth-century armies were so small they went in for the exhaustion not annihilation of their enemies, a gradual deterioration in the strategic balance which led to a negotiated peace. They tried to discourage the enemy from continuing operations, by fortifying fixed positions and so discouraging him from advancing. If the enemy did attack, the object was to draw the offensive army into a long and inconclusive siege. In the eighteenth century when the system of frontier fortifications reached its apogee, it resulted in the construction of elaborate systems of tunnels and trenches which were themselves major construction projects that rivalled in complexity the forts they surrounded. A successful siege might take months.

The air wars against Slobodan Milosevic and Saddam Hussein can be seen in terms similar to the investment of a fortress. The United States and Britain have effectively been at war with Iraq since 1990. NATO has effectively been at war with Serbia since 1994 when its planes first engaged in dogfights with the Serbian Air Force. Averaged out, President Clinton launched a cruise missile every three days of his term of office.

Between December 1998 and August 1999 the British and American Air Forces operating combat patrols in the northern and southern no-fly zones in Iraq faced more than 300 direct threats either from surface to air missiles or anti-aircraft artillery. There were also 200 infringements of the zones by Iraqi aircraft. During that period allied aircraft fired more than 1000 missiles at about 360 targets. Iraq's score against the coalition aircraft was zero, largely because the allied planes flew at 15,000 feet and thus had time to evade the missiles. Such operations are extensive, but they are attritional, and likely to remain inconclusive. All that air power can do is to contain a problem, not solve it. And since there is no end to enemy stereotyping, even if specific enemies themselves may be removed, since there is no end in sight to nuclear proliferation, ethnic cleansing or state-sponsored terrorism, siege warfare will probably continue well into the future.

One of the principal reasons why societies engage in siege warfare today is that they cannot tax their citizens as they once did. Nor can they print money, as the United States did in Vietnam, given the anti-inflationary economic strategies which are at the heart of modern economic planning. The shareholders have spent the peace dividend for the Cold War and have little enough money left for reinvestment except in technology. Nearly every society has seen defence spending reduced by around 40 per cent of Gross Domestic Product. Governments are also fast running out of soldiers. Manpower levels have been reduced by 25 per cent in the past ten years. Even in the United States, defence spending has shifted away from ground force to technology with the result that American forces have become increasingly weak on the ground. US Army active-duty divisions have been reduced from eighteen to ten, the lowest number since 1950. There are fewer infantry battalions than at any time since 1938 and ammunition stocks for the army and marines are nearly $2 billion under war requirements. In Britain, army strength is at its lowest since the last peace dividend at the end of the Napoleonic Wars when Wellington's veterans returned from Waterloo.

As military service is increasingly devalued by society, so the soldiers can read the runes for themselves. As more cuts are in the offing so they are leaving in larger numbers than ever. In 1999 the British Army was losing 120 trained men and women a month, an annual loss of 1444 of the most valuable personnel, the equivalent of two infantry battalions. The government announced some measures to staunch the outflow such as bonuses, incentive schemes and long release periods after unaccompanied and arduous deployments abroad, but these were stopgap measures which did little to increase morale. In the unresolved trade-off between technology and manpower, manpower has lost out.

Coalition warfare

Another feature of eighteenth-century warfare was the fact that nearly all conflicts involved opposing coalitions, and the problem with that was divided commands. It gave politicians an overdue influence in the micro-management of the battlefield. A decision to attack was often taken at home. and it could be a matter of days or weeks before it was communicated to the commanders in the field. Politicians tended to take decisions in the light of political calculations: the cost of prolonging a campaign or incurring even greater casualties. And the commanders themselves were politicians: they too were engaged in a calculus of costs and commitments to forestall campaigns from being cancelled or postponed.

In the absence of a strong ideological motivation to win or prevail, and given the small number of troops under their command, they were always wary of acting in a way which would ground campaigns. Coalition commanders were usually unwilling to seek a decisive encounter with an opposing military force. When in doubt they were inclined to demur.

The Kosovo War was unusual in that it involved an alliance of like-minded states bound closely together by their beliefs in liberal, and in this case humanitarian, principles. But if the war against Serbia did not find the allies deeply divided over ends, it found them divided over means. Those powers most in favour of the air war (Denmark and The Netherlands) were most opposed to a land campaign; and American public support for what was largely a US-led and run war was lukewarm to say the least.

The problem about eighteenth-century coalition warfare is that the allies could never agree on victory and, more to the point, on the cost of it, and therefore usually left conflicts unresolved. The problem, writes Robert Cooper, a British Foreign Office official, is the way western societies choose to fight their wars. Victory can no longer be an obtainable goal. For victory would mean empire, which is unacceptable, though NATO seems for the moment to be saddled with it in the Balkans.[25] The intermittent use of force, the pre-emptive attack or what he calls 'the rougher methods of an earlier era' are to be preferred. Even if coalitions could agree on ends they have difficulty agreeing on means. Humane warfare because it is risk averse does not allow a dialectic of victory and defeat. It seeks to ensure the temporary suspension of an opponent's will to fight in contrast to the destruction of a regime, or its territory, or its unconditional surrender. In the case of Kosovo, NATO achieved a military technical agreement whereby Serb soldiers withdrew from the province and coalition troops assumed a military presence on the ground whilst a trans-organisational administration was put in place to deal with functionally separated sectors of activity on a territory whose juridical status was left technically undefined.

The pattern of eighteenth-century warfare reflected the realities of eighteenth-century society. They were not societies in which social courage was demanded of the main citizen body, a fact which led commentators like Hegel to see Napoleonic warfare as distinctive and praiseworthy for that reason. Our idea of war as 'risk-management strategy with missiles' reflects our own social order and it is deeply worrying for that reason. History, of course, does not repeat itself, but it does rhyme. As T.S. Eliot wrote in 'The Dry Salvages' (the third of his *Four Quartets*): 'we had the experience but missed the meaning and approach to the meaning restores the experience in a different form.'[26] In war the central difference, of course, is the humane element. European armies 300 years ago were not renowned for their humanity, but at least they had achievements to show for their efforts.

Stress-free war

It would be much too premature, however, to suppose that we have really made courage redundant, and thus warfare humane for the soldiers who still fight it. When it came to the Cold War the modern world got off lightly. The ultimate inhumanity – a nuclear war – was always a remote threat, or one so appalling in its consequences that it was not worth worrying about it. It was better to live in a state of denial. Nuclear weapons themselves were too unpredictable and dangerous to use. It also counted for much that two Superpowers subscribed to ideologies of hope. They knew that war was no longer a historical shortcut; it was a historical endgame. Provided they prevented war from breaking out, both were confident that the market or the historical dialectic would deliver final victory. Capitalists and communists together both looked to the future with confidence.

However, what was true of the industrial powers is not true of others today. Instead we live in a world in which nuclear powers are proliferating at an alarming rate, and many of them will have the technology in a few years', time to target the West. Some of the countries which have weapons of mass destruction, like North Korea and Pakistan, can hardly face the future with confidence. Nor is the nuclear order managed by the established powers as it once was. The world is plagued by nuclear smugglers and deraciné nuclear physicists from the ex-Soviet Union who are both ready and willing to sell their expertise to the highest bidder.

In war, as in civilian life, technology has expanded exponentially like a recursive virus. The proliferation of high-tech weaponry and cutting-edge communications technology and their availability in the global market means than any person or country can now become a military power. In world arms markets vast weapons stockpiles are available virtually for the asking. Short-range ballistic missiles and information technologies have become commodities which enable new military powers to emerge extremely rapidly. Gary Stix sums up the dangerous situation faced by the western powers resulting from their own technological achievements:

Policy experts, technical gurus and defence contractors have begun to study a range of other potential threats, from a newly hatched super-power to a regional power with dramatically altered fighting tactics, to legions of mercenary hackers that bring down banks and stock exchanges with computer viruses and other malevolent software. The vast array of scenarios is a measure of the speculative turn that has gripped the military-planning establishments. Without the tangible presence of the superpower, new menaces can emerge from any quarter.[27]

Warfare has not only become increasingly technological; it is also becoming increasingly dirty. It is the *asymmetrical* nature of contemporary warfare which makes the use of weapons of mass destruction such as chemicals and biological weapons more likely than their use in the modern age which produced them.

Let me cite three examples of the latter:

1   At least seventy types of bacteria, viruses, rickett-siae and fungi can be weaponised. We can reliably treat no more than twenty to thirty of the diseases they cause.
2   In a simulated attack on New York in 1998 nearly all the members of the emergency unit 'died'. They did all the right things but the extent of the catastrophe defeated them.
3   The anthrax vaccine used in the United States has to be administered six times over an eighteenth-month period before it becomes fully effective and requires annual boosters thereafter.[28]

In a society which puts humanity first, which no longer asks great sacri-fices of its people, how do you react to inhumanity on such a scale? In the next Gulf War, entire societies may have to be vaccinated against chemical or biological threats. The real test of courage will come when an entire population has to be vaccinated, as may happen in ten or fifteen years' time when a number of countries will have the means to deliver a chemical attack on western Europe.

Past experience is not encouraging. In Britain the vaccination programme during the threatened swine flu epidemic in the mid-1970s was a failure. The government urged citizens to be vaccinated but few complied. In the event of a war, vaccinations would have to be compulsory, but how long would it be before the war started, and what would its effect be on national morale? The fact is that our citizens are no better protected against biological or chemical attack than they were when the research programmes began half a century ago. There may now be transgenic strains of disease that nothing can cure, in which case the nightmare millennium may be about to begin. The twenty-first century, like the fourteenth, may have its plagues, although they are likely to be of our own making and much deadlier than the Black Death.

A similarly bleak picture is in store for the military. You can vaccinate soldiers against biological agents, or even reduce anxiety levels with tranquillisers, but you cannot vaccinate them against anxiety itself. Like life in the post-industrial age, war is becoming more stressful not less, and one of the reasons for this is that soldiers now expect to encounter biological or chemical weapons at some point in their careers. A survey of 2500 soldiers in the aftermath of the Gulf War found that, of all their concerns, the fear of chemical and biological weapons was uppermost in their minds.[29]

This is not a new fear; its scale is. Let me quote two voices – one from the past, the other from the present. The first is taken from a fictional account of the man who invented the first chemical weapon, poison gas, that was used in the second year of the Great War. Fritz Harber is not much remembered today but he was one of the most important scientists of his time, and he appears briefly as the Professor in André Malraux's novel, *The Walnut Trees of Altenberg*:

'If you look at it objectively', said the Professor in a voice of authority, 'gas constitutes the most humane method of warfare. The gas, mind you, announces its presence. The opaque cornea first goes blue. The breath starts to come in hisses. The pupil – it is really very odd – becomes almost black. In a word, the enemy is forewarned. Now, if I think I still have a chance, even a faint chance, I am brave. But if I know in my heart of hearts that I haven't, then courage is no use.'[30]

To the officer the Professor is addressing, science has become as much an enemy as the adversary in the field. Malraux's picture of Harber is that of an intellectual who wants to do away with courage, one of the few factors which, even on the industrialised battlefields of the First World War, still made war heroic, if not humane.

The second voice is that of a contemporary journalist Molly Moore who accompanied the US marines in the Gulf War. In one of her most compelling reports from the front there is a description of the symptoms of an anthrax attack given by an instructor to the troops.

'With anthrax the symptoms won't start for two or three days . . . The first thing you will notice are little black dots appearing on your skin. You have hours or maybe only minutes to live at that point. You'll feel like you have a cold congestion. Then you can't breathe. When you're that bad you are probably going to die.'[31]

By the time the instructor had concluded his lecture, Moore recorded that she felt waves of nausea, headaches and lung congestion. Just *anticipating* a chemical attack had produced some of the symptoms.

The explanation for an increasingly pervasive anxiety about war on the eve of battle is to be found – as it is with all other risks – in the extent of our *success* in eliminating material scarcity (as I will argue in the next chapter) but also in confronting critical illness. At the turn of the century most people were at risk from acute illnesses. Forty out of a hundred patients could expect to die from injuries or diseases that required immediate hospitalisation. By 1980 that category constituted only 1 per cent of all causes of mortality. In their place patients began to experience long-term 'conditions'. The proportion of those who died of chronic illness rose from 46 per cent to 80 per cent. Today, by comparison, death tends to be preceded by a long period of illness. The success of medicine discharges people into a condition (or syndrome) which cannot be cured.

Such conditions are made more insupportable still by knowledge of the chronic conditions from which we suffer. In the past patients were largely ignorant; now they know everything. They join professional support groups; they read about their condition in the newspapers and view programmes on television in which it is the subject of endless and often pointless discussion. Such knowledge merely makes the condition worse, and gives rise to an even greater sense of victimisation. The condition, in short, becomes even more chronic. The constant dwelling on one's problems, the remorseless interrogation of oneself, the undermining of one's self-confidence and sense of being merely makes us more anxious than ever.[32]

Something not dissimilar has happened in war. One reason paradoxically why it has become so stressful is the higher rate of survival. The mobile army surgical units of the Korean War popularised by the film *M.A.S.H.* saw the average wait of soldiers for treatment reduced to one-and-a-half hours. Fifty-five per cent of the wounded were hospitalised on the same day they incurred their wounds. In Vietnam, helicopters which were used extensively for the first time enabled wounded soldiers to be hospitalised in under twenty-four hours. Only 2.5 per cent of those who made it to hospital failed to survive. An unprecedented 87 per cent were able to return home.[33]

In the Gulf War, government concern over casualties led to an extraordinary effort to treat soldiers in the field as quickly as possible. About a quarter of all British forces in theatre were medical or medical related. The obverse side of this, however, is that the chance of becoming a psychological casualty has increased exponentially. Overall, 25 per cent of all discharges during the 1914–18 war and between 20 and 50 per cent during the 1939–45 war were labelled 'psychiatric casualties'. Men fighting in Korea were twice as likely to become psychiatric casualties as be killed by enemy fire.[34]

Levels of breakdown in Vietnam, by contrast, were initially surprisingly low because of limited tours of duty, frequent rest periods and the absence of prolonged artillery or air bombardment. Indeed, less than 2 per cent of men *in service* suffered psychiatric breakdown. But of those who returned home – and it is this that makes the conflict so special – at least 54 per cent of veterans experienced Post Traumatic Stress Disorder (PTSD), the favoured term to describe panic attacks, the nightmares and dry dysphoria that takes the joy out of life and makes it difficult to associate with other people. This was also the experience of at least one non-western army. In Israel, 30 per cent of combat casualties in the 1973 Yom Kippur War were psychiatric. During the invasion of the Lebanon eleven years later, three times as many Israeli soldiers were killed than in all the three previous Arab–Israeli wars put together. Despite this fact the number of psychic casualties exceeded the number of dead by 150 per cent.[35]

The Gulf War, however, gave rise to something else quite different. One study found that of 4500 returning US veterans from the Gulf War, 9 per cent were affected by what was soon called Gulf War Syndrome. The figure rose to 34 per cent who reported significant psychological stress in the months immediately following their return. One year later 20 per cent more veterans reported moderate to severe family adjustment problems and 40 per cent cases of marital discord, one of the best measures of adjustment.[36]

Many veterans complained of rashes, fatigue, diarrhoea, chronic coughs, joint pain and memory loss. The military authorities originally thought that they might be the victims of infectious disorders, or exposure to smoke (from the oil wells which were set alight in the last week of the war), or from multiple chemical sensitivity from pre-treatment drugs, including anthrax vaccines, that were given to 150,000 soldiers. Important though the vaccines were, they probably did not reassure the troops. A soldier vaccinated against anthrax stands a greater chance of resisting the disease but the fit between the warfare agent and vaccine must be precise. Novel strains of the disease can nullify the effect. Whatever Gulf War Syndrome is, it is clearly not 'shock' or battle fatigue: it is physiological in origin, even if some of its symptoms are psychological, and as such it represents a disturbing new development.

This is the ultimate challenge facing a world that would like to make war more humane for itself, if not its enemies, that would like to make it less distressing for its soldiers, and for society itself. Will the other side play by the same rules? The rich man's option is to sanitise war; the poor man's is to make it even more horrendous than it is. This is the logic that both are pursuing and it is frightening in its implications for the future.

Indeed, if Saint Beuve is right in his claim that every age has its own special malady, then anxiety is likely to be the particular affliction of tomorrow's warrior. In this respect, Gulf War Syndrome belongs not to the 80,000 cases of shell-shock in the First World War – the casualties of industrialised warfare – but to a post-industrial world haunted by the disasters of Bhopal and Chernobyl, and, closer to home, Selafield and Three Mile Island. In future western armies will have to deal with a variety of new hazards: depleted uranium shells; pesticides; burning oilfields; chemical weapons and vaccines against their use which may even replicate some of the symptoms of the disease. For the infantryman as well as for the society from which he comes, war may become more inhumane, not less, precisely because it may demand even greater courage.

And that goes for society too, for which the ultimate challenge is no less demanding. There is a character in one of Victor Hugo's novels who dies in one of the anonymous barricades of the nineteenth century's many popular uprisings. His dying words are meant to be consoling: 'At least, the twentieth century will be happy.' Events turned out rather differently. In terms of probabilities denied and hopes extinguished, the world was fortunate to survive the twentieth century. Surviving the twenty-first century may require even greater good fortune.

4   War without hatred

'Anything worth living for', said Nately, 'is worth dying for.' 'And anything worth dying for,' answered the sacrilegious old man, 'is certainly worth living for.'

(Joseph Heller, *Catch 22*)[1]

'The Hate had started.' Thus Orwell in *Nineteen Eighty-Four* describes the ritual two-minute hate which the citizens of Oceania in London (renamed Airstrip One) are required to attend. And the man whom the citizens are required to hate is Emanuel Goldstein, the Enemy of the People, the counter-revolutionary who had once been a leading figure in the party. Even Winston Smith, the hero of the novel, the man who is turning against Big Brother, is caught up in the emotion of the hour:

> The horrible thing about the two minutes hate was not that one was obliged to act a part, but that it was impossible to avoid joining it. Within thirty seconds any pretence was always unnecessary ... and yet the rage that one felt was an abstract undirected emotion which could be switched from one object to another like the flame of a blow lamp.[2]

That too was the experience of many people in the twentieth century. The enemy today (the USSR in the 1930s) could become the ally tomorrow (in the Second World War) and the enemy soon after that (the Cold War). An ideological age required an almost visceral, even abstract hatred that could be applied against different countries or beliefs as and when required.

One of the reasons modern war was so inhumane was that hatred was very much part of the face of the modern era. The twentieth century compounded the fault, writes Eric Hobsbawm, in large part because with the Russian Revolution at its very outset, the world was encouraged to think in terms of binary opposites, of such mutually exclusive alternatives as capitalism and socialism.[3] We hated, Orwell wrote, because we knew 'socialism led to concentration camps, leader worship and war; capitalism to dole queues, the scramble for markets and war'.[4] Hating their enemies as they did, the democracies had no more compunction than totalitarian regimes in raining down death and destruction on to the heads of the citizens of the opposing side.

What made hatred in the modern era more terrifying still was the fact that enemies were hated in the abstract. The modern age hated internal and external enemies alike: the bourgeoisie, the malign revolutionary, the irredeemable native. All three, writes Peter Gay in *The Cultivation of Hatred*, the third volume of his classic account of the late Victorian mind, were theories justified by pseudo-scientific discourse. Even in the liberal West politicians contrived to discover great historical life-or-death struggles, whether between Aryans and Semites, whites and blacks, Anglo-Saxons and Celts. Indian-hating, Herman Melville put into the mouth of one of his characters, 'still exists and no doubt will continue to do so as long as Indians do'.[5]

The result was that we tended to demonise our enemies and demand their unconditional surrender. But hatred exacted a terrible price – endless conflict, permanent mobilisation for war, and a state-sanctioned licence to kill. Occasionally people recognised the irony of the situation. In 1942 the poet Robert Lowell found himself in a prison cell next to the Tsar of Murder Incorporated, Meyer Lepke. Lowell had been incarcerated for refusing to be conscripted. 'I am in for killing', Lepke told him. 'What are you in for?' 'I am in for refusing to kill', Lowell replied.[6] Many societies in the modern era seemed to be schizophrenic: they punished those who killed at home, and those who refused to kill abroad.

Our societies have changed profoundly. One of the main changes in the post-modern world is the absence of enemies. *Democracy Without Enemies* is the suggestive title of a book by Ulrich Beck.[7] Even in the democratic world we may still use the language of war in domestic politics. We may still employ terms such as 'going over the top' and 'defeating our enemies' (a language borrowed from the First World War), but the language is wearing thin. Perhaps the western world invests too much faith in the capacity of political will alone to solve the insoluble. Perhaps its conviction that all sides in the global community can co-exist without conflict is touching, if distinctly unfamiliar to the modern understanding of politics. It may owe more to wishful thinking than people are prepared to admit, but western governments appear to understand their nations' mood: there is no appetite for adverserial politics either at home or abroad. It is still possible to demonise enemies like Sadaam Hussein but difficult to insist on their unconditional surrender if this means prosecuting war to the bitter end. Failing to hate its enemies, the West has been singularly maladroit at removing them: Saddam Hussein remains in Baghdad. In short, it is becoming increasingly difficult to be permanently mobilised for battle.

Why no enemies?

> In America's attitude to the prospect of war, there is something deeper at work. Perhaps, the United States is no longer fitted for the part of global power because it now regards death as an unacceptable decline in the American standard of living.
>
> (Frank Johnson, *The Sunday Telegraph*, November 1990)

Most military histories, like most theories of war, present us with no psychologically sophisticated notion of why people fight, and most have little to say about the sociological conditions which predispose people to hate. Orwell was one of the few exceptions. His genius as a writer was to conceive of a society which, on one level, was not entirely unattractive. Although he envisaged a world of great power blocs engaged in a permanent state of war, very few citizens in *Nineteen Eighty-Four* get killed. They may be at war but there is no conscription. The only bombs that fall are dropped by a regime which wants to remind its citizens that there is still a war on.

There is also a social contract between the citizen and the state. There is no unemployment and few oppressive regulations. Indeed there are no laws to speak of at all. There is no inflation and no dole queues. There are cinemas and a state lottery as well as state-produced pornography (supplied by Pornsoc, a department of the Ministry of Truth). There is no racial discrimination either. Goldstein tells us, 'Jews, Negroes, South Americans of pure Indian blood are all to be found in the highest reaches of the party.' Interestingly, the book was published in the same year that baseball was desegregated for the first time in the United States. In Orwell's story the government has even eliminated the old agonies of family conflict. And it is a mark of its charity that in the end it wishes to cure Winston of his madness, not eliminate him or send him to a labour camp.

Orwell paints a picture of a world that, though permanently at war, offers its people some form of social security. Not too much of course, because a people too well-off materially would be disinclined to fight. Material reward, after all, provides people with a good reason for living. They have too much to lose. And a reason for living is also a good reason for not hating as well. It is a good reason for not getting oneself killed. Brecht put it rather well in a diary entry in 1920:

> [People] . . . are prepared to sacrifice everything for spurious, grandiose sounding platitudes. They'll die blissfully in pig sties if only they can be allowed to 'play a part' in the vast opera. But sensible ideas are something nobody cares to die for and even fighting for them is hampered by the possibility of death because people think it is more sensible to live, and you can die for 'nothing' but not for 'something' since it would be nothing if you're dead.[8]

In retrospect, we can see that the modern world had little time for humanity in war in large part, because it was preoccupied with material security.

That world is so far removed from our own that it is difficult to grasp how materially insecure people felt at the turn of the century. In 1900 a majority of Europeans lived in what we would now classify as Third World conditions. In Britain, one person in five could expect a solitary burial in the workhouse, poor law hospital or mental asylum. A quarter of the population lived in absolute poverty, including 40 per cent of all children. Destitution was still the outstanding feature of British life, despite the fact that it was the most industrialised society in the world, with the highest per capita income.

In 1914 very few manual labourers would have been without a neighbour, friend or relative struggling for subsistence. The infant mortality rate was 94:1000 for the middle class but no less than 24 per cent for those living in poverty. One baby in six died in a working-class family. What social researchers discovered at the beginning of the century was the cyclical nature of poverty: the succession of events in the lifetime of an individual working man which were likely to ensnare him at one point or another during his lifetime. One might escape poverty in childhood only to encounter it in childbirth or in old age. The fear of poverty and the insecurity which that fear generated was profound.[9]

It is against this background that we should read books like Ronald Blythe's *Akenfield* (1969), a portrait of an English village through the twentieth century. Even on a cursory reading the willingness to put up with the carnage of the Western Front appears less incomprehensible. Given a background of feudal brutality in the depressed countryside of rural Suffolk, war did not appear to be any more appalling than modern life. It is difficult even now, looking back, to grasp the dehumanising effect of poverty, the psychological wounds and the crippling mentality of resignation it caused, a subjection that was diminished only when people began to awaken to ideas of individual human dignity. As one veteran remembered:

> In my four months training with the regiment I'd put on nearly a stone in weight and got a bit taller. They said it was the food but it was really because for the first time in my life there'd been no strenuous work. I want to say this simply as a fact, the village people in my day were worked to death. It literally happened. It's not a figure of speech. . . . We were all delighted when war broke out on August 4.[10]

The condition of the working classes throughout western Europe was truly dreadful. One million British volunteers and conscripts had to be rejected by the War Board because they were found to be medically unfit to serve. A grim picture was painted by one writer of those who failed to pass muster, those battalions of colourless, stunted, half-toothless men from the hot, humid Lancashire mills: 'their staring faces gargoyles out of the tragical-comical-historical-pastoral edifice of English rural life.'[11] In a letter from the Front another officer wrote that the transformation of the new recruits in six months from stooped, wan, weak individuals to strong, well-fed, clear-eyed soldiers had almost converted him to socialism when he saw what industrialism had done to them.[12]

By the end of the war the soldiers were better fed and clothed. The British soldier in 1918 was served by a vast infrastructure of baths, brothels and canteens, and given long rest breaks behind the lines; he also knew the concept of leisure for the first time in history. For many, the camaraderie of their fellow soldiers, even the excitement of war, were not to be despised, however much they might complain about another aspect of the fighting: dying.

In a very early critique of the war, Virginia Woolf also asserted that what united women behind the war in 1914 was a wish to escape not their material so much as their psychological condition. So profound was their unconscious loathing for the private home with its cruelty, poverty and hypocrisy that they willingly escaped into the munitions factory, the hospital or the fields. They were willing to undertake any work that would improve their psychological condition. The theme of escape is so important in her analysis that she conceded that though more 'pacific' than their brothers or husbands, it would be true to say that women unconsciously desired the war.[13] They certainly gave it their unqualified support once it broke out, not simply filling the jobs they are known to have filled such as nursing and munitions-making but practically every other job as well – actual fighting aside – as spies, constables, messengers, and even chimney-sweeps. As the American journalist Mabel Daggert wrote at the time: 'On August 4 the door of the Doll's House opened. The shot that was fired in Serbia summoned men to their most ancient occupation and women to every other.'[14]

The aftermath of the war nevertheless posed additional problems of poverty for women. They were not emancipated after the First World War, even though they may have gained the vote. Perhaps three million of the nine million soldiers killed in the First World War left a widow behind. Six million children were deprived of their fathers. The war widows faced immense deprivation and poverty, despite the provision of state widows' pensions; and given the reduction in the number of single men, their chances of remarrying were slim.[15]

As late as the 1930s, one-fifth of the population of Britain still lived in conditions which are typical today of a developing country. The change came very suddenly – just before the Second World War. By 1950 it was no longer possible to tell a person's social class from their height. By then the life expectancy of the population was very similar (compared with the turn of the century when the rich could expect to live thirty years longer than the very poor).

Poverty was not the only problem. Material deprivation also bred disease. Prior to 1940 the population of Britain had had to live with the constant threat of illness. In 1900 13,000 people died of measles. Other infectious diseases terrified families with children. Here too a rapid change came about after the Second World War when the effect of sulphonamide drugs first began to be felt, and penicillin began to be widely administered. By 1948 deaths from measles had fallen to 3000; death from diptheria from 7500 to 150, and death from scarlet fever showed a hundredfold fall. Again the change came quite late in the day.[16]

Finally, the risks of childbirth also declined radically. At the beginning of the century the average expectation of life of a woman aged 20 was forty-six years (of which fifteen years were devoted to child-bearing). By 1940 the average life expectancy had risen to fifty-five years, of which only four were devoted to bearing children. The reduction in family size was due, in large part, to contraception and this in turn boosted disposable family income.

Visionaries, of course, had long dreamed of a world in which the basic needs of all would be met and the increasing consumption of material goods would give way to a more human pattern of activities. But it was not until the mid-1940s that the vision finally materialised. John Maynard Keynes, whose economic theories laid much of the foundation for twenty-five years of unprecedented economic prosperity after the Second World War, had hoped that: 'a point may soon be reached, much sooner perhaps than all of us are aware of, when (our absolute) needs are satisfied, in the sense that we prefer to devote our further energies to non-economic purposes.'[17]

Keynes' wish has now been realised. Most citizens of the western world will translate this century into the next feeling more *materially* secure than ever before from the everyday hazards that distinguish life in the developing world. Even though they may think of themselves at risk from the technological and economic forces that shape our world, they can expect to live to 80 (or even longer) – as they do at present in Japan – and they will expect to secure for themselves an agreeable environment in which to live. The difference between feeling secure and insecure is vitally important, for it has led to a shift from 'survival values' to 'well-being' values, to the search not for a more secure life but a *better quality* one.

This new world, writes the American sociologist Ronald Inglehart, is replacing the outlook that once dominated the industrial world. In the process it is transforming the basic norms governing politics, work, religion and family life. It represents, he contends, a later stage of economic development, but it is not a mere consequence of it. It is shaping the socio-economic condition of our world while being shaped by it in turn.[18]

Inglehart's views are important because they are based on a study of observed changes in over forty-three societies over a ten-year period: 1981 to 1990. He has been recording these changes for much longer, ever since he wrote his seminal work *The Silent Revolution* in 1973. What he charts is the emergence of post-material values within a much broader process of political change which is reshaping our political outlooks, gender roles, and even religious affiliations. His research is backed by a number of other studies which have appeared in recent years. They all identify major changes in outlook which stem from a radical improvement in material circumstances.

Political change

With a rise in the material standard of living the function of politics has begun to change. Rising income levels have helped bring about a decline of those great ideological positions which used to determine the high ground of political life. The old economically framed ideologies of Left and Right no longer carry the resonance they once did. The principal change is the disappearance of socialism and conservatism. There remain, to be sure, political parties of which these titles are used, either by the parties themselves or their opponents. But in both Britain and the United States New Right thinking challenges nineteenth-century conservatism in calling into question the competence of public bodies under government supervision including the great professions. It has little time for the paternalism of old. It wants to make every institution responsible for its own future.

Socialism too has lost much of its appeal. In the past it called for equality through government intervention in a society whose wants were assumed to be coterminous with its needs. Now the New Left wishes to offer people autonomy or the right of individual choice in a pluralistic society. The idea of society as a single entity is no longer fashionable. Multiculturalists, gay rights activists and feminists all claim that society is made up of individual communities with their own identities and needs. Politics in the larger sphere has become the adjustment of their respective claims and rights. The real challenge is not to find a third way that seeks to bridge the old economic divides of freedom versus equality but to answer a more fundamental question about the nature of government itself: the conditions of the contract between the government and the governed.

In the absence of a final answer comes a general decline in organised politics, as well as a general distrust of government. This trend was first noticed in the early 1970s when it gave rise to a variety of explanations according to political prejudice. Conservatives tended to attribute it to poor performance: the public, they claimed, was fed up with waste, corruption and inefficiency in the state sector. The Left tended to stress a psychological malaise: a tendency on the part of the public to expect too much of government and to be disappointed when it failed to deliver.

Inglehart provides his own explanation of what is happening, one that puts the main stress on the rise of post-material political issues. The post-material agenda is based much less on the redistribution of 'goods' (such as the ownership of property or the share-out of income) than the distribution of 'bads' – a subjective interest in security. There is now a growing emphasis on the subjective well-being and quality of life. Job satisfaction is all important. Human rights activists are increasingly interested in the ethics of foreign policy and security.

But he also finds another change at work. Declining trust in government is part of a broader erosion of respect for authority, be it religious, bureaucratic or government. Deference is eroding fast. Post-materialists tend to take their prosperity for granted and subsequently evaluate politics and the record of politicians by more exacting standards than in the past. Increasingly they see less need for discipline and self-denial demanded by governments in times of recession or slow growth. Correspondingly, they place an emphasis on self-expression and fulfilment. Hence the rise of citizen action groups and the prevalence of local community initiatives.

Between 1980 and 1993 the number of registered non-government organisations in the Northern Hemisphere nearly doubled, from 1600 to 2970. These bodies are now in the vanguard of a more forthright and proactive approach to human rights. Through involvement on the ground with refugees and other victims of conflict, they have been able to mobilise public sentiment together with the media, and to force reluctant governments to take a hand in relief work and protection, and often in conflict resolution too. Some groups are turning their attention not only to the exposure of political and human rights abuses; they are also setting their own agendas for peace by trying to tackle the causes of conflict as well.

One example at the grass-roots level is the work undertaken in Rwanda by the London-based organisation International Alert, which is seeking to foster a sense of intercommunal partnership. The Rome-based Catholic foundation, St Egidio, also played a significant part in reconciling the warring factions in Mozambique. But perhaps the most dramatic example of their activity so far is the role played by a collection of international organisations including the Red Cross in persuading governments to prohibit the use of anti-personnel land-mines in an attempt to reduce the incivility of civil conflict.[19]

Religious norms

Equally important are changes in religious norms. As we have become more materially secure, so God has come to play a decreasing role in our imagination. Where material insecurity is pervasive and a factor of daily life, religion still plays a vital role. When security increases, so does secularism.

In western Europe the churches stand empty. In Britain, only 12 per cent of people attend church on Sundays and only 14 per cent in Catholic France. What is happening is not so much the decline of spirituality as the decline of organised religion. Where religion is still alive in the West, organised religion is not. Christians in western Europe are now a moral minority whose status as a religious community is determined by what a largely secular society allows. To be a Christian in western Europe is to be an individual whose right to worship is protected by law.

Indeed, western civilisation in general no longer explicitly professes itself Christian at the institutional level, even though it is still profoundly shaped by its Christian heritage. And with the discrediting of the philosophical systems which claimed to have banished religion itself to the margins of social life – with the end of Marxism and scientific positivism – there is not even a strong philosophical reason to profess atheism or to dismiss religion as an error which is destined to succumb to scientific rationality. No one these days really cares – which is why Europe (if not the United States) tends to be called a 'post-Christian culture'.

Within the Christian world itself the transcendental, incomprehensible and mysterious (the mystery of God) is being removed from Christian dogma just as metaphysics is being removed from philosophy – and with them both the claim to have discovered the true 'nature' of humanity. No one is higher than the individual human being. Unlike Judaism and Islam, of course, the Christian faith is anthropomorphic. The figure of Christ still mediates God into humanity. It is proving difficult, however, to demythicise Christianity without disinventing Christ as a historical figure and/or a divine one. And once we do that there is very little left of Christianity but Christian humanism.

The demythification of Christianity will continue. It is required by the need to find a concordance between moral values and scientific knowledge. But as religion displaces God/Christ from the centre of the moral imagination, so it will re-centre man. Thus the individual will become of greater importance than ever. Christian humanism, not Christian dogma, is at the heart of the western world's interest in humanitarian warfare.

Humanism, after all, stems from a Christian impulse, and its central message: charity. Christians now accept charity as the supreme principle of their faith, not justice, or moral severity or the majesty of God, which is why they no longer find convincing the just war tradition. War has to be grounded not in justice but charity. Religious crusades died out 300 years ago; just wars have died out too. To be just, war has to be humane; it also has to be prescriptively humanitarian – an idea that stems from a Christian impulse and which could only have emerged from a Christian culture.[20]

Yet it would be wrong to conclude that those who profess no faith are unspiritual. In fact, most people have more time to think about the spiritual life, but their interest tends to be directed into non-organised religion, or into activities that are more private than public. It is hard to give this process a precise definition but essentially we are seeing a new inwardness, a new religious individualism that is generated less within the established religious organisations than among secular individuals who find 'New Age' religiosity more appealing. The very term 'religion' is now spurned by the evangelicals and most mainline Protestant denominations. What was once a religion is now a 'faith community' whose focus is spirituality rather than belief.

One of the most telling illustrations of this trend is the rise of environmentalism. The movements in the vanguard of the phenomenon show how the 'sacred' and post-material are more intimately linked than ever, even if they tend to de-link the citizen from the society of old. Environmentalism is one of the most effective faiths of our day precisely because it is 'a cry from the soul of modern man', a substitute for organised religion, one which stresses complexity as a positive feature of a world that wants to keep the truth of nature, like the truth of God, beyond our scientific, rational grasp.[21]

Indeed, environmentalism ultimately confronts science with the need to remember that the planet is fragile; that in material terms it is not only poverty or disease that is a problem; so too is the erosion of the natural world in which everyone lives. Satellite pictures have brought home to us the fragile position of humanity in a limitless universe. They have shown the planet in a new light, reformulating in the process the way we see the Earth in relation to ourselves. 'From space we see a small and fragile ball dominated not by human activity and edifice but by patterns of cloud, oceans, and greenery', observed the authors of *Our Common Future*, a report commissioned by the United Nations in 1983. Its opening sentence explicitly established the radical character of this change of perspective:

> In the middle of the twentieth century we saw our planet from space for the first time. Historians may eventually find that this vision had a greater impact on thought than did the Copernican revolution of the sixteenth century which upset the human self-image by revealing the Earth is not the centre of the universe.[22]

If we are to reposition ourselves in the picture (the task of humanism) it is important that we secure an environment in which human beings can develop and flourish. That is why we see the degradation of the planet as an act of violence against ourselves. In the words of René Girard:

> The sacred consists of all those forces whose dominance over man increases or seems to increase in proportion to man's effort to master them. Tempests, forest fires and plagues, among other phenomena, may be classified as sacred. Far outranking these, however ... stands human violence – violence seen as exterior to man and henceforth as a part of all the other outside forces that threaten mankind. Violence is the heart and soul of the sacred.[23]

Girard's point is compelling, for what humanity holds sacred is not nature but itself. In committing violence against nature we commit violence against the human race. Is not what is at stake the survival of a world that sustains mankind? Is not environmentalism, in that sense, the ultimate *humanist* project?

Individualism

The post-material world has also witnessed a declining respect for authority and a corresponding rise in autonomy, especially within the family. Insecurity tends to enhance the need for absolute norms of behaviour. Growing security is more conducive to a more permissive environment which is reflected in changing attitudes to abortion, divorce, homosexuality and extra-marital sex.

These, in turn, reflect a fundamental change in the structure of the family. The nineteenth-century Victorian family ideal, though culturally situated in a realm separate from public life, remained deeply committed to civic values and the goals of the larger political community. The 'nuclear family' made possible the stability of the family structure upon which the state relied for conscripting soldiers and mobilising women in wartime-related work. In the course of the twentieth century the patriarchal state and family were significantly undermined. Today in the West, no single family pattern is statistically dominant. Only a minority of American households, for example, still contain married couples with children, and many of these include divorced or remarried adults.

Divorce, in fact, has become so commonplace that today's families are frequently organised around relationships between ex-spouses and step-parents. Marriage is no longer the determining factor in family life. Couples live together much longer before marrying and single-parent families are becoming increasingly common. By 2020 married people in Britain will be in a minority, and within families stepfathers will outnumber fathers for the first time.[24] All the figures on marriage rates, cohabitation, the age of sexual initiation, divorce and birth rates suggest that the family as it is traditionally understood will become the favoured option of fewer and fewer people, for shorter periods of their lives.

Even the concept of 'parenthood' is being redefined. A child can now have up to five natural parents: a genetic mother, a surrogate mother, a nurturing mother during the day while the genetic mother is at work, a genetic father (or sperm donor) and a 'live-in' father who looks after the child while the other parent is at work. The full-time home-maker as well as the male bread-winner who earns the family wage now exist in fewer than 10 per cent of American homes.

Gradually the American family is beginning to resemble the patterns which are historically typical of traditionally marginalised groups such as African-Americans. Gradually they are being reformulated around kinship or fictive kins, and households are being determined by divorce rather than marriage. The white middle-class model is losing its place as a social trend-setter. Working-class African-Americans may be setting the pace for all of us.

Post-materialist war

These changes are likely to remain permanent. The shift from the politics of class conflict to the culture wars in the United States – the confrontations over gender, abortion and environmental protection – are likely to become even more marked. The changes are intergenerational. A long-term shift in prevailing attitudes will occur inevitably as the young replace the older cohorts in the post-industrial world.[25]

The post-material value system has already had an impact on attitudes to war and peace. In a world in which individuals must produce, stage and cobble together their biographies themselves, war has become a disorientating experience. Individuals have become the centre of their own universe, and this poses a challenge for today's armed forces faced with the proliferation of laws covering individual rights. By placing more emphasis on individual rights than on collective responsibility, much domestic and – in the case of Europe, European legislation – impacts adversely on the operational effectiveness of the army. Soldiers are still told that they have to be different from civilian employees because the success of military operations requires the subordination of individual rights to that of the unit or team. But they also need the reassurance that in bearing arms for their country the nation will look after them, and that is unlikely to be the case if they ride roughshod over individual rights.

Clearly, a society which puts a premium on individualism is likely to individualise every death – that of its own soldiers as well as the enemy's. Zero tolerance is already a problem when it comes to committing troops to open-ended conflict. Senior officers also know that public opinion at home will not accept high casualties. They have a greater interest than ever in keeping alive the men under their command and feel perhaps a greater responsibility than ever for their welfare.

Wars now have to be limited in duration in order to pose minimum risk to the soldiers themselves. Legislative bodies insist that governments commit themselves to 'exit strategies', guaranteeing that armies will be out of a conflict zone before they run into serious trouble. Casualty aversion may also be an aspect of a growing 'zero-deficit mentality' among senior officers who now believe casualties represent not only loss of life, but are also an indication that an operation has failed. To avoid 'failure' in Bosnia casualty aversion rose to an unprecedented level. 'Force protection' (the prevention of US casualties) became an explicit mission goal which superseded the primary mission of restoring peace to the region. As a result, war criminals were not aggressively pursued, community-building programmes were curtailed and every stray movement of a peacekeeper became a threat to the entire mission.

The rise of political subjectivity, namely the extent to which citizens now engage in what Beck calls 'subpolitics', is also transforming the character of the wars they are willing to be conducted in their name. Subpolitics is just another term for the shaping of politics from below. Professional and occupation groups, the technical intellegentsia in research institutes and citizen initiative groups are all reshaping political culture. There is a growing opportunity for groups traditionally outside the political system to have a voice in the shaping of their society.[26]

The emergence of one of these groups, aid workers, has already changed the political environment in which the military operate: 40 per cent of foreign aid is now channelled through private agencies. In Somalia, humanitarian organisations such as Save the Children confronted armed bandits and armies of warlords on a daily basis long before the Americans arrived in 1992. They did so without military training, the security afforded by armoured personnel carriers or a back-up force to call upon if things went wrong. Six years later more civilians working for the UN were killed in peacekeeping and humanitarian missions than were military personnel serving under the United Nations flag.[27]

Subpolitical groups in all walks of life have had a dramatic impact on international politics. Since 1992 in the form of non-government organisations, they have forced the World Bank to review its funding strategy; helped to create the post of UN High Commissioner for human rights; scuppered the Multilateral Agreement on Investment (which aimed to liberalise foreign investment and immunise it from the interests of national governments) and at the end of 1999 helped to win a pledge from Britain to write off the debts of the world's forty-one poorest countries.

They also have an interest in taking the citizen 'out of the loop' when it comes to war. In the modern era the industrial world used air power to wreck cities, regardless of the fact that it was making war on private life. It refused to draw a distinction between the two. The private was the public and vice versa. Even the democracies were indifferent to the fate of civilians. In the Second World War the allies claimed to be at war with the Nazi state, and not as in the Great War with the German people. This did not stop the US Air Force dropping 50 per cent of its bombs on civilians. (In the run-up to the D-Day landings 50,000 Frenchmen were killed in air raids designed to cripple the German army's ability to counter-attack.)

The figure for civilian targets went up to 70 per cent in Korea and 90 per cent in Vietnam. The apotheosis of this trend, of course, was nuclear targeting. In the Cold War – at least in the early days – hatred was a prerequisite of global conflict. As late as the 1960s it was possible for Thomas Schelling, one of the fathers of nuclear doctrine, to complain:

> I am struck with how customary it is to propose that advance warning be given to cities that are to be destroyed. This is going to extremes ... it seems to reflect a peculiar American penchant for warning rather than doing, for postponing decision, for anaesthetising the victim before striking the blow, for risking wealth, rather than people, and for doing grand things that do not hurt rather than small things that do.[28]

In all other respects Schelling was a humane man, with a reputation for imaginative thinking; but he lived in modern times. Today the West finds it difficult to target civilians. The mass media tends to magnify civilian deaths even when – as in Kosovo – most were unintended. Self-imposed restraints including restrictive rules of engagement during military operations have become a feature of recent conflicts.

One particularly vivid example was the use of human shields in Kosovo to deter the allied air forces from targeting Serbian armoured units. Another was the US F-117 strike on the Al Firdos bunker on the night of 13 February 1991 in which dozens of civilians who had been deliberately placed there lost their lives. Ultimately, the incident had little effect on public support for the Gulf War but the American political leadership took no further chances. The Bush administration, which had previously been committed to avoiding the micro-management of target selection that had bedevilled the Johnson administration's efforts in Vietnam, required all future targets in Baghdad to be cleared beforehand with the Chairman of the Joint Chiefs of Staff.[29]

It is not only the human cost of war which disturbs the conscience of the post-modern world; so too does environmental damage. Like civilian targeting this was not of great concern in the closing years of the modern era. In Korea after running out of civilian targets in February 1951, the USAF turned to bombing the countryside, especially the forests of North Korea. In Vietnam the use of herbicides began on an experimental basis in August 1961; six years later 1.7 million acres of land had been destroyed. Using defoliants including Agent Orange, the Americans sprayed 20 per cent of the country's jungles and 36 per cent of its mangrove forests, causing irreversible damage. Bulldozing vast areas also caused permanent devastation. Some 3000 sq. km. of land were ploughed under in the course of the war.[30]

Today, the western world knows that all wars by definition are harmful to the local ecology. Whoever employs chemicals or nuclear weapons or pollutes the sea, writes Umberto Eco, 'declares war not only on the neutrals but the whole earth'.[31] Consequence management groups in the United States are attempting to clean up the environmental damage in America, itself caused by the seepage of oil and other contaminating elements on the old Cold War military bases. As a concept, consequence management may be extended to cover the way the United States intends to fight its wars in future.

Uncivil society

The involvement of the citizen in politics is part of a broader movement: the rise of a politics of civility that is intent on redressing the large elements of incivility that are still to be found in social life. It is a movement that over the years has encompassed such diverse themes as the campaign against rape in marriage, as well as violence against children, together with the violence which is often still concealed in institutions such as prisons and schools. What these campaigns have revealed is the extent to which civil society is plagued by endemic sources of incivility, so much so, writes John Keane, that we might conclude that incivility is a chronic feature of civil society, if not one of its defining conditions.[32]

Perhaps the worst feature of all is violence against children. Modern society tended to suppress evidence of the phenomenon. First brought to light in Vienna at the very beginning of the twentieth century in a series of highly publicised court cases, the incidence of child abuse was denied for the next sixty years. The first steps towards general consciousness came only with improvements in X-ray technology after the Second World War. Radiology studies revealed mysterious recurring problems of bone fractures in children. But none of this came to general medical attention until 1962 with the appearance in *The Journal of the American Medical Association* of a breakthrough article entitled 'The battered child syndrome'. Before then it had been easier to accept Freud's contention that children unconsciously desired the death of their parents than the counter-proposition that parents were often responsible for the death of their children. Freud himself went to his grave denying that child abuse occurred.[33]

We know better, of course. In the past forty years the recorded number of children murdered in the United States during the first year of their lives has doubled. There has also been a quadrupling of the murder rate among 1–4-year-olds. Child abuse runs deep in the fabric of social life. Usually disguised, it erupts from time to time whenever a person's inability to cope with the demands of social life is combined with the chronic insecurity that arises from breaks in the regular pattern such as unemployment. Among African-Americans who represent the most dis-advantaged social group of all in the United States, the homicide rate is seven times higher than that of the rest of the population. More than twenty children in every 100,000 are killed. Sixty per cent of those charged with murder are usually parents of the child.[34]

In Britain the figures for child abuse are equally appalling. Every week one child dies of cruelty and neglect; 2000 more are sexually abused, and 3000 are physically abused in such a way as to leave a lasting memory of violence, usually at the hands of somebody whom they have wanted to love and trust. A quarter of all rape victims are children; a hundred a year are killed in their own homes; new babies are five times more likely to be murdered than adults; 35,000 children are on the child protection registers, although most cases of cruelty are believed to go unreported. The one inescapable fact is that 95 per cent of child murders are family matters: one-third of the killers are mothers, nearly half are their boyfriends or husbands. As for the victims, 40 per cent are not yet 1 year old, and another 20 per cent are under 4. And this is just the ones who die.[35] We live in a society in which children are tormented for showing an awkwardness or defiance which baffles their parents. We live in an era in which families are out of control, caught in a trap of poverty, boredom and futility, frequently drugged into a state of denial about the small child starving in a filthy back room.

Keane characterises this phenomenon as evidence of 'social fatigue'. The majority of perpetrators tend to be the victims of a civil society which does not work for them. They find themselves 'trapped within its high-tension zones'.[36] Of course, it is true that a century ago many more children suffered cruelty and neglect, but the vast majority did so in slum conditions of poverty and hunger we can hardly comprehend today, in which there was scant access to birth control, unwanted mouths to feed and no social workers or welfare benefits to ease the misery. Today's abused children are the products of a culture in which, although poverty is no longer rampant, all social and moral restraints have been dismantled: they are the victims of an anti-culture of fractured identities, violence and transient relationships.

But we also live in paradoxical times. Child abuse is rampant at the very moment when children are becoming even more important in private life. Indeed, in some cases they are the last remaining primary relationship which unites individuals. In marriage, partners come and go, but children remain. With the increasing fragility of relationships between the sexes the child is becoming the centre-piece of emotional bonding and practical companionship. If the number of births is declining in the post-modern world, the importance of children is rising. In the words of Ulrich Beck:

> The child becomes the final alternative to loneliness that can be built up against the vanishing possibilities of love. It is the private type of re-enchantment which arises with and derives its meaning from disenchantment.[37]

It is not surprising in the circumstances that western societies want to eliminate the incivility of warfare. Our citizens are now highly reluctant to see children or families targeted, however supportive they may be of a military campaign such as Kosovo. They want their pilots to disable, disrupt, neutralise or incapacitate, rather than to intentionally injure or kill. They prefer to nullify the fighting effectiveness of an adversary by robbing him of his capability or will to fight without the attendant harmful and costly effects on non-combatants. What they want most is a more discerning approach to warfare.

It is above all the scenes on television of the plight of children that prompt western audiences to demand that their governments intervene in the civil wars which plague the planet. Children have become a litmus test by which we judge not only the inhumanity of others, but our own ability to feel the pain of our fellow human beings.

The paradox, of course, is that civilian fatalities have climbed from 5 per cent of war-related deaths at the turn of the twentieth century to more than 90 per cent today. Over the past decade armed conflict has killed more children than did the two world wars. It has killed two million children, disabled five million more, and left twelve million homeless, more than a million orphaned or separated from their parents, and some ten million psychologically traumatised.

It is estimated that half a million children under age 5 died as a result of armed conflict in 1992 alone, and many more were wounded or deprived of essential supplies. In Chechnya, children made up 40 per cent of all civilian casualties in two months alone (February to March 1995). By the time peace came to Sarajevo, almost one child in four had been wounded. In Somalia half or more of all children under age 5 who were alive at the beginning of January 1992 were dead by the end of the year.[38]

The statistics are appalling. In their own way they are almost as shaming as the figures for the battle tolls of Verdun and the Somme. One way of arresting, if not reversing, this trend is to outlaw certain weapons. Recent initiatives on the part of the international community (by which we mean the West) have singled out, in particular, the indiscriminate use of land-mines and cluster bombs. A large number of the victims are children. Every month more than 2000 people are killed or maimed by mine explosions. At least, in 1997, more than 120 countries agreed to prohibit their use.

The next weapons to go are probably cluster bombs which were last used in Kosovo. Cluster bombs, in fact, are far more deadly than land-mines. When hidden (and in Kosovo 10 per cent failed to go off), they are far harder to detect and dispose of than land-mines. Indeed they were considered so dangerous that the US military would not allow their own troops to disarm them. The Pentagon refused to allow its professional personnel to dispose of them. The job was dumped on under-funded civilian teams largely staffed by the very people NATO went to war to defend from Serbian aggression.

The feminisation of society

One of the most important social changes in the course of the twentieth century was the decline of masculinity, and with it the decline of confron-tationism in politics. One of the last times men asserted themselves self-consciously as a gender was just before the Great War. Looking back on the nineteenth century, Bernard Shaw thought the first half was the most impressive and creative of all, the second the most wicked. 'The great convictions of the nineteenth century,' he wrote in 1912, 'were not convictions of individual but of social sin.'[39] The sin of aggression had been assumed not only by individuals but also by classes and nation states, and even by a gender – in this case, men.

Nietzsche spoke for many when he identified what he thought to be a disturbing trend, a feature of mass society: the 'feminisation' of Europe, to which he referred disparagingly in the course of condemning what he called the 'emasculation' of European culture. The castration metaphor is vivid in his writing. In his eyes what made it worse was that it was a self-inflicted wound. What he directed his polemics against was not so much the militancy of the 'new woman' as the demise of masculinity. A society that preferred tranquillity and self-indulgence to the assertion of the will was bereft of 'manlier drives and virtues'. 'There is little manliness here', says Zarathustra of the ambient 'herd' society of the masses.[40]

In Nietzsche's writings (misread though they were), the cult of masculinity did not matter much; but when taken up by political figures it did. 'Alibis of aggression', the historian Peter Gay calls them: the great alibis that led nation states in the course of the next fifty years to go to war on the grounds of nationalism, race and masculinity. The cult of manliness at the end of the nineteenth century made men more violent, dangerous and aggressive. Manliness, writes Gay, represented one of the most dangerous alibis of all for aggression, for it involved the largest social group.

Every culture, of course, constructs its own distinctive alibis, and each of these defensive strategies has a history. What made the twentieth century unique was that the liberal European world dressed up its aggressive instincts in a pseudo-scientific gloss which legitimised and even sanctioned violence against other races, classes or nations. With its belief in natural selection Darwinism seemed to confirm that the tougher, manlier races were more likely to succeed in the struggle for survival.

It was a view which penetrated the domestic realm as well. Looking back at the pre-war years when the cult of masculinity was at its height, Leonard Woolf explained the influence it had during his own adolescence and that of his contemporaries:

> I suspect that the male carapace is usually grown to conceal cowardice. It was the fear of ridicule and disapproval if one revealed one's real thoughts or feelings and sometimes the fear of revealing one's fears, which prompted one to invent the kind of second hand version of oneself which might provide for one's original self the safety of a permanent alibi.[41]

Whether political or personal, the cult of manliness was deeply destructive. For one of the problems of manliness, of course, was that it was best demonstrated in war. Indeed, in Greek the word for manliness, *andreia*, is also the word for courage. And as Aristotle tells us, courage is best shown in battle.

Yet after the First World War men increasingly lost both the confidence and will to test each other's manliness in the battlefield. Well before the war, in fact, it had become a platitude that aggression against others was only likely to end in even greater aggression against oneself. In the 1920s Virginia Woolf launched a particularly virulent attack on the cult of masculinity and its contribution to war, as did Aldous Huxley, who memorably attacked the male ethos in his novel *Crome Yellow*. In Woolf's case she was merely keeping faith with the tradition of her own family, for her father Leslie Stephen had consistently derided the 'muscular Christianity' of the male public schools and the emphasis on manliness put by nineteenth-century evangelists.

By the time Woolf was writing, however, society was beginning to change. As early as the 1920s Wyndham Lewis (one of the few British writers to celebrate heroic manliness) was complaining that the pass had been sold. 'The feminisation of the white European and American is already far advanced, coming in the wake of the war'.[42] But if this was true of the democracies it was not true, alas, of the totalitarian world.

Totalitarian ideology promoted the cult of aggressive masculinity. Hitler's state thrived on its values; indeed they were a distinguishing feature of post-war German writing. 'The air was charged to overflowing with manliness,' wrote Ernst Junger in his account of his own wartime career, *War as an Inner Experience* (1922), 'every breath was an intoxication.'[43] Contemporaries later noted the aggressive masculine imagery in the national socialist writing of the period which extolled the self-sacrificing and danger-loving individual – the hero who incarnated in his own person the ancient virtues of courage, hardness and discipline. That was the creed of the Third Reich; that is what it lived – and died – by.

To challenge the rise of fascism in the inter-war period was to challenge the logic of a revolution which Hitler boasted would be an entirely male event. The purpose of every totalitarian system was subordination, and women were subordinated more than men in the Third Reich. Among the many criticisms Hitler made of the Weimar Republic, one of the principal ones was its advancement of women's rights. Once in power he dismissed all the women Reichstag members and most women doctors. In the Nazi paintings and propaganda posters of the period, women were depicted with softer lines and gentle contours (all sexuality denied), the image of devotion and co-operation. They were an object to be looked at and fertilised; they were there not only to breed for the Reich, but more important, to breed true.

In Soviet Russia their plight was different but equally demeaning. 'We must create a new type of Russian Revolutionary woman', remarked one of Trotsky's admirers. 'The French Revolution created its own type; we must do the same.'[44] The story is recorded by a woman of rare courage,

Nadezhda Mandelstam, the wife of one of the Soviet state's greatest poets who died in the gulag in 1938. The twentieth century was a revolutionary age and it had its full complement of women heroes. Mandelstam was merely one of a number of indefatigable women who placed such high hopes in the Russian Revolution. But although the USSR promoted the image of female heroes, the reality was very different. Early on, revolutionary leaders like Rosa Luxemburg were confirmed in their suspicion that women's rights could not be left to men, even revolutionaries. In the new Soviet state women may have won legal equality and the right to abortion and divorce, but economically they remained the subordinate sex. Politically, the Soviet state was a patriarchy. In its seventy-four-year history not a single woman achieved high office.

Looking back, the struggle for women's liberation in the first half of the twentieth century can be seen on one level as a struggle against its twin patriarchs: Marx and Freud. Both created systems, each with their high priests and dissenters, their martyrs by the thousand as well as their dubious prophets. Both mapped out a whole way of life from mass to individual psychology, from the conscious to the unconscious, from political to psychic alienation and from society to self. In their different systems there was no role for women except as servants of the dialectic or as a repressed gender. Marx and Freud were both misogynists. Both were prepared to accept that women should have the vote but neither could accept their wish to be self-fulfilled.

The position of women in western societies has changed so much that the politics of masculinity is being replayed once again – but this time from a position of even greater weakness. A deep crisis would appear to be engulfing a significant if increasingly marginalised part of the male community. In the closing decade of the twentieth century the two largest demonstrations in Washington were staged by men. A million protesters gathered in the Mall in October 1995, and 750,000 staged a similar protest two years later. The first were black militants, followers of the fundamentalist preacher Louis Farakhan's 'Nation of Islam'; the second were slightly overweight, middle-aged, lower-middle-class white members of an evangelical movement called 'The Promise Keepers'. Both were all-male movements of a kind not seen before. Both reflected, or appeared to, a deepening of the gender war.

For despite their racial and religious differences, they had much in common: the belief in the supremacy of men in the home; the stark difference between male and female roles in society; and a fierce hostility to abortion. Both groups were deeply troubled by the mounting evidence of male dysfunctionality in social life: illegitimacy, violence, addiction and disease. The 'Nation of Islam' may have been the more radical in its analysis of racial injustice, but it was profoundly conservative on the issue of the sex war. It segregated women at its meetings, and the white evangelicals banished them altogether. Both offered women a better deal in terms of male responsibility in the family, but one that would be compensated for by a restoration of male authority in general.

It is not clear, writes Andrew Sullivan, whether both groups are expressions of male chauvinism or whether they are uttering a genuine cry for help. It is not clear whether greater male social irresponsibility is related in some subliminal way to the progress of women in the past fifty years. In the African-American population women have been gaining ground in the marketplace at exactly the same time as black manhood is threatened by criminality, illegitimacy and addiction. And this has occurred in a culture that socially is profoundly conservative and in which women traditionally have played a subordinate role.[45]

Is male dysfunctionality related to a crisis in self-confidence? Are men still more at risk from themselves as a result of their own failure to adjust to the new times? Biology, concludes Sullivan, teaches us at the end of the twentieth century that men have become the weaker sex. Sociology tells us that they are the inferior sex as well in terms of higher incidents of suicide, alcoholism, drug addiction and cardio-vascular disease. As the new millennium opens, men appear to be the most threatened as well as the most threatening sex. Are they also becoming a socially maladjusted sex? For they tend to be emotionally volatile and more prone to promiscuity and physical risk, which account, of course, in part for a reduction in their life expectancy. In the larger social context, the decline of male self-confidence may be a response to 'the feminisation' of the western world. Indeed some sociologists would contend that the two are intimately linked.

For society itself is changing, and with it gender roles and relations. In that context 'the feminisation of society' reflects the 'third wave' of women's emancipation. The first involved gaining the vote, the second securing the end of discrimination in the workplace. What this last phase represents is a transformation in the way that both men and women look at the world, and a challenge to the 'masculine' stereotypes which once dominated political life.

We must return to the early twentieth century. 'What do women want?' Freud famously asked. Well, even in the 1920s they wanted more than the vote. They wanted to express a distinctive feminine point of view. And we see it emerge seventy years later in the world of war as well as business. In the latter, globalisation has improved their position greatly. The restructuring of western economies in the 1980s as the manufacturing industries of the past gave way to the service industries of the future favoured the recruitment of women employees. Male employers valued the skills which they considered to be especially 'feminine', such as flexibility, communication and teamwork. A new business ethos favoured the restructuring of the old hierarchical status system and the emergence of a more egalitarian management style.

With the end of the Cold War the rise of 'feminine' values has also begun to change other institutions, including the military. As Aristotle tells us, men find it easier to be courageous, women to be moderate. The 'feminine' virtues of empathy and caring, caution, protection, apology and sentiment are regularly exalted above the 'masculine ones' of heroism, daring and endurance. Today the very word 'manliness' seems obsolete. The women's revolution has succeeded to a degree that even now goes unacknowledged. We are in the process of making language gender-neutral. As for manliness, the quality of one gender, or rather of one sex, it seems to describe the essence of the enemy which is being attacked: the social evil we are intent on eradicating. This is the face of 'humane warfare' too: 'humanity', rightly or not, is associated with women more than with men. Of all the factors I have discussed, the increasing influence of 'feminine' values in civil society may encourage the West to invest even more time and effort in fighting wars 'humanely'.

In the absence of the hatred that distinguished much of modern warfare, the West may be predisposed to favour the use of new technologies that will allow it to destroy an enemy's production facilities and R & D assets, not its forces in the field; to target its economy rather than its citizens; to dismantle its technological infrastructure, not its cities. What the new technologies promise is to neutralise the enemy, rather than maim or kill him. Humane warfare is likely to be the future of war. In the absence of hatred what other way is there to fight it? Killing is beginning to lose its appeal.

Non-lethal warfare

As long ago as 1959, Maj.-Gen. William Creasy, former Chief of the Army Chemical Corps, suggested that the development of psycho-chemicals might provide a means of waging war without killing the enemy. As early as 1965 military writers were beginning to look at the technological options they called euphemistically 'non-lethal violence'.[46] It is only in recent years, however, that technologies have begun to come on stream which make possible its application. In September 1992 the US Army issued a draft paper which advocated minimising large-scale casualties in future wars, as well as the damage to the local environment. With the publication of that paper the age of non-lethal violence can be said to have arrived.

Some of the main examples of non-lethal weapons (NLWs) include:

1   *Accoustics*. Sound is produced by waves of energy passing through the air at speeds of about 300 meters per second. The Los Alamos National Laboratory and the US Army's Armament Research, Development and Engineering Center are trying to develop a tuned beam of low-frequency, high-intensity sound which by disorientating large numbers of people may enhance crowd control. Russian researchers are also developing pockets of sonic energy (sonic bullets) which can be directed against an enemy in a lethal or non-lethal fashion.

2   *Chemicals.* These can be used to glue enemy vehicles to the spot or foul the turbine blades of hydroelectric power stations, or the engines of enemy planes. In the words of one US official, 'against people, polymer agents (i.e. super adhesives) could be employed to glue a person to almost anything that he or she may touch, including another person.'[47]

3   *Electromagnetic.* The Electrical Power Distribution Munition (EPDM) was used on the first day of the Gulf War. Long conductive carbon fibres were dropped over Iraqi power lines and distribution points, causing massive short-circuiting.

Other NLWs include sleep agents (introducing dimethyl sulfiride into air-conditioning systems); strobe lighting (the Lawrence Livermore laboratory has already built a prototype that can induce epileptic fits), and liquid sten guns, a step-up from water cannon with an electrical charge. In addition, the US military is working on super acids which will form alloys with the metal structures of targets under attack, creating a material which is much weaker than the original.

These technologies, though still in their infancy, are limitless in nature as well as appeal. Both the United States and Russia are investing huge sums in them. The proliferation of new systems answers a public need: that governments should take firm action without attendant loss of life. In the words of the defence analyst James Adams, they represent the face of warfare in the future.[48]

For non-lethal weapons make possible (in principle, at least) the use of more discriminate force by providing an escalating, sliding scale of force options. What they promise, in the words of Col. Michael Stanton, who saw them used for the first time when the US Marines returned briefly to Somalia in February 1995, is 'gentler operations other than war'. 'We would like to see the development of non-lethal weapons as proof of civility and restraint. Non-lethal weapons show our reverence for life and our commitment to the use of minimum force.'[49]

Two key words spring out from Stanton's statement: 'civility' and 'restraint'. Another, perhaps, is the word 'gentle'. All three are evidence of 'feminisation'. This is what humane warfare promises: the chance for the first time to eliminate the incivility of modern warfare. As Alvin and Heidi Toffler write:

> Non-lethality emerges not as a simple replacement for war, or an extension of peace, but as something different. It is something radically different in global affairs – an intermediate phenomenon, a pausing place, an arena for contests where more outcomes are decided bloodlessly.[50]

These weapons are still in the very early stage of development. Their use in a discriminate fashion begs many questions for the future; but claims that their use will make soldiers 'soft', or undermine their self-esteem, seem ungrounded. In Somalia the US marines did not seem any less ready to use lethal force when required to do so.

On the basis of that experience, the US Army is already pioneering 'virtual peacekeeping' too, in which non-lethal information technology could be used as a deterrent or confidence-building measure. Information technology can be used to distract, pacify, intimidate, immobilise, confuse or mislead an adversary with no loss of life. In the Dayton negotiations which brought the war in Bosnia to an end, a system called 'Power Scene' (an advanced software program for visualising terrain) allowed the negotiators to fix the inter-ethnic border. But it also had other uses, including a veiled threat to the Serbian, Croat and Muslim leaders that NATO was capable of precisely hitting targets if the fighting did not stop.[51]

The advocates of virtual peacekeeping hope for much from the new technology. They hope that societies about to become involved in a conflict could be shown a simulation of the consequences of their deeds. Such a simulation may not necessarily show their destruction, only the path leading to war and its consequences for the economy against the path leading to peace. They hope that CD-Rom games which are beginning to show the faces, even personalities of the players, could be utilised during negotiations or initial discussions. It might allow both sides to witness at firsthand some of the distress or pain their future actions might cause. Computer-aided design (CAD) software allows designers to make three-dimensional models of almost anything as part of a virtual reality climate in complex negotiations.[52]

Through virtual peacekeeping the world may be able to transcend, if not hatred, the binary way of thinking which holds societies like Serbia and Bosnia together and at the same time tears them apart. It may break the vicious circle of inflicting death and yet suffering it (martyrdom), and introduce the world to a third way: living. In theory this is all very promising. In practice the real challenge is whether the peace can be kept in this fashion. As Bismarck once remarked, 'Just because you wind a clock forward three hours does not mean that you shorten time for others.' In future the West may find itself fighting societies which still hate their enemies no less passionately than in the past and that are prepared to make war more inhumane, not less. It is that challenge which I will address in a later chapter.

5   The humane warrior

It was Machiavelli who noted that once a man became a soldier 'he changes not only his clothing but he adopts attitudes, manners, ways of speaking and becoming himself quite at odds with the civilian life'.[1] This quotation is taken from John Hale's classic account of Renaissance warfare. In those days, despite the prevalence of violence at every level of society, soldiers and civilians were worlds apart – as distinct, in fact, as the clergy was from laity. Hale records that contemporary writers criticised members of the Imperial Army in 1528 for letting their beards sprout and their hair grow long – through this inversion of the clerical tonsure they were signalling their entry into a separate way of life and, like the clergy, their form of dress focused attention on their difference from other men. From the late fifteenth century, anti-soldier attitudes swirled easily along the grooves cut by centuries of anti-clericalism.[2]

It should not be thought that the clerical analogy distances us entirely from our forebears. As late as the 1960s, a British general wrote that service under arms had been seen 'at some times and in some places as a calling resembling that of a priesthood in its detachment'.[3] The professional soldier, he added, had become a citizen in the modern era but had not yet – and never would – become a civilian. In the words of a noted American sociologist, 'military service stands by itself. It has some of the qualities of a priesthood. . .'[4]

What most commentators on military life accepted without question was that even in the liberal, democratic West the subordination of the military to civilian authority and its growing reflection of civic norms could not and should not turn the soldier into a civilian. In our more secular times the analogy with the priesthood may have lost its appeal, but the difference between the civilian and military worlds is still considered to be absolute.

In reality, concludes John Keegan, soldiers are not as 'other' men. In that sense, like the clergy, they are indeed 'unworldly'. War is fought by men with different values and skills. The military world may exist in parallel with the civilian, but it does not belong to it. Both worlds, of course, change over time, and that of the warrior must adapt to the civilian. The post-modern warrior is not a modern soldier but the distance between the civilian and military can never be closed.[5]

Counter-culture

Is this, in fact, the case today? It is a question which is beginning to be asked with increasing concern by many professional soldiers especially in the United States, where many writers now talk of a growing 'rift' between the two. The last time they did so was during the Vietnam War. They called themselves the 'counter-culture': the student radicals and activists on the left, the *jeunesse dorée* of the young generation. Not only were they critical of military values, they were also loud in their condemnation of the 'militarism' which they claimed permeated American political life: the military-industrial complex, the CIA and the culture of secrecy it fostered. For many young people the United States itself was a 'national security state', permanently armed not only against external enemies, but also against radicalism at home in its many forms.

Today it is the military which now calls itself a 'counter-culture' (to quote a former American Under-Secretary of State).[6] According to a former Secretary of the Navy, John Lehman, the US military represents something more: 'a separate caste', cut off from the civilian population.[7] In a post-heroic age the military is deemed to reflect the qualities of 'decency' and 'honour' that are no longer to be found in public life. Many soldiers find themselves at odds with a country in which crime is rampant and drug dependency apparently a norm, a society in which there seems to be little trace of the traditional values that officers still try to inculcate in the ranks. Clearly, many soldiers really do feel they are members of a counter-culture in their attachment to a value system which still honours courage, heroism and, above all, honour itself.

In opposition to this view there are those who argue that the gap between the two communities is narrowing. The post-modern soldier, writes the sociologist Charles Moskos, is much more in step with civilian attitudes than his modern predecessor during the Cold War years. The distinctions between the civilian and military worlds are diminishing, as are those between military functions and their civilian equivalents. Military culture is challenged by the relativistic civilian ethos from without and by increasing civilianisation of military functions from within. As long as the West faces no clearly defined *existential* threat to its security in the future, considerations other than military effectiveness will assume greater importance, especially with regard to questions of force structure.[8]

Indeed, what, for want of a better term, may be called 'the post-modern military' is being transformed in far more profound ways than Moskos and others acknowledge. Two parallel movements are challenging the armed forces' traditional understanding of their role and social function. First, the arrival of what Martin Shaw calls a 'post-military society' has undermined the Clausewitzian understanding of the relationship between state, people and army in a way that challenges our late nineteenth-century understanding of military service.[9] Second, what one writer terms 'the revenge of civil society' – that is, the reassertion of civil values and attitudes – is leading to the civilianisation of the armed services.[10] The military is now expected not only to share the values civil society holds in high esteem, but even in the way it prosecutes war it is expected to reflect civility and compassion – in a word, humanitarianism.

Both of these developments have hollowed out the warrior ethos which has been celebrated since the French Revolution. But so too has the demise of the 'post-traditional' military, which has been highlighted, most of all, by the admission of women into the armed forces since the early 1970s. Indeed, it represents the most profound break with tradition in two thousand years. Traditionally, war has been an all-male activity. Whether the introduction of women threatens to 'de-gender' war is not the question. What it has done already is in itself profound enough – it has further obscured Machiavelli's distinction between the civilian and military worlds, and in the process given rise to the 'humane soldier'.

Post-military society

One of the main features of modern warfare was the distinction between civilian and military culture. It was in one sense much more pronounced than in the pre-modern era. Medieval society, for example, at every level, was permeated by the ideology of violence and inspired by its ethics, and one can find copious evidence of its expression in the literature, liturgy and iconography of the period. One of the most irritating things about the medieval cliché which divides the community into those who prayed, those who worked and those who fought is that it gives an utterly misleading impression. The reality is that nearly everyone had to engage in hard physical 'work'. Those who 'worked' could be called to fight upon occasion; those who 'prayed' justified and managed the use of force because their security depended upon it. And those who 'fought' were often pious, could envisage the act of war as an act of devotion, and even served in military orders such as the Templars.[11]

One of the defining features of the modern era was that although the citizen was conscripted to fight for the first time, even then the military retained a distinctive ethos. The military was not democratic but national service was. National service was considered not a burden but a privilege, for it embodied the three principles of the French Revolution: liberty, equality and fraternity.

With regard to the first principle, even authoritarian governments found it necessary to reward conscripts for their service to the state by giving them the vote. Even Austria-Hungary extended universal male suffrage in 1907. Every European power did so with the exception of Russia, which is one reason, perhaps, why it was the only twentieth-century European power to experience a revolution.

No modern state, moreover, could be secure – or feel secure; no modern state could enjoy peace of mind if it was not at peace with itself. No state could be secure if its citizens did not feel they belonged to it and it to them. Conscription created a feeling of common endeavour in the face of a common enemy. It was the indispensable unifying myth of fraternity. Finally, the identification of equality with arms bearing – the fact that in the eyes of the enemy state all were equal – carried with it the idea that to serve as a soldier made a man more, not less of a citizen. To sum up, the mass armies of the late nineteenth century were instruments of social cohesion. From being an anonymous member of a national community the citizen was forged into a member of a nation state.

Today, the military plays no role in nation building or civic consciousness, and in the absence of a clearly defined threat it is being democratised from within. The citizen is no longer expected to be a soldier. Instead, the soldier is being required to act more and more like a citizen.

The end of the military-civic role has also heralded the end of Clausewitz's trinitarian nexus between the state, the people and the army, although to listen to many generals one would not know it. Colin Powell, for example, continues to argue that the armed forces of the United States occupy an ontological rather than strategic space: they are part of the fabric of American values.[12] 'In a society that seems to have trouble transmitting values, the marines stand out', adds Thomas Ricks in his book *Making the Corps*. The military is an educative organisation because it transmits values to the 'Beavis's and Butthead's of America': 'the side that isn't surfing into the twenty-first century on the breaking wave of Microsoft products. It takes kids and nurtures them.'[13]

Translated into the language of an earlier period in history, this is Clausewitz's concept of the relationship between the military and civil society. For both Clausewitz and Hegel, and even the liberals who came after them, keeping the military and civil society distinct, but in a working partnership, was vital to the 'ethical health' of the nation. For both men the state was a spiritual, not merely a territorial entity. Both advocated a citizen army because of their belief that the fighting spirit of a people was crucial in legitimising the role of the state itself. State institutions were only as strong as the spirit of the people who served them, manifest, of course, most expressly in war. The collective identification of citizen and state presupposed an Enlightenment understanding of society and citizenship. For Clausewitz, service in the army was an ontological commitment, for war – or the preparation for it – created the conditions for the maintenance of a virtuous community through which subjectivity could be experienced, *existentially* for the citizen, *collectively* for the state.

And in the ethos of the professional soldier (the soldier who served exclusively in the military profession), both Hegel and Clausewitz also saw something new, or something specifically modern. The character of war had changed, for it was now waged not by feudal retainers of the king or even mercenaries, but by professional soldiers who saw themselves as public servants. The warrior no longer served his own selfish ends or those of a feudal master. He served society, and derived his self-esteem from his willingness to sacrifice his life for his fellow citizens, or what Hegel called 'an ethical idea'.

Today, the relationship between the military and the state and the society from which its members are recruited has once again become contractual as it was in the eighteenth century. And it is this development which marks a decisive break with the trinitarian system, which so concerns politicians such as the US Defence Secretary William Cohen who has called for the American people to be 'reconnected' to the military that serves them.[14] In France, Regis Debray wants the citizen to be put in touch with the military in the same way that distinguished life in the Third Republic.[15] Both would like to preserve the division of labour on which the old version of civil society was based. Being 'reconnected' means state, society and army all recognising their mutual claims on each other.

It is much too late for that. War is no longer a subjective experience for society or even for the professional soldier as Clausewitz understood it – 'a duel on a larger scale' or 'a trial of moral and political forces'. For some time the discourse on strategy has borrowed heavily from the civilian world – from the theatre, organised sport and the marketplace. Generals talk of scenarios, theatres, game plans and assets. Sir Charles Guthrie, the Chief of the British Defence Staff, employing the language of the times, insists the military can only do what the 'market' will allow.[16] And it is to the market that the military is increasingly turning. When the US Marines go to Wall Street to learn about decision-making, and when the military turns to Wal-Mart to learn about logistics, a new era has clearly dawned.[17]

In their own work, Charles Moskos and his collaborators who have looked at fifteen different military establishments around the world, generically described as 'post-modern', have shown how the ethos of the armed forces has also changed. Distinctive military values still predominate but the occupational incentives of the marketplace have begun to compete with normative considerations of the military in the post-Cold War world. The structure, makeup and purpose of the armed forces, as well as its values, have begun to change significantly.

To appreciate this better, let us look at something that neither Moskos nor his collaborators address: the growth of a post-traditional military culture, a term I take from Anthony Giddens, even though he has not addressed the military as a social organisation. Post-modern times produce post-modern mores, and what Giddens tells us is that while traditions were an intimate part of modernity, what makes our times post-modern is the de-traditionalisation of social institutions.

What makes it so is that social bonds are effectively forged rather than inherited from the past; soldiering has once again become a career, not a calling. It is also de-centred in terms of authority but re-centred in terms of opportunities, now focused on new forms of interdependence with civil society. But as Giddens insists, neither the military nor civilian world should see this in terms of decline. To regard narcissism, or excessive individualism, as being at the core of a post-traditional military would be a mistake. As the American sociologist Ronald Ingelhart concludes at the end of his survey of post-modernisation, our societies have moved away 'from an emphasis on economic efficiency and bureaucratic authority and scientific rationality that characterised modernisation towards a more humane society with more room for individual autonomy, diversity and self expression'.[18] Reflecting new civil values, it can be said that we are witnessing the rise of a new kind of soldier, not one who has gone 'soft' but one who has become, by necessity, more *humane*.

Post-traditional military

Every culture has its own ethos, its value system and behavioural norms. The military is no exception. Indeed, with their traditional emphasis on obedience, loyalty, honour and the need for self-sacrifice, the armed services have been distinct from civil society precisely because they draw upon a tradition which is presumed, often mistakenly, to go back a long way.

Tradition is a belief in a set of practices which resist the challenge of change. It is a medium of identity, and the maintenance of an identity is the principal prerequisite of ontological security. It helps define what makes a soldier a soldier. This psychological need for differentiation is historically what has allowed traditions to create such strong emotional attachments. Threats to the integrity of a tradition are often experienced as threats to self. And the self-worth of the soldier in the past has been dictated, even in a liberal society, by the gap between the civilian and military professions.

So William Cohen may complain that the military and society are disconnected, but the prospect of being too connected is also a threat. This explains the outcry that followed the remarks of a former Assistant Secretary for War who accused the marines of being 'extremists': 'Whenever you have extremes you have the risk of total disconnection from society.'[19] Although subsequently forced to resign, her resignation did not resolve the debate. Many soldiers who no longer feel secure in their profession no longer feel their profession is as 'exclusive' as it once was.

And that, adds Giddens, is what a tradition involves: exclusion of those outside it. It consists not only of a collective memory and ritual, but also of a formulaic notion of truth interpreted by the 'guardians' of the tradition. It is the connection between the last two that gives a tradition its qualities of exclusiveness. A tradition always distinguishes between insiders and outsiders, in this case between soldiers and civilians.

What has happened is that exclusiveness and the ability to exclude, whether on grounds of race, sexual orientation or just plain civilian values, is melting away. I will highlight each of Giddens' categories in order to test how far they have been hollowed out.

Collective memory

There can no more be a private tradition than a private language. Every tradition is social and based on or involves socialisation, and collective memory is geared to social practices.[20] This is why collective memories are not set in stone. They are revised and reinterpreted to legitimate the present. Memory is collective because tradition is so short; it serves a social purpose, and what marks it out as social is the continuous reinterpretation of the past which takes place.

Many of the armies' most cherished memories about self-sacrifice, for example, did not survive the First World War or the mechanisation of warfare in the early twentieth century, and tradition was revised to take account of that fact. The very fact that society honoured 'the unknown soldier' after 1918, the very fact that on the industrialised battlefield death was anonymous not individualised, reinforced the collective ethos.

Today's soldiers are individualised as never before. Danish Army cadets, when asked which of the following items they felt they most related to, 71 per cent answered 'yourself'. Only 14 per cent identified a collective entity – in this case not the army, or their unit, or even country, but their native city. It was a response which indicated that cadets perceive themselves as individualists governed by private beliefs and norms.[21] Similarly, after interviewing Italian soldiers who had served in Somalia and Albania, another researcher discovered that their main motivation in joining up had been not patriotism or even an occupational incentive, but the wish to have a meaningful personal experience.[22]

In Britain, which boasts one of the most professional armies in the world, the High Command has been forced to introduce the first ever military 'covenant', spelling out the realities of serving in an army that no longer feels it can take for granted that the young men and women coming into the forces from different parts of a rapidly changing society will understand the need for 'high degrees of personal and collective commitment [and] self-sacrifice'. Soldiers are warned that they have to be different from their civilian employers because the success of military operations requires the subordination of individual rights to the needs of the task and the team.[23]

Yet, when it comes to one's family rather than one's 'unencumbered self', it is the occupational incentives that now define military service more than ever. In part, this is a structural phenomenon. Marriage is now a norm in military life; it was not so in the past. Indeed, we forget that conscription for the first time removed women from the battlefield.

Whether because the growing militarisation of rear services rendered their presence redundant or because the introduction of railways for strategic movement made it impossible to transport them free of charge, the hordes of female camp followers who traditionally accompanied troops throughout history disappeared. On the way the First World War linked war and masculinity ideologically and culturally in a way that had not been seen since the Greeks. Perhaps at no time were the armed forces so exclusively male as during the decades immediately before and after 1914.[24]

This has long ceased to be the case. As late as 1950 fewer than one in ten drafted men in the US forces were married. By 1998 at the pre-grade level of corporal, one in three were married. And in the striking reversal of the past, soldiers in the AVF were more likely to be married than their civilian counterparts.[25] And married soldiers produce children. Indeed, today's fighting machine in America is the largest daycare provider in the world. Active duty personnel have 1.6 million children (half of whom are under age 6). Good pay and generous benefits have made military service an increasingly attractive option for single parents. Indeed, for many, war has become an optional 'add-on'.

A nationally released survey of GI attitudes in the summer of 1997 revealed that only one-third of female and just under half of male soldiers believed the principal mission of the army was to fight and win in combat. More remarkable still, the same survey found that only 37 per cent of men and a quarter of women would 'feel good about going to war with [their] company'.[26] Whether it is personal fulfilment, or professional advancement, or increasingly social security, collective memory with its emphasis on self-sacrifice in actual war-fighting no longer seems to have much appeal. In that respect too, soldiers and civilians are becoming more alike.

Ritual

Just as collective memory has given way to individual subjectivity as fewer soldiers than ever – of both sexes – join up to fight, so has ritual, for which there is little need or demand in today's military. It is ritual which enmeshes traditions in practice. It connects continual reinterpretation of the past with practical enactment and is seen to do so. Ritual enhances present performances by conferring upon them temporal autonomy beyond the mundane routine act which addresses present needs.[27]

Late in the history of the US military, for example, the rituals of West Point (most nineteenth-century inventions) were still employed to build up the character of soldiers and denote the practice of soldiering. They were found to be of little use in Vietnam and many have been abandoned since. Many West Point traditions and those learned in other institutions like the Naval War Academy in Annapolis, which fell under intense and critical public scrutiny in the same period, were relics – signifiers of a past that could no longer be reinterpreted because it had too little to say to the present. Or, at least, its connections to the present were no longer part of what gave them identity. A relic, writes Giddens, is 'a memory trace shorn of its collective framework'.[28]

Worse still, they were no longer even useful rituals. Ritualism had been replaced by ritualisation. Ritualism is a state of mind in which ritual activities are bound at, at least, with mystical notions of a formulaic truth. Ritualisation is a state in which social interaction has taken a purely standardised form. It has been adopted as a way of defining roles which people have on certain ceremonial occasions and the occasions on which ceremony (which has always had a distinctive role in military institutions in the past) are progressively declining. Ceremony has little place in a post-modern military.

Today's soldiers are not trained in arcane rituals any longer or expected to learn practices distinct from society as a whole. Their culture is now a business one. Business management did not die in Vietnam; it has been reborn, though in a different context from the corporate strategies of the early 1960s. And it involves far more than introducing business management into military decision-making in the cause of greater efficiency. It means narrowing the distinction between the civilian and military worlds.

As early as the 1960s the social penetration of the armed forces by a civilian mentality was noted by sociologists and social scientists, and there is a large literature that can be invoked, from Morris Janowitz's seminal book *The Professional Soldier* to Jacques van Doorn's classic work of the 1970s *The Soldier and Social Change*. Van Doorn observed that the state of civil–military relations was in many western countries the exact opposite of the 'militarisation' of the social world that had characterised the era of total war. And it was the economic dimension which struck him most when he wrote about the 'process . . . of social penetration into the armed forces', which had resulted in 'a high degree of civilianisation'.[29] When using the term, he had in mind the introduction of managerialism into the US military at the time of the Vietnam War, associated with the disastrous stewardship of Robert McNamara.

More recently still, the term has come to be associated with the market reforms of the 1980s and the neo-liberal insistence that every organisation should pay for itself. In the Anglo-American world in particular, competitive tendering, privatisation and decentralisation have markedly changed military culture, so much so that the military may soon begin to think in terms of such commercial concepts as productivity and performance-related pay.[30]

But to confine an analysis of what has happened purely to the economic sphere is to miss the point. Historically, the 'civilianisation' of the military has been happening for some time, though the speed of the past twenty years is without precedent. The reason for the transformation is that the military failed to maintain the distance, both political and cultural, that Machiavelli identified four centuries earlier.

One Canadian expert, for example, describes the ethics preserved in his own country's military as a 'dysfunctional form of tribalism' whose norms and values had become so distorted internally that in Somalia they led to disastrous results. And it is in Canada that there is an ever-increasing emphasis in the military on business process re-engineering supported by computerised information technology and applications responsive to personnel management and administrative problem-solving. The emphasis is now on producing 'corporate level officers' and restructuring the armed forces at the senior officer level.[31] The Canadians, indeed, have gone further than others in suggesting that the civil service and military ethos, while distinct from one another, are also *complementary*. Current trends in reducing the number of uniformed personnel may see the introduction of a greater number of civilian employees at lower levels of military decision-making and not just the National Defense Headquarters.

Guardians of knowledge

Rituals, of course, have to be interpreted. Hence the evolution of what Giddens calls a 'formulaic truth' – a truth which renders certain aspects of tradition 'untouchable'. Only certain individuals are considered to have access to the truth and only they can understand certain words and practices. Traditionally, the guardians have stood between the civilian world and access to military understanding, even in the age of the citizen soldier and total war.

Guardians are not experts as we understand the term today. They have status, not competence. It is not possible to acquire their knowledge or skill; it is given by status. Their knowledge is not communicable to the outsider. War (as Clausewitz told his readers) was not a science, and as such was not accessible to universal understanding; it was an art. The skills of the general were a craft, taught by apprenticeship in the field and experience, plus intuition, and the knowledge claims they incorporated were protected as arcane and esoteric.

In short, the guardians of tradition were not experts. An expert is a bureaucratic official, performing the specialised duties of his office. Personal loyalty is downplayed, with the emphasis instead on due process of law. The guardian's authority, by contrast, is moral – wisdom and expertise are the keys. But as Giddens adds, the difference between expertise and tradition is much more profound than this. Expertise is disembedded – it is universal, not local, and not centred on a specific culture or organisation. It is not tied either to a formulaic truth – for the experts, knowledge is always corrigible; it is always open to challenge and always suspect until tested. And although certain intuitive or emotional values still adhere to the expert – we trust one rather than another because we recognise he has 'flair' (as Clausewitz's general had 'genius') – these qualities, though important, are the qualities of a particular expert, not of expertise itself.[32]

Above all, it is the feature of expertise that no two experts can ever agree. 'It works in principle, but does it work in practice?' This suspicion which is universal among the lay public illustrates what makes expertise different. It relies on a mixture of scepticism and universalism. We may disbelieve an argument in a particular context while acknowledging the truth of the principle it incorporates. Experts themselves disagree with each other precisely in order to overcome differences and disagreement and attempt to win an argument, and thus establish their own universalistic credentials. This they do through public discourse; experts have to explain themselves to the public, these days through the media.

Today's military, of course, is no stranger to the media. Since the 1980s it has become sensitive to public discourse, perhaps more so than any other organisation. In Germany new army service regulations on the conduct of operations (HDv100/100) make media relations a vital task of today's commanding officers. Indeed, the ability to convey the right information at the right time in the right place has been elevated to a basic quality of military leadership.[33] Officers are no longer guardians of a knowledge which is arcane and impenetrable to the public; they have become experts. Shorn of the status of a formulaic truth, military expertise is now corrigible. A general is capable of being corrected. The military as a profession is now accountable to the public in a way that was not true before.

Like most other experts as well, they find they are no longer taken at trust or at face value. Science no longer has the unquestionable authority it did in the modern era. In our post-modern times all claims to knowledge are suspect. We do not trust bankers or economists or lawyers as we once did, and since Vietnam the US public no longer trusts its generals. 'Every man a soldier', Keegan tells us, is no longer conceptually possible in an information age. But every man now feels confident to challenge military advice or to choose those generals he wants to listen to.

One reason for this, on which Giddens, with Ulrich Beck and many other contemporary sociologists find themselves in agreement, is that we live in a risk society, and that is vitally important; for one reason our societies are post-traditional is that the past has lost its power to determine the present. Instead, the future has taken its place as a determinant of present action.

Calculating and managing risk has become a main political and social preoccupation. Citizens expect governments to avoid or minimise future risk and to compensate them when they fail. The ancient Greek thought of the *polis* as an active, formative training for the minds and characters of citizens has given way to a machine for the production of safety and maximisation of convenience.

Risk calculus now dominates our lives, Nickolas Luhmann, Germany's most influential social thinker, reminds us. We experience the future in the form of risk – the risk of taking a particular decision. Risk is now an aspect of decision-making, and risks concern the possible but not yet determined losses that result from the decisions we take. Those losses can be effected by particular choices and would not result from any other decisions – for example, whether to press ahead with building a particular chemical plant. Every decision we take contains unwelcome consequences.[34]

Politics and war have become forms of insurance. We cannot, in insuring ourselves, of course, create any certainty that a disaster or accident will not happen. The only guarantee is that an accident will not affect the financial status of the victim. Therefore all the dangers which we can insure against (disarming Saddam Hussein through UNSCOM, or quarantining Milosovic through war) are transformed into risk. The risk lies in the decision to insure, or act, or not to do so. And we incessantly search for decisions that can minimise a risk or neutralise a problem. We define as a risk, in short, not doing something that might help.

Not only do we go to war to avoid risk; we also fight in a risk-aversive manner. And in our desire to minimise risks we have become more sceptical of terms employed by experts such as 'adequate proof', 'truth', or even 'justice' which once sanctioned the blank cheques we gave to politicians and soldiers alike. Lawyers now sit in on briefings to determine the legality of targets. Environmentalists and aid agencies sit in on war-games in the Pentagon and are likely to do so increasingly in real life as armies seek to limit the damage to the environment caused by their own operations or to civil society which has to be reconstructed once war has ceased.

One consequence of all of this is that the previously depoliticised areas of decision-making (such as war) in which the authority of experts was rarely questioned (at least until after the event, as in the First World War) now find themselves politicised through the public awareness of risk. They now align themselves to public debate and media attention. Economic investment decisions, the chemical composition of products in medicines, the wisdom of pursuing particular scientific and research programmes – all are now publicly debated. So too are military crises and operations.

This politicisation of the non-political sphere has been assisted by technology. Where television led in the 1960s and especially real-time transmission in the Gulf War, the internet will further redefine the root definition of a news story. Internet users of the future, tracking military forces in a conflict, will be able to switch on not just to a textual account of the war or a digital photograph on a screen, but to an integrated package of both. In the next war, the citizen-subscriber to the internet will be able to connect to a computer simulation of a bombing mission and then switch to a live satellite image of a battle zone. Further subject familiarity and thus confidence to critique what he/she sees will come from accessing a three-dimensional topographical map of the target area. Using all these data, the subscriber-citizen will be able to e-mail his comments on the operation to the White House and join a chat room of citizens discussing how to prosecute the war. The internet will do much more than television to involve the citizen as never before in critiquing the operations of the armed forces in warfare as they take place.[35]

One of the outstanding features of our post-modern societies is that previously depoliticised areas of decision-making now find themselves politicised by public awareness of risks. This includes what Clausewitz tells us is the most risky activity of all: war. In the face of resistance, the armed forces are being democratised beyond the scope of what Morris Janowicz would have imagined possible in the 1960s when he wrote his seminal study. That too is part of our detraditionalised military culture. What this may herald is a more responsible military, or one more responsive to civil concerns and values, one more self-critical than in the past precisely because the tradition no longer excludes civic involvement.

The feminisation of the military

So far I have tried to establish a link between changes in society and the post-traditional military. As Giddens argues, tradition and modernity were not opposed or mutually exclusive. The modern army of the late nineteenth century was modern because it was traditional. Pre-modern traditions could be incorporated into the process of modernisation. The legitimacy of science and knowledge as a system perpetuated ideas of unquestioned truth which retained strong links with formulaic truth. Military science might have been a late nineteenth-century invention but it did not challenge the guardian ethos. Its term notwithstanding, officers were taught that war remained an 'art'.

Tradition also provided identity which modernity made not only desirable but necessary. As so many old certainties were challenged or questioned in the modern era, so the sociology and politics of identity became more important than ever. In the modern era societies spent a great deal of time trying to understand themselves in the hope of imposing some order on the chaos of their subjective growth.

It was in the nature of modernity to provoke crises of identity. That is what was modern about it. That is what constituted, also, its inventiveness. Without such crises there would have been no self-questioning and therefore no change. But this is also what produced the terror of modernity. Rapid social transformation left few areas of certainty or arenas in which individuals felt in control of their destiny, which is why they held to their traditions all the more tenaciously. Hence Eric Hobsbawm's 'invented traditions'. Indeed most military customs are late nineteenth century in origin (like most ceremonial uniforms). As armies became more mechanised and civilians penetrated through conscription, the more the past was reinterpreted to provide continuity with the present.

The post-modern era has very little need of traditions and what it provides: fixed identity. And it no longer allows social exclusion. The reassertion of civil social values (the end of trinitarian politics) is the historical context within which this transformation of culture must be seen. Nowhere is this more true than the most startling break with tradition of all: the admission of women in combat-related (and in some cases even combat) roles.

This development has been called by its critics (of whom there are many) 'the feminisation of the military'. Its importance is precisely that it is seen to threaten the traditional military culture. In the words of Congresswoman Pat Schroeder, 'what you've got is . . . culture cracking'.[36] For her, the 'de-gendering' of war is to be applauded. For many enlisted men who see their admission as the enfeeblement of national defence it has generated frustration and anger. Thousands of women are sexually abused every year – ten times more than women outside the ranks. As one US Army study on sexual harassment concluded, the victimisation of women soldiers was clearly considered by many male soldiers to be 'a normal part of army life'.[37]

We know the old arguments. The average woman has less height, upper body strength, muscle mass, skeleton weight, aerobic capacity and endurance stamina than the average man. Women do not meet the standards for 70 per cent of army specialists. Female recruits are injured at twice the rate of male. The critics, however, should remember that women only began entering the US military in serious numbers between 1971 and 1972 because not enough men could be found to serve in the All Volunteer Force (AVF) which was then in the process of being established. As male recruitment continues to fall at the very time, of course, that the overall size of military forces is rapidly decreasing, so women have been further integrated into the services. Starting in the early 1990s, basic training was gender-integrated in all the armed forces except the Marine Corps and ground combat arms of the army. Beginning in 1995 navy women were allowed to serve on warships (excluding submarines) and as combat pilots aboard aircraft-carriers, and in the USAF they were allowed to fly bombers and even fighter planes.

But this further integration has also been met by the complaint that the US military is now facing declining combat effectiveness. It has been turned, the critics argue, into a safe haven for young mothers (their average age being 22 to 23 at a time when the average female has her first child at 29).[38] It can even be argued that many women, especially the enlisted, are entering the military precisely because they expect not to fight.

According to a Harvard study carried out in the mid-1990s, only 3 per cent of army women believe they *should* serve in combat on the same terms as men. Given the opportunity only 11 per cent of enlisted women and 14 per cent of female officers would volunteer for combat and 52 per cent (or more than half) of all army women would 'probably or definitely leave the service if forced into combat positions'.[39] This 'combat-shyness' is also reflected in public attitudes. It is part of the 'humanity' of civil society that 64 per cent of people polled in the Gulf War opposed sending single parents of young children to the war zone.[40] A number of bills were even prepared by Congress to prevent women from being deployed, but the war came to an end before they could be enacted. When they do so some do not serve for long. In Bosnia between 1995 and 1996 one woman was evacuated every three days because they became pregnant. Many reportedly conceived to avoid 'hell-tours' abroad.[41]

Not all these criticisms are unfounded but we should also look at the feminisation of the American military in much broader historical terms. Whatever the arguments, the development is yet another manifestation of the closing of the gap between the civilian and military worlds; it is another feature of 'civilianisation'. And with it has gone one of the most cherished features of the traditional military ethos, although in one respect a very recent late nineteenth-century one: the end of the ideal of 'manliness'. In turn this has transformed not only the character of the warrior but also *her* nature.

Case study: the end of the manly warrior

Modern society was self-consciously gendered. Certain values were appropriated by, or considered unique to men: work, politics, public affairs, and moral codes based on principle. Women were allotted the private sphere: ordinary (domestic) virtues and the morality of sympathy. Only comparatively late did society begin to recognise that just as human biological life needs the two genders to sustain it, so does social life need an interaction of masculine and feminine values.

Feminisation does not mean masculine values giving way to feminine ones – it means that the 'space' of public institutions, the cultural and social organisations including armies, must incorporate aspects of private life: conversation, caring, compassion, social attributes which being 'left' to women had not been thought worthy, until recently, of philosophical or moral reflection. Tztevan Todorov puts the case very well. What the post-modern world concedes is that it would be disastrous to align only with masculine values or even, in a less likely scenario, feminine ones. When we are asked to be more 'humane' we are asked to take into account 50 per cent of humanity that has been traditionally excluded from the discourse of war.

> It follows that each individual must accept him- or herself – as a heteroclite being irredeemably imperfect with respect to the terms of each set of values, and that we must each – in the way we live – accept this alternation (or androgyny) along with the necessity of compromise.[42]

As Todorov concludes, the traditional gender-based division of values is not unavoidable. Gender, after all, like the cult of 'manliness' in the late nineteenth century, can often be a social construct. It does not automatically follow from the biological fact of sex that women cannot be tough or men compassionate, that neither can perform well in each other's traditional spheres: the public and private. Second, those values known as 'feminine' have been undervalued throughout western history, more so than in many other cultures, perhaps in part because what the western world has done well is war.

Yet it was only in the West (at least since the Greeks) that women have been traditionally banned from the battlefield.[43] And even then – at the height of the modern era – the old warrior ethos (especially the masculinist image) was not always considered desirable or helpful. Indeed some would claim that industrialised warfare rendered the manliness cult redundant long before the testing ground of the Somme or Iwo Jima. Before the war, wrote the infantry platoon commander Sidney Jary, he would have listed such masculinist qualities as physical stamina, a competitive nature, hunting and aggression, as the necessary qualities of a good soldier. After experiencing war from Normandy to north-west Germany in 1944 to 1945, his ideas changed radically. He now recognised that good soldiering depended on:

> Suffrance without which one could not survive. . . . A quiet mind which enables the soldier to live in harmony with his fellows through all sorts of difficult and dreadful conditions. . . . There is simply no room for the assertive. Thirdly . . . a sense of the ridiculous which helps the soldier surmount the unacceptable.[44]

Given the choice, in fact, between selecting sportsmen or poets for a dangerous mission, Jary declared he would have preferred to have recruited the latter; and that would appear to be our case too. We judge warriors by this new standard or at least encourage them to judge themselves. Ian Long, one of the first Tornado pilots to take part in the air war against Iraq, was applauded by one British public relations executive as presenting 'a relevant, caring, 1990s face' to the camera, rather than the historically sanctioned military mode of aggressive jingoism.[45]

All of this begs the question: Is the feminisation of the military consistent with the continuation of 'the western way of warfare'? Traditional military culture supplies one answer; post-traditional another. Is the military being emasculated, is that the meaning of civilianisation? It all depends on what we mean by manliness and what we mean by the culture of war. The question is indeed one of military culture. 'We bring young men and women into the armed forces to be warriors in a warrior culture', Colin Powell told the *New Yorker*. Soldiers are 'not social workers'.[46]

In traditional societies warrior cultures have always been all-male, based on honour codes, male prestige and competition for retaining self-esteem. Women have sometimes played an important role in this, from the Spartan mothers who demanded their sons should either come back with their shields or on them, to the Chechen rebels of today. Wiry and resilient and disciplined, young Chechens pick up their military skills when they are children. Men are not allowed to display emotion or affection for their children in public; but they may teach their sons the workings of a Kalashnikov early in life, before they reach adolescence.

Western armies, of course, have long ceased to be based on the warrior castes which traditionally composed them. Today we do not have warriors, we have soldiers. And the advent of humane warfare has transformed the military ethos in further ways still. Our information societies put a premium on technical versatility and knowledge rather than muscle as a source of power. Western soldiers, like citizens, interface with computers. Databases, simulation programs, expert systems, holograms – all cast doubt on traditional categories of analysis and thought such as the value of a job, the ownership of merchandise and the copyright of ideas. And all cast doubt on the traditional understanding of war, *devaluing* the job of the soldier as traditionally defined in the eyes of some.

But perhaps what is happening is that soldiering in the western world is being *revalued*. Even in the twenty-first century it is difficult to imagine that western armies will not be predominantly male or that they will be effectively de-gendered. But women will significantly change attitudes to war itself, which is why their presence in uniform is so important.

This is still very much in conflict with the *spirit* of the traditional military ethos, which is one explanation for the controversy excited by the presence of women in the forces. Most western armies are still tied to a traditional code which is *non-material*. Generals still talk of honour and tend to play up or talk up the irrational and emotive, as if dying for a material interest is somehow demeaning. What this amounts to is putting the biological above the social and treating the military as being different from civil society precisely because civilian life relies on social and materialist constructions such as wealth creation as opposed to those 'human' attributions – hatred and courage – which Clausewitz identified as being intrinsic not only to the character but the nature of war. One of the intrinsic consequences of civilianisation (and feminisation that accompanies it) is that military culture is beginning to turn its back on the biological (which of course has traditionally excluded women) and is focusing on the rational and material instead.

In a discussion of military codes, Francis Fukuyama takes a very 'modern' view which sits ill with the post-modern military in arguing that what distinguishes the human from the non-human is that the former are not programmed to act by instinctual behaviour. They are prepared to die for honour or a flag. But is the warrior who dies for honour necessarily a moral agent because honour is something that lies beyond the instinctive realm of self-preservation? Are mercenaries any less 'warriors', for example, because they do not fight for honour, certainly not their own, even if they fight for the honour of their employers? Is materialism in war (i.e. fighting for money) necessarily *dishonourable*? Fukuyama's argument would appear to be predicated on the proposition that civil society has triumphed at last and that the evidence for this is to be found in the civilianisation of military codes.

Fukuyama's reading of history is influenced by Alexandre Kojeve's reading of Hegel in the 1930s which put an emphasis on the existential nature of life, the constant fight for recognition. Man is not an animal, for though he too fights for self-preservation, he rises above his nature by showing a willingness to risk his life for a non-material reward. The two examples Kojeve cited in defence of his thesis were both military: 'a medal or the enemy's flag'. Soldiers fight to secure both not for their intrinsic usefulness but because they are desired by others, by the society they serve. Soldiers live in the recognition of their fellow citizens, in the 'soldier's tale' told of their lives after their death, and in warrior societies they even live in the esteem in which they are held by their enemies.

Moreover, Kojeve's Hegel tells us, we want to be recognised by other men because we want to be recognised as *men*.[47] It is this which holds the key to one of the objections against women soldiers. Until recently what made a man superior as a human being was his willingness to risk what we all, as human beings, value most: his own life. One of the foremost sources of self-esteem which the soldiers still derive from their service is the oldest of all, which dates back to Homer: the belief that society is divided into two, between those willing to risk their lives and those who are not, for with it was born 'the warrior's honour' (the warrior being a more honourable man than a civilian, and a woman).

Talking about his own combat experience in Vietnam, William Broyles wrote: 'If you come back whole you bring with you the knowledge that you have explored regions of your own soul that in most men will remain uncharted.'[48] Broyles' comments are quoted in an article in *Harpers* subtitled 'Is America's military training warriors or humanitarians?' For many officers it is a timely question because fewer soldiers than ever are being asked to put their lives on the line. In 1998 more civilians working in NGOs died than peacekeepers. The 10,000 civilians sent on essential war-related work to the Gulf showed much greater discipline than the soldiers: fewer were sent home for disciplinary problems.[49] In Kosovo civilians have to diffuse unexploded cluster bombs dropped by NATO planes because of the refusal of the Clinton administration to allow soldiers to carry out such work.[50]

It is precisely the individual right to life itself that is causing so much anguish among high-ranking officers in the US Army. Brig.-Gen. William Boykin admits that the US Army has gone too far, that it has allowed its soldiers to think that their mission is not to get hurt. Excessive force protection is eroding the 'warrior's honour' . Many generals are becoming increasingly critical of civil society's reluctance to allow soldiers to take risks. As one unnamed Lieutenant-Colonel complained after the Kosovo War:

> I hate to say it but there seems to be a parting of the ways between society and the military. We're citizen-soldiers, but we're used to getting on ships and sailing away from society taking care of ourselves. We're asking nothing from our country but to be allowed to go to the forefront and fight without complaint.[51]

Many soldiers are angry at the civilians for quarantining them from danger even if they often have their reasons for doing so. But there is an increasing belief in civilian society at large that even when it comes to fighting wars – from a distance, by remote control – the materialist ethos of zero casualties is increasingly defining military service anyway. New weapons systems are designed to ensure that risks are minimised and casualties kept to an absolute minimum.

Even Fukuyama regrets the fact that:

> In our world there are still people who run around risking their lives in bloody battles over a name; or a flag; or a piece of clothing; but they tend to belong to gangs with names like the Bloods or the Crips, and make their living dealing drugs.[52]

For Fukuyama, as for Hegel, a man is most human when he risks his life, when he allows his human desire to prevail over his natural instincts. In showing his contempt for life at any price, he puts his dignity first and in so doing becomes a true moral agent.

But it can also be argued that this ideal of honour speaks to an era which has long passed. Is not the equation of the nobility with non-utilitarianism socially conditioned too? Is it not in this regard dangerous because it is fundamentally inconsistent with the liberal ethos of our societies at home? As one of the principal liberal philosophers tells us, our first priority must be to avoid pain.[53] That includes soldiers as well as civilians. Should not the liberal experience of war be liberal too? Should we not fight for a material cause, a reason grounded in biology: to spare others pain or to terminate oppression? Should we not renounce once and for all fighting for an existential end, or a metaphysical principle that reduces humanity itself to an agent of history? War can be a perfectly rational activity, and to seek to minimise death or undue suffering is surely the only response such acceptance can sanction. In such a moral universe there is no room for the exaggerated 'manliness' of all-male gangs in Miami or LA Central which Fukuyama celebrates for their 'humanity' (for being more human, for showing themselves 'moral' agents even though engaging in an amoral trade).

The repudiation of manliness in the post-traditional military is therefore a reflection of its repudiation in society too. Like everything else it was grounded in a late nineteenth-century idea. So too was the Clausewitzian ideal of subjectivity: war as an existential experience which separated the civilian from the soldier by opening up those 'uncharted regions of the soul' that soldiers like Broyles lauded as a reason for serving in the military as late as the Vietnam War. This was an era that believed humanity had no biological purpose, only an existential or metaphysical reality with which it should remain in tune. 'I see many soldiers, would that I saw warriors', Nietzsche has Zarathustra complain about the soldier-citizens who were being enlisted even in his day to fight in the era's nationalist wars.[54] Today he would be even more alarmed for the soldiers, even the professionals, now outnumber the warriors who have been banished by Alvin and Heidi Toffler (in a book lauded by the US military) to a minor niche in the warfare market. The marines and special services, they conclude, have become pioneers of 'niche warfare'.[55]

6   Zoning the planet

> From the right angle the world could be seen as one large and magnifi-
> cent firework display.
>
> (Madison Smart Bell, *Doctor Sleep*, 1991)

So far I have discussed the changing character of war and concluded that
the West is trying to make it more humane, to put humanity back in the
picture. The West even fights wars for humanity – not as an abstraction
as in the past but as individuals and peoples. At the same time, however,
war is becoming increasingly inhuman in many parts of the world, and
this presents the western community with a dilemma.

The West may have lost a few hundred casualties in the Gulf and none
in Kosovo, but the death-toll in the rest of the world is telling: 150,000 killed
in Sierra Leone (1990–97); 45,000 in Chechnya (1994–95). The Americans
call it asymmetric war, others call it hell. Unfortunately, the rules and
conventions which apply in our world do not seem to apply in others.
Indeed, for much of the world the nature of war has not changed at all, and
if its character has it is because it is becoming more uncivilised.

In a world without metaphysics we have to fall back on humanism –
but that is problematic when human violence is as devastating as it is. Is
humanitarianism strong enough to sustain a moral consensus for war?
Whenever we are confronted by awful acts – genocide in Rwanda, ethnic
cleansing in the Balkans, or the gassing of Kurds, or Islamic fundamentalist atrocities in Algeria – our first thought is that they are meaningless.
We call them irrational, barbaric and nihilistic, or a mixture of all three.
We find them unintelligible; we find our belief in humanity challenged.

Such was the case in Rwanda where the world community looked on
uncomprehending at the slaughter. In three recent studies of the genocide
the killers who took part were described as 'ragged and illiterate peasants
. . . easily roused to hatred'; 'illiterate and impressionable peasants'; and 'a
wretched people . . . credulous and naive, a primitive peasant mass'.[1] To
describe the killers as barbarians not only evades the more difficult question
of why ordinary human beings can be roused to kill so wantonly; it also

dehumanises them and thus almost absolves them of responsibility for their actions, and absolves us too, of course, from holding them to account.

'We are not here to save the Somalis, we are here to redeem them', declared the Under-Secretary of State Lawrence Eagleberger when the United States sent troops to Somalia in 1993.[2] But what if people do not wish to be redeemed? What happens if they reject humanitarianism? Redemption suggests a metaphysical principle and Americans still use the old language of religion, and the secular faiths of the nineteenth century. But that is the problem: we no longer have absolute faith in humanity. The moment 241 soldiers are killed in a car bomb attack in an evening, or eighteen lose their lives in a fire fight in an afternoon, public clamour to pull out the troops tends to be irresistible.

We are faced, in short, with a serious dilemma: to have meaning it is necessary to ground an act in an absolute, or universal principle. It is useful to believe in the one true God for that reason or the global vision of history called 'the future'.[3] But it looks as if humanitarianism is a principle which cannot always survive the first contact with inhumanity. This is the problem: we live in a world divided into different time zones. Our rules of engagement are not necessarily those of our enemies.

Humanitarianism seems to have limits. The West may have turned its back on the Hegelian dialectic of History, on the grand narratives which once engaged its imagination, but something of the Hegelian 'world view' still lingers on and is all the more pervasive for being unacknowledged. From a reading of the three writers I cite below one would come to the conclusion that 'humanity' in war is limited to those who have a history, as opposed to those who have rendered themselves 'history-less'. In addition, the inhumanity of warfare in much of the world – such as mass rape in Bosnia, the mutilation of fingers, hands and ears in Sierra Leone, and widespread looting in Liberia – is often taken as a sign of nihilism, barbarism or anarchy. And history – we are told, or tell ourselves – is neither anarchical nor nihilistic. It is rational; it has a theme. Above all it is ordered.

Keeping the peace

The first of the three writers is the South African poet Breyten Breytenbach, who writes of a world in which the prophets and charlatans and the ideologies they once espoused, such as communism and fascism, have been discredited at last. The world he paints, nevertheless, is one in which little has changed for the disenfranchised and the dispossessed. It is a world in which one ideology – liberal internationalism – now dominates, masking the exploitation carried out by the hypertropic rhetoric of liberal leaders. It is a world in which a new 'ism' – globalism – merely cloaks 'private estrangement' at home. It is a world in which the industrial societies of east Asia and the West confront the inhabitants of the rest of the world with a bleak future: 'those exotically miserable continents constituting the ghostly sub consciousness of history'. Africa has 'time but no history'. It is in grave danger of being rendered 'history less'.[4]

In an article entitled 'The coming anarchy' which appeared in *The Atlantic Monthly* in February 1994 Robert Kaplan painted an even more disturbing picture of a world fast regressing into barbarism, a world which was about to be reclaimed by a history we thought we had escaped. Kaplan offers a nightmare vision of an age in which the past has returned in the shape of disease, criminal anarchy and the breakdown of the state system, a world in which groups we used to think we had seen the back of – warlords in Somalia, bandits in Liberia, private mercenary armies in Sierra Leone – have stolen back into our consciousness. The vision Kaplan offers is 'an epoch of theme less juxtapositions in which the classificatory grid of nation states is going to be replaced by a jagged glass pattern of city states and nebulous and anarchic regionalisms'.[5]

The rich countries, he warns, will ignore the plight of the poor at their peril. For poverty fosters international criminality, and criminality, in turn, spills over the frontiers of the First World. Unlike Breytenbach, Kaplan suggests Africa will play a major role in the future, if only as a model of what is to come. Kaplan has been criticised for ignoring what has gone wrong and focusing only on what will get worse. And what will get worse will be criminality and the movement of refugees. In Bosnia the mafia gangs that bid for the cellular phone contract were one of the only truly ethnically mixed organisations, intermingling Croats, Bosnian Muslims and Serbs all working in harmony towards one end: their own profit. In other words, far from being a special case, the African continent may be as relevant to the future character of world politics as the Balkans were a hundred years ago.

A final description of the pre-modern world comes from the pen of the eminent political economist Susan Strange, who paints the picture of a world which is just as violent as Kaplan's and just as unjust as Breytenbach's, but one which is far less dangerous to those who matter most: the countries of the post-industrial world. If the danger of war between advanced powers such as the United States and Japan, and the next wave of countries coming on stream such as China and Brazil, has greatly diminished, then perhaps the world market does not need universal peace or collective security against aggression. 'Let us not assume,' Strange insists, 'that because preventing war between the great powers was the main issue of world politics in the twentieth century, that it will also be the main issue in the twenty-first.'[6]

The favourite model for the 'losers' in this world is that of the under-class, a term which was first coined by Oscar Lewis in the 1960s to describe the poor in Puerto Rico and Mexico City, a self-perpetuating class for whom dependency on the hand-outs of others had become a way of life. In Lewis' account the poor were characterised by a set of attitudes that were bred by the struggle to survive. The culture of poverty placed in a class of their own those whose behaviour and values converted their poverty into a self-perpetuating world of dependence.

Since then the term has come to be used of the poor in America's inner cities, and the black poor at that, who are the chief victims of crime as well as its chief agents. Africa too has come to represent an underclass in recent years. If the association of urban poverty and race in the United States is relatively recent, a product of the migration of African-Americans into the northern cities after the Second World War, Africa too did not emerge into the world's consciousness as its most troubled continent until the 1980s when it produced three out of the world's four major famines. Today, the continent accounts for two-thirds of the world's refugees.

By the end of the twentieth century Africa had been reduced to the status of a victim in its own imagination as well as that of the outside world. Television images of refugee camps in Ethiopia and southern Sudan appeared to show a people beyond hope or even despair, a people beyond redemption. There is an echo here of Conrad's novel, *Heart of Darkness*, and Marlow's encounter as he sails up the Congo river and sees the destitute natives on the bank:

> Black shapes crouched, lay, sat between the trees leaning against the trunks, clinging to the earth, half coming out, half effaced within the dim light – in all the attitudes of pain, abandonment and despair. . . . They were dying slowly . . . nothing but black shadows of disease and starvation . . . bundles of acute angles sat with their legs drawn up . . . I stood horror struck.[7]

In Marlow's account the natives cease to be human. They are reduced instead to 'angles', 'shadows' and 'shapes' which cannot be seen very clearly. The difference today is that we can see them all too clearly through the camera's eye. Yet it is a difference which rebounds on the continent. In Conrad's tale, at least, they represented disease, abandonment, despair and starvation, the legacy not so much of the continent itself as the darkness of colonial rule. Today, in a continent that it supposedly independent and sovereign, they have become the products of the African condition. The problem is not that the European powers have done so much but that their African successors have done so little.

All three writers offer us a version of the contemporary scene in which the people of an entire continent have become 'local', trapped in a time that is outside universal history. Breytenbach writes of a world in which some societies have time but no history, in which they are excluded from the historical consciousness of the rest of us. Kaplan paints a picture of a world in which the big themes have been replaced by a mosaic of unclassifiable confrontations. It is a world which is themeless – 'a themeless juxtaposition of events' – and what is history, of course, if it has no theme?

Strange writes of whole societies which are no longer progressing into the twenty-first century but which are apparently marking time. As the hero of Saul Bellow's novel, *The Dean's December* (1982) remarks, the underclass is a redundant one. When referring to its plight one cannot even use the term 'culture': 'There is no culture there. It's only a wilderness and damned monstrous too. We're talking about a people consigned to destruction, a doomed people.'[8] When we think of Africa too we think of a continent in which millions of people are sleep-walking to destruction.

None of these accounts of the world are untrue because they assert that the world is now divided into three different time zones. Where their analysis is questionable is their implicit claim (a Hegelian one) that there has been a major transformation in the structure of world history. When western commentators look at countries like Liberia and Sierra Leone, what they see is a disaster zone, one so unrelentingly bleak that much of the world can be said to have no future. To use the colloquial meaning of the term, 'the future is history'.

This explains the demoralisation of western forces when they finally intervene in societies such as Somalia. For the future is no longer what it was. In the Cold War years we lived in a single historical time zone – the future, or more pertinently, the passage to it from the past. Today we appear to live in two. History is no longer a dialectic within one zone: a struggle between communism and capitalism for the high ground of history. Instead, it appears to have become a dialectic between the future and the past. If one has to limit the occasions on which one intervenes, it is better to fight for those people with a future. That is the logic of triage, of humanitarian warfare.

An insecure world

The western world faces a dilemma. Its commitment to make war more 'humane' is intimately tied to its faith in humanitarianism. But the latter is a universalistic faith that has little sympathy for particularism of the kind the pre-modern world is witnessing: the growth of a neo-feudal security regime in which the only protection against violence is membership of gangs, clans, or allegiance to personal warlords or leaders with their respective feudal affiliations and ties. The problem is that gang membership can create a strong sense of identity. Neo-tribal affiliations can provide what spirit of community there is in much of the world, and that spirit often feeds off war.

Humanitarian intervention (in the form of peacekeeping or even humanitarian war) is not always calculated to make people feel less insecure. Writers who were fortunate enough to survive the Second World War should know this better than writers who were born after it. For until 1945 insecurity was a fact of life in much of the western world, as Sigmund Freud knew well. Freud was the first man to propose writing a history of the phenomenon to show how in certain periods people felt more or less secure, and how insecurity took different forms in different historical eras. In his 1920 study *Beyond the Pleasure Principle*, he went to great lengths to distinguish between fear, fright and anxiety.

Fright refers to the state we fall into when suddenly confronted by a dangerous situation for which we are unprepared. Fear presupposes a definite object of which we are afraid. Anxiety refers to a state of mind when we prepare for a danger we know we may not be able to avoid. Freud stressed the fact that in common usage the three terms tended to be used interchangeably. People tended to use each word as a synonym for the other. It was a mistake he wanted to redress.

While pre-modern societies were more fearful and frightened of early death, for example, or supernatural events which were deemed to presage natural catastrophes, modern societies were more anxious. What made them especially anxious in the twentieth century was the threat of war.[9] The poet W.H. Auden called the twentieth century 'the age of anxiety', and the world was no less anxious after the Second World War than it had been before it. For the next forty years it lived in the shadow of a nuclear holocaust. What Freud set out to ask in his book was what made the modern age different from every other. If he were writing today he would probably ask: What makes the West, or what some call the 'post-modern' world, different again?

The post-modern world is still *anxious*, mostly about crime and terrorism at home. By contrast, modern societies such as the Czech Republic are still *fearful*, and what makes them most fearful is whatever may prevent them from joining the post-modern community, or may make them revert to the pre-modern condition. For a people such as the Czechs security involves a very narrow set of issues: developing stable market economies; building up social safety nets; integrating the country into the world economy – in other words, successfully transiting the old Second World into the First. The traditional threats – war, revolution and invasion – have been replaced by economic challenges. 'The Challenges of Modern Society' is the suggestive title of one of the committees which make up NATO's Partnership for Peace Programme.

And what of the pre-modern world? It is still *frightened* of day-to-day death in the form of war, poverty or rampant disease. Survival cannot be taken for granted. It is estimated that nearly 100 million people are caught in a cycle of civil strife and hunger. About 50 million have been forced to flee their homes. The conflicts which have driven them out take many forms, from random acts of violence by individual groups or rival criminal gangs with no aspiration to control the state, to sporadic incidents of violence by organised groups seeking greater political participation.

Faced with such permanent sources of insecurity, many people choose to pursue individual strategies of survival. Many more are forced to align with whoever will protect them. It is a condition with which Europe itself was quite familiar until recently. When Arthur Ransome, a British Foreign Office official, travelled through Galicia after the outbreak of the First World War, he noted that:

> The peasants working on the land were very unwilling to identify themselves as belonging to any of the warring nations. Again and again on asking a peasant to what nationality he belonged Russian, Little Russian or Polish, I heard the reply 'Orthodox' – and when the men were pressed to say to what actual race he belonged, I heard him answer safely, 'We are local.'[10]

The peasants, in other words, were whatever it was safe to be. They were the product of centuries of proverbial native guile. The story has the singular merit of identifying what is so important in pre-modern communities. No definition of security, no idea of what an armchair strategist thinks should make people feel more secure, will necessarily make them less frightened.

The humanitarian military ethos

If the West has little sympathy for particularism, it has absolutely none for the inhumane way in which particularist warriors fight their tribal wars. Indeed, whenever the post-modern world intervenes in the pre-modern – mostly in the form of peacekeeping – it has to confront what the Tofflers call 'a collision of war forms'.[11] Post-modern societies fight their wars in their own fashion. Pre-modern societies tend to do the same.

What makes the latter appear so undeserving of respect – what appears to make the pre-modern warrior a man without honour – is the increasing *inhumanity* of contemporary conflict at a time when the western military are being trained to become not warriors but humanitarians. What concerns western observers most is that the violence in a society like Liberia appears to be 'autistic'; the belligerents appear to be unable to distinguish between destruction and self-destruction, or to conceive of the consequences of their acts. Their inhumanity, it is argued, is not a contingent factor – a result of brutalisation stemming from the lengthy nature of the wars. It is endogenous, the fact that the wars represent a Hobbesian struggle of all against all. The irregular who fights in such conflicts, writes Michael Ignatieff, ignores human rights, adheres to no standards of warfare and rarely comes under the military laws devised by states. The result is a descent into excessive violence, barbarism and genocide.[12]

The West, of course, has confronted 'barbarians' before. In a letter home from the Sudan where he served as a reporter-cum-soldier, Winston Churchill wrote that the whole campaign reminded him of a 'pantomime scene at Drury Lane'. What had etched itself so vividly on his imagination was the colour of the campaign. The enemies of the British Empire tended to emerge 'one by one from the dark wings of barbarism up to the bright footlights of civilisation. Perhaps, the time will come when the supply will be exhausted and there will be no more royal freaks to conquer.'[13]

In those days the 'barbarians' came dressed to kill. Today the way they dress is still taken to be a sign of their barbarism. The very spirit of war, writes Barbara Ehrenreich, once associated with national honour, has become a commodity available in the global consumer market. With Rambo, Hollywood offers a denationalised generic warrior hero suitable for universal emulation. What struck an American journalist about the Russian special forces in Chechnya was that they had clearly been influenced by the Rambo films:

> The soldiers were dressed in preposterous Rambo outfits: headbands, mirrored shades, sleeveless muscle-shirts, bandoleers, belts packed with hunting knives – [they] wanted nothing more than to look like their movie hero.[14]

The influence of Sylvester Stallone's crass representation of the all-American soldier hero did not stop at Chechnya. Serbian soldiers fought in Rambo-style headbands; a Liberian guerrilla fighter called himself 'General Rambo'. Within the United States itself Rambo culture has inspired the militia movement in defence of the citizens' rights to bear arms.

What most distinguishes yesterday's imperial warriors from today's peacekeepers is that the former respected their enemies, or at least claimed to. The extent of that respect is vividly illustrated in Tolstoy's last novel *Hadji Murad* (a copy of which Wittgenstein gave his friend Norman Malcolm to accompany him into military service in the Second World War). Murad was a hero of the resistance to the imposition of Russian rule in the Caucasus. In December 1851, however, having fallen out with the Iman who was the political leader of the resistance movement, he deserted to the Russians, only to be killed in action four months later.

He may have been an unlikely hero, but Tolstoy, who served as an artillery office in that war, saw him as the ultimate Chechen hero, a man who dies courageously with his identity not only uncompromised but enhanced. In his novel, he makes him the master (which in real life he was not) of every attribute that mattered: including resourcefulness, leadership, horsemanship and vision. No other hero in western literature, claims Harold Bloom, America's most distinguished critic, is quite like him. No member of another warrior caste was ever paid such respect by a western writer.[15]

Respect for the enemy was at the very heart of the western warrior ethic. One of the most moving passages in literature is to be found in a concluding chapter of *The Seven Pillars of Wisdom* in which T.E. Lawrence praised the valour of a German detachment and wrote that he was proud of the men who had killed his brothers: 'they were glorious'.[16] Nietzsche claimed it was the confrontation with one like oneself, with an enemy worthy of respect, that defines the warrior above all else. The enemy as peer is a theme of much of his writing. The true warrior is one who can 'endure no other enemy than one in which there is nothing to despise and very much to honour'.[17] It was a passage invoked by Ernst Junger, one of the great European soldier-writers of the twentieth century, in an entry in his diary in May 1917. While serving on the Western Front with the Hanover Fusiliers, Junger encountered his first Indian soldiers – Rajputs from one of India's military castes or 'martial races' – men from the First Hariana Lancers. As a member of a military nation himself, Junger considered himself privileged to fight them:

> What does Nietzsche say of fighting men? 'You must have as enemies only those whom you hate but not those whom you despise. You must be proud of your enemy and then the enemy's success is your success also.'[18]

For even defeat, of course, provided it is at the hands of a worthy opponent, need involve no shame. The stories of heroic defeats are often as stirring as those of heroic victories; for both involve what is at the centre of the appeal of war: victory over oneself, the overcoming of fear, as well as the wish not to dishonour oneself in the face of the enemy. When fighting a despicable opponent, of course, none of these factors apply.

Why do western armies respect their adversaries so little today? One explanation is sociological; the other is moral – humanitarian armies cannot stomach inhumanity; modern armies could. Let us look at the sociological explanation first.

In India, wrote Hegel, every caste had its special duties and rights. While the Europeans said bravery was a virtue, the Hindus said, 'bravery is the virtue of the Cshatryas – the warrior caste'.[19] In some parts of today's world the situation has changed very little. The Indian Army still recruits from its military castes, as befits a modern rather than post-modern nation. It still recruits from the same 20 per cent of the population, the Rajputs, Sikhs, Dogras, Maharattas and the people of the North West Himalayan Frontier. Similarly, the Chechens tend to fight with the same ardour as their ancestors. Fewer than 15,000 of them resisted a 100,000-strong Russian army for months in the second Chechen War (1999–2000). Wiry, resilient and disciplined, they pick up their military skills when they are children. Men may not display emotion or affection for their children in public, but the fathers teach the sons the workings of a Kalashnikov early in life. Engagement with the Russians over three centuries has fostered qualities ideal for guerrilla warfare: respect for seniors, group loyalty, no alcohol. Their inspiration comes from a militantly purist Wahhabism.

Even late into the twentieth century western armies recruited from a class, if not a caste. In a letter which Churchill wrote to General Alanbrook on his appointment as the Commander of the Imperial General Staff in November 1941, he reminded him of his friendship with his two brothers. One he had met in the Fourth Hussars while serving on the North West Frontier, the other while fighting in the South African war at Spionkop.[20] Churchill came from a military class himself, from a family that by tradition had sent its younger sons into the army. From the moment he left Sandhurst and obtained a commission in the Fourth Hussars he did his utmost to get into the fight. Within a few years he had seen fighting on the North West Frontier, the Sudan and South Africa, and taken part in the last great cavalry charge in history by the Twenty-First Lancers at Omdurman, a charge he described so vividly that it came to appear to be a greater episode than it actually was.

As a member of his class, Churchill believed war to be character forming. He regarded it as a form of nurture. In the first book he ever wrote, his account of his first campaign, that of the Malakand Field Force, he extolled war's moral virtue. What struck him most forcefully was how 'the uncertainty and importance of the present reduced the past and future to comparative insignificance'.[21] Such sentiments were not untypical either of his class or his times; and 'the times' lasted much longer than we might suppose. Two-thirds of Britain's generals and 56 per cent of its colonels before the Great War came from the ranks of the aristocracy or gentry. After the war the number of officers who were the sons of gentlemen entering the military academies may have dropped significantly, but the sons of officers rose appreciably so that the overall military background did not change much. Even after the Second World War the officer corps was able to socialise with those who were not from public schools so that the British officer corps still retained the vestiges of the original aristocratic system.[22]

Today, the situation is very different. Western soldiers are no longer drawn from castes or classes or the traditional social groups which made up the modern army. In the British Army 58 per cent of generals and field marshals came from one of the leading public schools; in 1999 this was true of only 33 per cent as well as a mere 6 per cent of major-generals. The army is more like a business which needs skilled people to manage finances, human resources and technology. Managerial techniques and an increasing emphasis on technical skills makes for a more meritocratic military much more interested in information warfare than in policing or patrolling distant frontiers in faraway places around the world. Western armies increasingly recruit men and women wholly absorbed in the world of computer algorithms and software networks for whom the military dimension is no more than a 'add-on'. They are a world apart from the soldiers of the past.[23]

For the most part, nineteenth-century warriors respected each other not only because they both thought of themselves as warriors, but also because they lived in a *mental* world which was not entirely different. What was extraordinary, writes Philip Mason, about the Pathan (Anglo-Indian for Pukhtun) wars was that the players on both sides admired much the same qualities: courage, loyalty to the side on which a man happened to be fighting, and the defence of personal honour. As one ex-serving soldier wrote:

> There was among the Pathans something that called to the Englishman or the Scotsman – partly that the people looked you in the eye, that there was no equivocation, and that you couldn't browbeat them even if you wished to. When we crossed the bridge at Attock we felt we had come home.[24]

The British respected the Pukhtuns as 'sporting' adversaries. War on the north-west frontier involved its own honour code and rules. There was no malice when the whistle blew and the game was over. Frontier officers were a special breed among the British and sometimes they were almost converted to the Pathan sense of honour and usually to his sense of humour. Of course, Mason adds, 'It did not often happen the other way round.'[25]

Finally, the warrior castes of the nineteenth and early twentieth centuries – whether they hailed from Europe or the non-western world – also lived in the same technological environment. Western armies, contrary to popular belief, were not distanced from the societies they conquered by technology, as are many today. One recent study argues that the British did not possess a technological edge of any value against their Afghani adversaries until the third and last Afghan War (1919) when they were able to use portable radios, air power, lorries, armoured cars and mobile machine-guns.[26] In the first two encounters the imperial forces fought with similar weapons to their enemies', which did much, of course, to narrow the cultural gap between the two.

And that, of course, was the point. If the lawless tribes on the north-west frontier did not romanticise the British as the latter romanticised them, they did, at least, respect their fighting qualities. By contrast, many of the communities the West now faces in battle have little or no respect for the managerial techniques of its armies or their increasing preoccupation with media management. This is an issue for many senior American commanders who are concerned that recruiting advertisements at home tend to focus on humanitarian assistance rather than combat skills. The nation, they claim, needs warriors, not humanitarians. As General Peter Schoomaker, Commander of US Special Operations, explained in 1999: 'We have a fundamental problem in the western world dealing with warrior-class cultures.'[27]

This was especially true of the American experience in Somalia (1993–94). From the beginning, the Somalis did not take them as seriously as they took themselves. They were not overawed by the size of the American presence. They were not impressed either by the daytime patrols by helicopter gunships. Even the way the Americans dressed communicated the wrong signals. They always went around in flak jackets and wore helmets, and were described by the Somalis as 'human tanks'. Without the Americans realising it, this was a constant irritant and a definite factor in Somali aggressiveness towards them in the summer of 1993. The Americans both inspired fear and were perceived as being fearful: a fatal combination.[28]

Even America's allies were scornful of the way US forces conducted themselves. The French were confirmed in their suspicion that the operation had been hijacked by the Americans when they decided to put up a $25,000 reward for Aideed's head with a wanted poster in the best Tombstone-OK Corral tradition. It is not always, however, the regard or lack of it that a western force shows for its enemies that is important, so much as the seriousness with which it is taken by the locals. The Somalis themselves had no objection to the Hollywood touch that the French found vulgar. Indeed, the most popular film in Mogadishu for years was Sylvester Stallone's *Rambo III*, in which the eponymous hero helped another people, this time the Afghans, to liberate themselves from oppressive Soviet rule. The film may have bombed at the box-office in the United States but it never left the screens of downtown Mogadishu. Unfortunately, it merely served to highlight the contrast between the Somali conception of the US Army before and after its arrival.

Turning to the other side of the equation, western soldiers have little if any respect for their adversaries either. In part this arises from the unbridgeable gap between today's 'technological' imperative in war and the old martial values. Information societies put a premium on technical versatility and knowledge rather than muscle as a source of power. Western soldiers, like western citizens, interface even more with computers. Databases, simulation programs, experts systems, holograms – all cast doubt on traditional categories of analysis and thought, such as the value of a job, the ownership of merchandise and the copyright of ideas. They also cast doubt on the value of war. They tend to *devalue* the job of the soldier as traditionally defined, as well as the traditional idea of warfare.

The soldiers who now know the old conflicts and act by the old moral codes tend to be special forces: the SAS, the G9 in Germany, the Rangers in the United States, who are engaged in what the Tofflers call 'a niche market'[29] – or niche warfare. Operations behind enemy lines tend to capture the public imagination, for they are still part of the old way of warfare and appear more intelligible and familiar as well as intrinsically more romantic to an audience at home that knows war largely from what it sees on the screens or reads in books, a public that enjoys the Rambo films.

Most other western soldiers have little respect, professional or otherwise, for the people who fight the new wave of ethnic and other conflicts. Indeed, one of the chief paradoxes of humane warfare is that they regard them not as fellow soldiers but as 'warriors'. In the words of one American soldier, many are 'erratic primitives of shifting allegiance habituated to violence with no stake in civil order'. His portrait of them is unedifying indeed:

> When we face warriors we . . . face men who have acquired a taste for killing who do not behave rationally according to our definition of rationality, who are capable of atrocities that challenge the descriptive powers of language and who will sacrifice their own kind in order to survive.[30]

In his book *The Warrior's Honour*, the Canadian writer Michael Ignatieff writes in different terms. Both the western and non pre-modern worlds breed warriors: the difference is that the military code which combines a code of belonging with an ethic of responsibility applies less and less in both worlds. Modern technology is steadily increasing the distance, both moral and geographic, between the warrior and his enemy. In other parts of the world where the state has lost control, war has become the preserve of private armies, gangsters and paramilitaries. As a result, the distinction between battle and barbarism is beginning to be blurred.

But then Ignatieff's idea of soldiers is a very western one. 'Armies train people to kill but they also teach restraint and discipline; they channel aggression into ritual. War is redeemed only by moral rules.'[31] Western soldiers still see war as a *schooling* in which training and judgement are given time to develop before being put to use. By contrast, in Sierra Leone 80 per cent of rebel soldiers were between the ages of 7 and 14, and the government relied on children as well. Both sides used them to commit the kinds of atrocities that even adults might have been reluctant to carry out. That is why there are 300,000 child soldiers at large in the world. Violence often serves as an initiation for the new recruits; acts of violence bind the youths together, creating a permanent rift between those who commit the acts and the communities from which they come. No wonder western peacekeepers see so many of their potential enemies as barbarians. Child soldiers are used by all accounts for their ruthlessness, their lack of moral inhibitions, their lack of restraint. Nothing is more terrifying than a child wielding a gun who is still officially below the age when he is meant to be developed enough to assume responsibility for his actions.

Whether their role is evidence of nihilism or barbarism is another matter. Medieval armies were made up of irregulars who were bound by no code of honour worth discussing. We should not be fooled by the 'humane' code of chivalry. What we see as a redeeming feature of warfare was probably that of a guild rather than a force motivated by Christian compassion. The laws of war were the rules by which it was safer for men to fight, as well as the rules which made war profitable. Given the acquisitive nature of medieval warfare, it made no sense killing off nobles in battle when they could be ransomed instead. War was a business. Like other enterprises, staying in business was important. Enjoying a string of good years (an ongoing pillage) was more profitable than having one great day (a decisive battle) – though on the big day the ransoming of prisoners usually ensured the death-toll was low. That made chivalry an evil not a panacea in at least two respects.

First, it prolonged war; second, it permitted the application of double standards. For there seems to have been no apparent incongruity between the notions of chivalry and acts of pillage. There is little reason to suspect that the code of chivalry that limited the horrors of battle was ever really intended to extend to non-combatants. As one of the principal English historians of the Middle Ages writes:

> Chivalry with its idealisation of the freelance fighting man, could not be a force effective of limiting the horrors of war; by prompting men to seek wars and praising those who did. Its tendency, for all its idealism and because of it, was rather to help make these horrors endemic.[32]

Warfare in Sierra Leone shares much with medieval warfare in Europe. The experience of weak governments, the phenomenon of 'strong men' within wider 'jurisdictions', the battle-avoiding strategies and the burden of war heaped upon the non-combatant all echo medieval warfare. The various factions that are fighting for profit are aware that others are doing the same. None of them has any confidence in the potential outcome of the conflict. The majority are trying to make the most of the situation while it lasts and would prefer it to last for as long as possible.

It is this economic rationale that makes warfare in much of Africa not only endemic but also inhumane, because it is disproportionately aimed against civilians. Indeed, it has resulted in an extremely cynical endgame in which there appears to be some complicity between government and rebel forces. A typical scenario would involve government forces withdrawing from a town, leaving arms and ammunition to the rebels they are supposed to be fighting. The rebels pick up the arms and extract loot, mostly in the form of portable and easily disposable items from the townspeople before they themselves retreat. The government forces return in order to loot larger items and partake in more illegal mining. Whether the 'rebels' truly are rebels, and not, as is perhaps the case, government troops in disguise, the economic rationale is clear. The irony of the situation is that civilians increasingly have less reason to remain non-combatants. It is often safer to be a member of an armed band, and nearly always safer to attack civilians than to attack armed opponents.[33]

Looked at in this light we can conclude that war is inhumane in much of Africa precisely because it is so 'rational'. Inhumanity serves a purpose. As long as they label the violence 'irrational', western societies are unlikely to fight many humanitarian wars in the future. They refused to intervene in the Great Lakes crisis in 1996, or Sierra Leone a few years later. Clearly, humanitarian war has its limits.

Humanitarian imperialism

The trouble is that humanitarianism does not seem to convey the same moral urgency and moral strength of the old *mission civilisatrice*. Without an imperial ethos (or something very like it) it is difficult to justify casualties, and more difficult still to keep the peace in the way that imperial armies once did. For behind the bravado and romance of Britain's little wars there was a great deal of violence. There was nothing romantic about fighting on the north-west frontier in country which was harsh, fierce, jagged and unrelenting. Frequently, British soldiers had to slog through valleys, or found themselves penned up in the hills in searing heat, engaged in a war of sniping and ambushes and long marches at night, always facing the fanaticism of an enemy that was proud to die for the faith.

Nor did the British in their more reflective moments have any illusion about the way they themselves conducted war. Even a romantic like Churchill never deceived himself that the wars which the Empire fought to keep the peace were brutal. 'Of course it's cruel and barbarous', he once conceded after his unit had burned down native houses as a punishment for a raid. But then, he added, 'Everything else is in war.'[34] Whenever the British burned villages in winter, they effectively condemned civilians to either starvation or a lingering death from the cold.

There is also little self-deception in Churchill's account of an incident involving the 11th Bengal Lancers:

> No quarter was asked or given, and every tribesman caught was speared or cut down at once. Their bodies lay thickly strewn about the fields, spotting with black and white patches the bright green of the rice crop. It was a terrible lesson, and one which the inhabitants ... will never forget.[35]

What made the cost of imposing peace acceptable was a sense of duty. The role of the white man, Kipling wrote, was 'freedom' – the righting of wrongs and failing freedom, war. 'Savage wars of peace', he called them, because though savage, they brought the defeated peoples within the imperial peace, the Pax Britannica. It followed that war itself was necessary, a job that was heroic because it was dogged and unpraised. 'The old grim, thankless task of ruling heedless of praise or blame', *The Quarterly Review* defined it in 1919.[36]

As Kathryn Tidrick points out, what is interesting about British campaigns in the Punjab was that whenever they burned villages and crops in reprisal for raids – that is, whenever they employed the same methods as the conquerors of centuries back – they *denied* that they did so. They were proud of their military record, and anxious to stress that India owed little to the sword and everything to the moral force or character of its rulers. None of this was cynically intended. The modern age was not cynical about such matters. It sought to invest war with an authentic moral character. The British believed that in the long term severity saved life and would render unnecessary more severe punishment later.

This, adds Tidrick, may seem a curiously pessimistic view of human nature for a people like the Victorians who were so preoccupied with the improvement of their subject peoples. But it was rooted in their belief in the weight of original sin which tended to detract from the moral optimism and belief in progress that was such a feature of those years. It endowed violence with a moral quality which gave it legitimacy. It allowed them to treat the subject peoples as errant children, Kipling's 'new caught, sullen peoples/half devil and half child'. Ultimately, 'to be cruel in order to be kind,' writes Tidrick, 'is to inflict legitimate punishment rather than to practise illegitimate oppression.'[37]

Today's soldiers have no metaphysical beliefs to sustain them when the going gets tough; they only have their humanism. This is why they often cut and run at the first sign of trouble, or intervene reluctantly when much of the damage has been done. The western soldier may complain of his enemies' lack of honour but it would be wrong to attribute to them mind-less terror or nihilism, or an interest in war for its own sake. In the end they must recognise that every warrior's code reflects the ethos of war; the reason men fight it determines the means by which it is fought. A western army tries to employ humane methods especially when it is fighting for humanitarian ends. A society trying to factor out incivility in warfare will be horrified by the inhumanity of Serb paramilitary groups, or the child soldiers of the RUF. The latter, by comparison, are in the war business for very different ends, and the methods they employ are not necessarily at odds with what Clausewitz called war's 'true nature'. Ultimately, the problem is compounded by the fact that western soldiers have no metaphysical beliefs on which to rely, and which would allow them to act cruelly – if only to be kind. Western soldiers are not Tidrick's nineteenth-century warriors. Cruelty is no longer part of their vocabulary or sense of self.

Humanitarian war and the loss of metaphysics

Nor for that matter is history; and it was history which invested the western moment in the developing world with *meaning*. The imperial powers in the nineteenth century may not have been motivated to expand by anything other than greed, or the struggle for political advantage, but they invested their intervention at least with meaning: they located it in the post-Enlightenment belief in progress, and war as its medium. By contrast, life in the West today is becoming 'post-historical'. Western societies, writes Jan Patocka, represent the triumph of historicity and its implosion, the human turn from metaphysics – from reaching for a life lived in the perspective of truth and justice – to the mundane satisfaction of mundane needs. In our attempt to make life more humane we live life merely for the sake of catering to it.

Patocka's work is interesting in this respect because it challenges the grandiosity of the humanitarian project. It suggests that it devalues if not diminishes man. We no longer value others so much as *pity* them. Societies no longer aim for a new utopian project. There is no project. Humanitarianism has become not an end but a means. I think Patocka puts it particularly well. We do not live in a post-modern age. We live in the modern world but 'the question is whether historical humans are still willing to embrace history'.[38]

From one perspective humanitarian warfare can even be seen as a rejection of history. One person who shares that belief is Patocka's fellow Czech, Vaclav Havel, who fears that the West has become a risk society increasingly unwilling to take those great leaps in the dark that Heraclitus thought made conflict the father of all things. 'Beset by so many threats to civilisation . . . it is seemingly incapable of confronting these dangers.'[39] In a plot line which might fit one of his own absurdist plays from the 1960s, he believes that the end of the Cold War has given the West a chance to put humanity back into the centre of the picture just at the moment when the western powers have lost their ability to act. In a risk society history is of no significance. As every outcome has unforseeable consequences, especially war, we fight wars with such minimal risk to our soldiers that they fight sometimes to little purpose. There is no project. Instead we are in danger of fighting what Michael Ignatieff calls 'drive-by wars' like Kosovo, in which we can strike anywhere in near certainty that neither its civilians nor its soldiers will ever again be put at risk.[40]

What do I mean by a historical project? For much of the twentieth century its leading power, the United States, never questioned the need to forge a world order; that was its historical mission. Liberalism claimed (and still claims, of course) that all human beings share a fundamental rationality, and that if left unchecked people would recognise a Kantian interest in not resorting to war to settle their differences. Liberal societies believed in the application of liberal laws that would allow freedom of the individual, a freedom which would only end where the freedom of his fellow human beings began. Since war is fundamentally unreasonable it followed that it could be found in the illiberal status of states. When Wilson took the United States into the First World War he did so to end the reason for wars – 'the German feudal system'.[41] In 1917 when the United States finally entered the war, it identified the defeat of Prussian militarism in terms of a *modernising* project.

Many British writers thought in similar terms. In his book, *The Common Sense of War and Peace*, H.G. Wells exhorted his readers to remember their essential humanity and to suppress their miserable differential traits, no matter how genuinely held. Writing in 1940 he suggested that the British people's defiance of Hitler was not a national quirk – the British people were at that moment in history 'the battle front of humanity. If they are not that front they are nothing – that duty is a privilege.'[42] Here was a strong belief in a historical project, as well as a striking affirmation of the unity of mankind. When Britain yielded that 'front line' to the United States the Wilson project was reaffirmed. The Cold War gave the Americans the opportunity to advance beyond the present.

To provide a meaning in history is no small matter, writes Zaki Laidi. It is to make the world a problem to be studied. It is also to advertise a claim to universal validity; the right to speak not only on one's own behalf but also on that of the human community. Laidi's own book, *A World without Meaning*, was a bestseller in France, and in it he accused the United States of projecting its military power around the world in the absence of a concrete project. No longer interested in *making* history, the West sends forces into societies like Bosnia, not to realise a project but to manage a crisis. Unfortunately, humanitarian intervention loses any meaning if it becomes autonomous from politics, or detached from a project. In Somalia the upshot came at the end of Operation 'Restore Hope' when humanitarian bodies had to intervene to care for the victims of humanitarian intervention. And 50,000 soldiers were sent to Bosnia not to ensure the country's political existence but to manage the humanitarian consequences of its partition.

Laidi concludes that humanitarian warfare has three requirements which make it a contradiction in terms. First, it rests on spontaneous legitimisation that is hard to reject (the wish to save human life) despite the fact that governments are often forced by public opinion into adventures they would rather have avoided. Second, action has to be kept to a limited time span to reduce the cost of the operation, including the cost in life to one's own forces. Third, it requires evading serious solutions to the problem, because this would call for military means incompatible with humanitarianism. One reason, for example, why NATO did not drop food supplies for the thousands of Kosovars displaced from their homes was the fear of flying below 15,000 ft which would have put its pilots at risk of being shot down. Instead it leased the operation to a consortium of private NGOs.[43]

In a word, the United States has no grand *purpose* in mind. If, as Laidi argues in his book, we understand 'meaning' to consist of three interrelated notions – a foundation, a sense of unity and a final goal – then humanitarian warfare can properly be described as 'meaningless'. While the need to project ourselves into the future has never been so strong, we have never been so poorly armed on the conceptual front to conceive this future. We have no foundation except pity for our fellow human beings which Nietzsche considered, probably rightly, to be an insufficient ground for action.

And we have no sense of unity any longer because we are forced to be selective in the tragedies in which we find ourselves engaged, so much so that in Rwanda the State Department found itself involved in a semantic debate as to whether or not the massacres that so outraged public opinion constituted 'genocide'. And we have no final project in mind other than the rescue of the dispossessed. We have no ambition to construct a new world order or to put a different society in place. War is becoming remedial as well as reactive.

The problem is that this does not make war particularly humane, for we delimit the scope of our concern. The marginalised societies of the globe are an embarrassment. At best, they are seen as useless; at worst, threatening. By labelling the poor as an 'underclass' as many observers now do, we institutionalise their place on the fringes of the 'civilised' world. The rich occasionally salve their guilt with what Zygmunt Bauman calls 'occasional carnivals of charity such as humanitarian wars'.[44] But that is the point: the carnival moves on to the next town or mission, often leaving the dispossessed as powerless as they were before (as in the case of Somalia).

This in turn can lead to 'seductions of disgust' when the people we try to redeem remain, or when they present themselves to us as being irredeemable.[45] It is easy to become disillusioned when confronted with the media representation of contemporary civil wars. As Nietzsche once put it: 'together with the fear of man we have lost our love of him, our reverence for him, our hopes for him ... The sight of man now makes us weary – what if nihilism is not *that*? – *What if we are weary of Man?*'[46]

Or perhaps this is the wrong question. Without losing our interest in humanity will we lose interest in helping it? Certainly, we make fewer demands on ourselves. We are increasingly reluctant to allow our soldiers to take risks even on behalf of those whom they are trying to assist. Of course, there is no particular virtue in risking one's life for the sake of it. If it is possible to reduce casualties to a minimum, one should try to do so. But in an attempt to minimise risks the West is in danger of distorting its own 'humanitarianism', and, worse still, of confusing moralism for morality. For apart from the fundamental distinction between good and evil – between helping and hurting – there is another ethical distinction which is central to the moral imagination – between giving things and giving of oneself. To work for the happiness of others may require us to risk our own. In refusing to do so we run the risk of replacing the abstractions of old – the social myths of class, nation and race which sanctioned inhumanity in war with another social myth – that of 'humanity', defined in such abstract terms that we are asked to sacrifice very little.

Moralism favours abstractions which cost little. Morality by contrast is subjective not objective: it involves the willingness to run risks for other people. The post-Cold War impetus to conduct wars for humanitarian ends tends to contend with the impetus to 'humanise' their means. With its new 'post-modern military' culture, the West appears intent upon transforming war into something new: an operation for the immediate purpose of crisis management, rather than a struggle against adversaries for competing notions of the future.

US military involvement in the post-Cold War world reflects an assumption that technology can compensate for the anaemic humanitarianism currently dominating the foreign policy discourse which is, in turn, reflective of a 'degraded liberal creed' that appears incapable of sustaining a vision beyond the immediate crises at hand. As Adam Wolfson noted at the time, the Clinton administration's reaction to ethnic cleansing in Kosovo had no sense of political vision beyond the here and now:

> Where most people are dying is where we should be, regardless of interest, politics, or even ideals. There is no sense here, as perhaps there was among an earlier generation of idealists, that our liberal-democratic principles are of universal validity. What remains of the liberal creed is only a blind belief in human equality and a feeling of compassion for those who are suffering. Not that there's anything wrong with equality and compassion, but today's liberal humanitarians have little else to offer.[47]

'Having little else to offer' is symptomatic of a *biological* approach to humanitarianism which is consistent with the claim I made in Chapter 5: our wish to re-ground the humane soldier in a non-ontological discourse that puts life above metaphysical identities of anything 'higher' than individual life. If it is consistent, however, it renders western armies incapable of accomplishing much more than alleviating the immediate images of death and suffering. As laudable as these sentiments may be, the impulse to alleviate suffering does not make for a sustainable solution to humanitarian crises and may indeed exacerbate them.[48]

Unfortunately, current military thinking favours stasis over transformation, or immobility rather than action. Whereas the modern ethos encouraged attempts to transform situations, the post-modern condition is altogether suspicious of radical change. The attempt to take the metaphysics out of warfare (as I will argue in Chapter 7) reflects and reinforces a preoccupation with trading in only one tense: the present. It allows the American military to 'restore' order (even if there was no previous order to restore) and 'keep' the peace (regardless of whether there was actually ever any peace to keep).[49]

In short, there is reason to suspect that in our risk-averse cultures humanitarianism does not run very deep. When we do intervene our operations are usually limited. We no longer fight our enemies to the end or demand their unconditional surrender. Even the instigators of genocide and ethnic cleansing are usually left in power, even if indicted at the War Crimes Court of the Hague. And because the wars the West fights are usually limited, it tries to quarantine the nihilistic regions of the world, to seal them off or at least attempt to. It tends to divide the globe into various time zones defined in part by their humanity or inhumanity, their civility or barbarism. And that, of course, has the paradoxical effect of diminishing our own humanity by calling into question one of the cardinal beliefs of the modern era: the universal nature of the human condition.

7 Humane war and the moral imagination

Lin Yutang and humanised thinking

During the Nuremburg trials Hermann Goering spent much of his time in the dock reading a work of philosophy, a contemporary bestseller, by a Chinese philosopher, Lin Yutang. His book, *The Importance of Living*, went into several editions in the 1930s. It was rarely out of print. One of its principal contentions was that nations, like individuals, have their own conceptual understanding of the world.

It is difficult to know what Goering made of the philosopher's discussion of national characteristics in an era which took them for granted. Taking R for a sense of Reality (or Realism), D for Dreams (or Idealism), H for a Sense of Humour, and S for Sensitivity, he rated the three main protagonists of the twentieth century thus:

R3	D3	H2	S2	=	Americans
R3	D4	H1	S2	=	Germans
R2	D4	H1	S1	=	Russians

In all three protagonists, humour was low. It might exist but it did not include irony, defined as a wish to put some distance between oneself and one's ultimate beliefs, and to see those beliefs (and oneself) through the eyes of others. Sensitivity was low too, except perhaps in the arts. Even in the liberal world which did not censor modern art as 'decadent' or condemn it for being contrary to 'social realism', the artists challenged the humanism of the Enlightenment. They were no longer prepared to take on trust the old assumption that the autonomous subject was the measure of human perfection. In the sciences too, people were prepared to accept a degree of discipline and conformity formerly rejected as incompatible with human dignity.[1]

What is most striking about the above table, however, is that the dream quotient was high for all three countries, and the reality quotient low. The problem with the latter was that it was assumed even in the United States that provided a people had the will to succeed – which meant acting collectively – they could overcome every obstacle, especially material ones, a fact which explains why materially weak societies like the Third Reich (and later the USSR) felt confident enough to challenge the United States, the strongest power of all.

More pernicious still, when people dreamed they dreamed in abstractions. What distinguished the past 2000 years of warfare was the mythical reduction of complex political situations. In the pre-modern era men had invoked the myths of God or the Divine Right of Kings or the Great Chain of Being (the ordered hierarchy of the commonwealth). What defines all communities are their beliefs and their willingness to fight for them. The only difference in the modern era was that the myths were secularised. God was replaced by History with which nations were either in or out of step, which 'crept' up upon them, or 'stole' their future (the metaphors reinforced the immediacy of the myths themselves as well as the need to fight one's corner: to fight one's way into history, or sometimes out of it).

In addition, the West used to mythologise entire social groups – the bourgeoisie and the proletariat and their polar opposites – which it conceptualised as 'malign' or 'progressive' or 'revolutionary'. Myths represented the temporal incarnation of the creative and moral component of humanity, the abstractions with which it engaged emotionally. They took concrete personified shape and entered into conflict with each other. And it is significant how often the roles the myths asked people to assume – hero, victim or crusader – were drawn from the metaphor of war.

The values which Lin Yutang ascribed to each nation were (as he was the first to confess) rather crude formulas by which the mechanism of human progress and historical change could be expressed. But they all related to war, or the reasons which drove men to fight it. The world that he described is now three generations away. War no longer figures very prominently in the collective imagination. It no longer forms what William James called 'the stuff of experience', any more than it is the subject of epic stories or tales of human endurance and heroism.

When we go to war we see the world in a very different light. When we talk of reality we talk in utilitarian terms, in an inverted Benthamite desire to impose minimal suffering on the minimum number. We are committed to limiting the human costs of war too. No longer interested in utopia we dream more limited imaginings, and ask less of those who still dream. Our sensibility has made us more sensitive to the plight of others, our enemies as well as our friends. It is our humour, however, which has increased most significantly. When we look at war we find it increasingly ironic. We have become intensely self-conscious of our own actions, driven as we are by memories of what injustices we committed in the past in the name of our own rather recondite understanding of progress, or a liberal world order, or civilising mission.

Our own times, of course, may appear shallow. Indeed, it is often claimed that we are no longer willing to fight for anything of spiritual or intellectual importance. Our reluctance to do so, however, can also be taken as a sign of what Lin Yutang called 'humanised thinking'.[2] As the title of his book asserts, life should be lived in the real not the abstract. We have exposed what Hannah Arendt called the 'vicious interconnection' between abstract notions and abstract emotions to which much of the inhumanity of the modern age can be traced.[3]

In the attempt to make war more humane, the West is also addressing its moral imagination. In the past the legitimacy of conflict was rooted in religion and metaphysics. Societies derived or purported to derive their beliefs about how they should behave from God's intentions for man, or from the nature of the world and our understanding of it. Science challenged many of these beliefs in the early years of the modern era, but not all of them. For many referred to an order of reality which was supposed to be beyond the reach of science itself.

What distinguishes our present world is the death of metaphysics, and with it has gone a revaluation of war as a moral concern or activity. We no longer fight for History, or a class, or race. We fight for others, or ourselves. We fight against inhumanity. And that is difficult, of course, because war requires that we act cruelly towards others, that we inflict pain on other people. We can only do so if we are self-consistent – if we fight for humanity; if we fight humanitarian wars.

The post-modern age fights humanitarian wars because we have renounced metaphysics. Man is now responsible only for himself, and his main responsibility is to pursue policies which reduce human suffering. The moral injunction of our times is to avoid acting cruelly towards others. We must attempt to transform war in a way that eliminates what Grotius considered to be one of its most enduring features: its cruelty. That can best be done, contends Richard Rorty, by putting the individual – both the soldier and the civilian, the belligerent and non-belligerent alike – at the heart of the war equation. And that, in turn, requires us to repudiate the concept of a humanity higher than the individual human being – or a principle higher than humanity itself – such as an idea, or historical principle, or divine force.

The problem with Rorty's position is *not* that it prevents us from going to war. We can reduce suffering significantly by preventing people from behaving cruelly towards others. But in a world in which others are seeking to revalue war in the name of a 'higher authority' including God, humane warfare may devalue the warrior in the eyes of our enemies.

Richard Rorty and the end of metaphysics

> Weapons have become godless since then. Weapons have
> lost their religion.
>
> Don DeLillo, *Running Dog*, 1978

Rorty bases his own humanitarian project on a rejection of metaphysics. Instead, he looks forward to what he calls the closing down of metaphysics, which, he adds, was 'one of the less important side shows of

Western civilisation'.[4] Whether this was true in the twentieth century is another matter entirely. For metaphysics was one of the most important features of that most defining of human activities, war. Dislodged from the modern consciousness, God was replaced by metaphysical abstractions that retained a tenacious hold on the western imagination.

Although modernity is usually associated with the eclipse of religion by secular concepts, these secular concepts none the less retained a faith in the immaterial and abstract principles characteristic of the West's Judao-Christian inheritance. Metaphysical principles offered a way of abolishing God with the least possible expense by substituting an Enlightenment faith in mankind, or a Hegelian concept of History. Life continued to have meaning, therefore, in relation to something transcending the material existence of each individual; it followed a mythic grand narrative that extended beyond the realm of everyday experience.

Metaphysics offered a concept of the Absolute that demanded sacrifice. War once again took on the crusading character of the religious wars of the past, where participants on both sides had managed to convince themselves of the righteousness of their cause. Martin Van Creveld contends that this willingness to die 'represents the single most important factor' in modern war, and is even more crucial than the willingness to kill. 'War', he writes, 'does not begin when some people kill others; instead it starts at the point where they themselves risk being killed in return.'[5] Conceptions of freedom and equality provided more compelling motivations for sacrifice than naked *raison d'état*. Metaphysics provided a purpose for war that transcended the importance of individual life and imbued fighting with a significance that made the destructiveness of modern warfare possible.

But metaphysics provided more than the actual purpose for warfare. Hegel's teleological concept of History also provided a grand narrative that promoted the future over the present tense, and in so doing made war the agent or locomotive of History.[6] Modern warfare was inextricably linked to a future-oriented ethos. The immediate horrors of war were only bearable if 'modern man' was willing to surrender the present tense. Since History now had a theme, events could be 'historic' rather than simply 'historical'. Sacrifice was legitimised through an emphasis on the ends of warfare rather than the means.[7] Individuals played an active role in this historical 'world process' as the agents of History. History did not simply happen; it was something that was *made*.

History as a metaphysical principle

> Walking back to the porter's lodge of Churchill College, Cambridge, [George] Steiner and I returned to the subject of the historical Hitler in particular, his fabled charisma. 'I used to ask my students,' Steiner said, 'if Hitler walked into a room would you get up?' 'Would they get up meaning?' 'Would one sit in the presence of World History?'[8]

It is a telling anecdote from one of England's leading literary critics. Hitler, of course, saw himself as a world historical figure from the first because he believed he had understood 'the meaning of history'. This claim appears in *Mein Kampf* and it was not a throw-away line, for when he was later asked which of the many statements he made in the book was the most self-revealing, he replied, 'a short sentence at the very beginning in which I say that as a youth I learned the meaning of history'.[9] Until the end of his life Hitler believed implicitly in the self-creating power of the imagination and will, in the cult of the hero and the world historical figure he believed himself to be.

What this anecdote captures is the extent to which war has changed as has the world we live in: few of us, if any, think in such terms today. As Steiner admits, he *used* to ask his students that question; he does so no longer. Our world has no time for great historical themes, still less for Hegelian heroes. It has become distrustful of history.

The Enlightenment, of course, was critical of the metaphysical systems of thought of antiquity and the Middle Ages. It rejected divine revelation. It looked forward but it re-invented God. It anchored social life to a new metaphysical system. To error, wrote d'Holbach, 'we owe the religious terrors which freeze human beings in fear and make them slaughter each other for the sake of figments of the mind.'[10] But as Voltaire had recognised, if God did not exist humanity would have to invent him; and this is what happened. Metaphysics was re-grounded not on God but on History.

One especially revealing example of this is to be found in the work of the philosopher Maurice Merleau-Ponty who, like Jean-Paul Sartre, became a fashionable writer on the Left in the 1950s. Looking back on the Second World War he concluded that it had precipitated a process of Hegelian education. It had been an educative experience that had moved men closer to universality and self-consciousness. It had established a 'ground of historicity' between combatants and non-combatants alike which they had not freely chosen: between Aryan and Jew, Frenchman and German. They had found salvation in becoming 'European', and in doing so they had moved a little closer to the brotherhood of man – the 'end' towards which History was moving.[11]

War was central not only to the Hegelian dialectic but also to the reaction to Hegelianism, to the three 'schools' of dialectical materialism, liberal pragmatism and existentialism. All in their different ways tended to subvert humanism. All three, in subordinating the individual, allowed recourse to cruelty and misanthropy. In the struggle for progress, human emancipation and personal authenticity, everything was permitted.

Even Marx, in the last years of his life, believed the proletariat would only realise its destiny through war. It needed war because it was the only class in history to recognise that it was in its own interests to seek its own abolition. It could only prevail by transforming society and thus transforming itself. This idea had an appeal that survived the carnage of the

First World War. In the Spanish Civil War those who fought on the Left found a cause which they believed to be historically sanctioned. What is remarkable about the poetry of the conflict is that unlike that of the First World War, the poets located the struggle in history. And although they did not gloss over the violence, what is remarkable is that the phrases they used which had been discredited in the trenches – such as 'valour', 'pride' and 'the glorious dead' – resurfaced in the poetry of the Civil War. And the reason for this was that a new myth had revalued war, and with it the willingness to die for a cause.[12]

Even liberal writers who were less interested in abstract ideas than their illiberal critics invested war with a metaphysical importance that it had never had before, for they derived it from their own belief in progress. 'There are some battles ' wrote the mid-Victorian writer Edward Creasy, 'which claim our attention on account of their enduring importance and by reason of the practical influence of our own social and political condition which we can trace to the results of those engagements. They have for us an actual and abiding interest.' Battles have always fascinated historians in the past, of course. What changed in the nineteenth century was that the most 'decisive' were now considered historically important not only for deciding things, but also for *improving* them.[13] What changed was that they became a medium of the pervasive modern belief in progress.

All fifteen of the battles which Creasy told his readers were the most decisive in history were chosen for their political consequences. As a thoroughly 'modern' man he was not interested in religion, he was interested in progress. If he had been interested in the former he might have chosen the Milvian Bridge at which Constantine established Christianity in the Roman Empire, or Vouillé where Catholic Christianity became the faith of the successors of Rome; or Lutzen which produced a religious stalemate between the Protestant and Catholic faiths, and which persisted up to Creasy's day. But as a modern man, he was not interested in the salvation of the soul. He was interested in war as a progressive force, and he chose Marathon, the first on the list, because it had 'secured for mankind the growth of free institutions (democracy), the liberal enlightenment of the Western World and the gradual ascendancy of the West.'[14] His last battle, Waterloo, had been fought in his lifetime and confirmed that Britain had once again defeated the forces of tyranny in defence of liberal values. For Creasy, writing as he did in 1851, this was the Grand Narrative of History.[15]

Finally, war could also be experienced existentially, a theme which was particularly prominent in the work of the liberation war theorists of the 1950s, especially the most famous, Franz Fanon. Sartre believed that if Sorel's fascist utterances were set aside, Fanon could be acknowledged as the first writer since Engels to bring the process of history into the clear light. But Sorel's thought was different from Fanon's. He embraced violence as a social end grounded in a social 'myth'. Fanon's starting point was personal authenticity. You can be what others want you to be: a slave, a Jew, or member of a minority. Or you can be yourself through an act of self-assertion. Violence, claimed Fanon, was a medium of political consciousness; it was a way by which a colonial subject could become a hero, and thus gain self-respect. It was a view which found particularly forceful expression in his contention that, for an African, every white man he killed was a double profit: the act brought him to the awareness of his manhood and rid the world of a racist at the same time.[16] To quote Judith Shklar, 'As a world history class victim he must learn to play his part cruelly.'[17]

Today we have grown weary of grand narratives, or what Arendt called 'abstract notions' such as History. We no longer believe that history has a goal or a purpose. No single configuration or historical narrative appears to constitute a theme. However we choose to phrase the problem, the conclusion is the same. If we no longer allow ourselves the comfort of a teleological view of history which gives it a goal and a purpose we must accept that cruelty, pain and suffering are part of the human condition. They can be reduced but not eliminated at the 'end of history'. We can no longer go to war to advance that end.

And if history is cruel we must blame not some mythical force but ourselves. We no longer have a historical sanction to act cruelly towards others. To quote a passage from Thomas Pynchon's novel, *The Crying of Lot 49*, 'Power, omniscience, implacable malice, everything they had thought to be an historical principle, a *Zeitgeist*, are carried over to the now human enemy.'[18] Humanity has been given back its historical subjectivity; in so doing history has become humanistic – if not alas humane.

We have reached the end of an era. With its threat of total war through nuclear annihilation, the twentieth century represented the apotheosis of a 'High Modernity' that also anticipated its own collapse. For nuclear deterrence could only 'work' by holding the future hostage. Unlike the wars of the past, the logic of nuclear deterrence required a resolute *un*willingness to 'make History' for fear of bringing history to an abrupt conclusion.

The 'balance of terror' was not the only threat to the metaphysics of History. Another process was also working to elevate the private over the public, the present over the future, and the individual over the tran-scendent: market capitalism. Self-regulating markets tend to foster the pursuit of private, immediate, material gain, and have little interest in considerations beyond the individual pursuit of pleasure. They tend to make 'the long-term appear futile, perspective an illusion, patience useless, versatility indispensable.'[19] In the United States, the market's emphasis on efficiency appeared to render metaphysical speculation an altogether inefficient waste of time, while America's success in achieving those material comforts removed the impetus to enquire too deeply into the human condi-tion.[20] Together with a corresponding 'preoccupation with happiness', most

Americans took little interest in the 'big questions' served by metaphysical speculation. By the end of the 1970s, the sociologist Christopher Lasch noted a growing 'culture of narcissism' in the United States, fostered by market capitalism and characterised by a 'survivalist ethic' that encouraged Americans 'to live for yourself, not for your predecessors or posterity'[21] Similarly, the idea of transcendence detached itself from any coherent set of symbols; 'vivid' and 'ubiquitous' corporate symbols could no longer 'deliver the indispensable feeling that the world does not end at the borders of the self'.[22]

This seemed to be confirmed even in the way the Cold War came to an end. Instead of culminating in a dramatic Armageddon, perhaps appropriate for the end of an epoch, it ended on a muted note. With the collapse of the Soviet Union and the end of the Superpower rivalries, warfare finally entered the discourse of 'humanised modernity'. Unfashionable in private as well as public life, metaphysical principles have all but disappeared from the discourse on politics.

We are left with only one metaphysical principle: our obligation to Humanity (the injunction of Christian humanism). We find a compelling version of it in Vaclav Havel's defence of the Kosovo War:

> The bombardment of Yugoslavia . . . elevated human rights above the laws of states . . . [this] was accomplished out of respect of the law, a law that is higher than one guaranteeing the sovereignty of the state. The alliance has intervened out of respect for human rights. This right has its roots outside the physical world. While the state is a product of man, man is a product of God.[23]

In metaphysical thinking there is always a higher reality beyond the real world we observe every day. As Plato argued, it is impossible to know that one is living in a city unless one has an idea of what a city is. Likewise it is impossible to fight for humanity unless one has an understanding of a higher moral injunction to be humane. In this case Havel's 'higher law' – 'human rights, human freedoms and human dignity . . . have their roots somewhere outside the perceptible world'.

Such metaphysical thinking Rorty would consider self-defeating, not least because in the western world belief in God is unlikely to be sufficiently persuasive to legitimise war. And he would have little truck with Havel's belief, expressed in an earlier speech, that the West should have 'a metaphysically anchored sense of responsibility' without which Havel claims it would remain 'unanchored' in a chaotic and violent world.[24]

Rorty is probably right to consider that the attempt is unlikely to succeed, not least because we would seem to have turned our back on all metaphysical propositions. We no longer believe in myths, pre- or post-enlightenment, whether they take the form of God, the nation state or progress. We no longer find war 'progressive' or 'ethical' or 'holy' – in fact, we find it increasingly irrational, uncivilised and inhumane. Our attempt to humanise war by rejecting myths is more than just a break with a tradition which assumed that war was necessarily inhumane. What we are attempting to do marks a decisive break not only with the modern era but with *every* era of history.

The demise of metaphysics is important for that reason. We have no myths on which to rely; we have only ourselves. Instead of metaphysics Rorty urges us to embrace a pragmatic philosophy which accepts that humanity does not have an essential nature, namely that there is something unchangeable called 'the human'. In challenging this assumption we should recognise that humanity is an open-ended notion, that the word 'human' names a project, not a God-created essence as Havel conceives it.

At the heart of Rorty's philosophy is a refusal to regard humanity as the incarnation of something larger than the individual: the Movement, Reason, God, the Holy. Instead we should accept our human finitude. We should accept that we have obligations to other people (not to bully them, but to join them in overthrowing tyrants). And that does not require that we share with them any greater existence. What we share with them when we are aware of such moral obligations is not rationality, human nature, or the fatherhood of God, or even the knowledge of moral law. We share instead the ability to sympathise with their pain.[25]

Rorty calls himself a liberal ironist. He is a liberal because he believes cruelty is the worst thing that one human being can do to another. He is an ironist because he faces up to the historical contingency of his own central beliefs; he does not believe that they refer back to something beyond the reach of time (like God). He is therefore not a metaphysician for he grounds the belief in not inflicting pain on the human imagination. 'Imagine me,' Humbert Humbert enjoins his readers in *Lolita*. 'I shall not exist if you do not imagine me.' In other words, if we are not novelists in our daily lives we will not understand much of anything, which is why Rorty advises philosophers to turn to works of the imagination, especially literature. For only through our imagination can we 'see strange people as fellow sufferers'. Once we increase our sensitivity to the pain and humiliation of others we find it difficult to marginalise people different from ourselves, by suggesting that 'they' do not feel pain as we do.[26]

Our obligation to other human beings means expanding our sense of 'us' as far as we can. As Patocka argued, over the centuries our sense of common humanity has been expanded from clan or kin to the community, to the 'imagined community' of the nation state and further afield still, to the 'global village' which encompasses East Timor and Rwanda. Rorty is of course right, to remind us that we still have far to go, for we have not yet even begun to extend our sense of brotherhood to the marginalised class in our own inner cities.

The right thing to do, he tell us, is to create a sense of solidarity with mankind. The wrong thing is to follow Havel and 'recognise' it as something

God-given that exists antecedent to our recognition of it. Instead of meta-physics, we should accept that the renunciation of cruelty has a corollary: the search for truth is not distinct from the search for human happiness. A true belief is an instrumental one. The desire for the 'truth' of the human condition cannot take precedence over the desire for happiness. And happiness is merely an extension of the liberal agenda like votes for women, and equal rights for blacks, and multi-cultural values. Humanitarianism is a political invention; it is a political project which may indeed require the citizen to be schooled in what Martha Nussbaum calls 'a cosmopolitan education'.[27]

In the end, Rorty would challenge Zaki Laidi's discouraging picture of a world that has surrendered the Enlightenment project altogether. For his appeal to freedom can be defended in an anti-foundationalist manner on the basis of efficiency.

> It would be more efficient to do so because it would let us concentrate our energies on manipulating sentiments or acquiring a sentimental education. That sort of education sufficiently acquaints people of different kinds with one another so that they are less tempted to think of those different from themselves as quasi-human. The goal of the manipulation of sentiment is to expand the reference of the terms 'our kind of people' and 'people like us'.[28]

There is much in this which seems humane, and even humanising, but there is much that also seems to be questionable. Can we make war part of the humanitarian agenda, can we humanise it as we are trying to do with the rest of the modern (liberal) project? What happens when taking the metaphysics out of life means taking the metaphysics out of war? Can war even exist in the Rortyian universe?

Of course, since Rorty himself does not address the subject of war in any of his writings, one might be forgiven for concluding that non-metaphysical liberalism will somehow dispense with warfare altogether. He alludes to the peaceful relationships that would result if individuals saw each other as 'fellow sufferers', but he does not bother to think through the implications of 'putting cruelty first' on the liberal agenda. Does this mean that liberals should forcefully intervene on a fellow sufferer's behalf if necessary?

Rorty simply maintains that liberals can recognise 'the contingency of their own consciences' and yet remain 'faithful to those consciences at the same time'.[29] Sacrifice may be necessary, but he does not see sacrifice as much of a problem for the liberal ironist. Instead he points to the Europeans who risked their lives to rescue Jewish families during the Holocaust as an example of liberal sacrifice, implying that it was their solidarity with other human beings as biological creatures that encouraged them to risk all in order to save others.[30]

It is a questionable conclusion to reach. As Barbara Elshtain remarks, the personal reminiscences of the rescuers tend to suggest that 'ironical reasonableness didn't have a lot to do with risk-taking'.[31] She contends that Rorty ignores their self-proclaimed commitment to religious or meta-physical ideals, especially insofar as they included notions of morality and goodness extending beyond the realm of human biology. Rorty's assumption that sacrifice is still possible without a metaphysical purpose follows from his scorn for eschatological issues altogether. In eschewing the 'big questions' of life and death as unnecessary for everyday living, he still assumes that liberal ironists would be willing to defend their values if the situation demanded it. Again this is open to question. Indeed, this blithe failure to think through the implications of non-metaphysical living indicates what Elshtain calls 'the unbearable lightness of liberalism', where concerned citizens such as Rorty have tried to jettison 'the metaphysical underpinning of the don't-be-cruel rule' without even deliberating on the relationship between that metaphysical underpinning and sacrifice.[32]

Writing during the throes of the Second World War, Lewis Mumford pointed out how this kind of superficial approach to life and death rendered the earlier generation of American pragmatists at a loss when confronted with the question of war:

> The pragmatic liberal's failure to confront except in a hurried, shame-faced way the essential facts of life and death has been responsible for much of the slippery thinking on the subject of war that has weakened the moral decision of millions. The present crisis compels democratic peoples to sacrifice everything – or to accept servitude, hoping that by shamming dead they may escape notice and avoid actual physical death.[33]

Mumford's criticism is perhaps even more relevant today than it was in 1941. America's involvement in the Second World War indicated that it was prepared to sacrifice lives before sacrificing ideals. More recently, however, 'slippery thinking on war' has flourished. Whether consciously adopted or not, Rortyian-style liberalism has generated a confused attempt to reconcile an emerging humanitarian conscience with a reluctance to confront the cruelties of war.

Instead, the United States has tried to resolve this dilemma by attempting to take the cruelty out of war altogether. Unfortunately the new humanitarianism does not include a vision of any transcendent ideal that extends beyond the immediate crisis, and therefore fails to offer a compelling reason to endure the cruelties that war usually brings. Similar to Rorty's non-metaphysical take on human rights, the humanitarian conscience does not seem to be based on anything other than the desire to alleviate immediate physical suffering. Aided by television images (which sanctify the immediate over a 'big picture') and abetted by a minimalist approach to liberalism, the American foreign policy discourse now treats humanity in the same way that Rorty conceives of the concept: as 'a biological rather than a moral notion'.[34] Taking the cruelty out of war, therefore, makes perfect sense when saving individual lives becomes the goal of military intervention. Without its metaphysical foundations, however, humanity fails to justify the sacrifice and bloodshed which is innate to warfare, or which has been hitherto. Instead the means of war begin to take precedence over the ends.

War and sacrifice in an ironic world

Rorty agrees with Nietzsche on the contingency of the historical character of our sense of moral obligation. The seventeenth century with which I began this book also knew of humanitarianism, of course, at least in its vision of a better future. What is remarkable about the manifesto written by Milton to justify England's declaration of war against Spain in 1655 was that it was the first state paper ever to make a public grievance out of the mistreatment of a non-European people by a European power (in this case that of the Indians by their Spanish conquerors in the New World). The grounds for that grievance were quite explicit: 'All great and extraordinary wrongs done to particular persons ought to be considered as in a manner done to all the rest of the human race.' Whatever the motivation of Cromwell's government in going to war, Milton like many others took the principle of human brotherhood seriously.[35]

But the seventeenth century which David Ogg described so vividly was, for the most part, a cruel age which produced Grotius and Milton but only to mock them – there was little humanity in the way it practised war. Milton's poetry might have appealed to his contemporaries, but not his politics. It is our age which has given rise to the humanitarian agenda, and we should seek out the reasons why this is so. It is important to acknowledge that our wish to humanise war is historically contingent.

Humanitarianism itself, we are told by Rorty, like peace, is an 'invention'. As a concept it is deeply rooted in the society of the day: in the post-materialist, risk-averse cultures that we have become. To understand humane warfare we have to understand the needs, fears and aspirations of our own citizens (no longer citizen-soldiers) who support Kosovo-style wars. Like maxims in the philosophy of Keats, humane warfare is valid for them only when they 'feel it on their pulses' – when it rings true, when it captures in their imagination the reality of what 'war' has become.

But if 'humane warfare' is a historically contingent phenomenon, it would be irresponsible to ignore what is happening elsewhere on the planet where war is being revalued in terms of the politics of identity or ethnicity. *We* may see war as an obstacle to self-creation because it denies difference and 'otherness'. Others still see war as a form of self-creation, or a source of spirituality, or a way of forging a more 'authentic' social life. In other words, if war is no longer part of our moral imagination it is still part of theirs. We may have taken war out of the equation, but nothing can justify it now in terms of the name of the will of God, or a moral law, or a form of Darwinian selection. Nothing can justify war except the suffering of man. This is certainly noble, but it is unlikely to appeal to societies in which God still enjoins people to go to war.

In the end, the problem of attempting to humanise war is twofold. First, it encourages us to indulge in what the historian Daniel Boorstin calls 'the myth of popular innocence' – the illusion that adversary peoples are passive victims of cynical leaders when, in fact, many support war, and fight it with passionate commitment.[36] Second, the danger is that in fighting as we do we run the risk of devaluing ourselves in the eyes of others. In finding politics ironic we are in danger of making it appear self-serving. Indeed, the way the West chooses to fight its wars is becoming increasingly 'unreal' for much of the non-western world: for the Islamic fighters fighting for the faith; and for the faithless (but not irrational) young bloods of West Africa from the rural slums inspired by the writings of Marcus Garvey. For the former, war has no legitimacy without metaphysics; for the latter, humanity has no place in war. The moral economy of humane warfare rings false for both of them. It is not part of their moral imagination.

Much of the world still believes in myths and fights for them. Some societies find deeply offensive what they take to be the West's attempt to devalue war by taking metaphysical principles out of the equation. Far from revaluing war, they think the West is in the process of devaluing it at the very time that they themselves are re-invoking the 'sacred' or 'metaphysical', at the very time that they are rediscovering just or holy wars or wars which affect to be spiritual. It is our enemies who find 'humanitarian war' more ironic than we do ourselves.

Other societies have little time for liberal irony or our contempt for cruelty, or our distaste for myths we consider atavistic, irrational or inhumane. Many of the people with whom western armies find themselves in conflict are indeed barbaric: the men who put a K47 in the hands of a 9-year-old child; the Indonesian militias in East Timor; the Montenegrin reservists who laid waste Croatia's Dalmatian coast in 1991, looting the tourist resorts and bombarding historic Dubrovnik. But not all the people we find ourselves fighting are barbarians, and not all of them are 'barbarous' because they are contemptuous of our way of warfare. Many do not see our soldiers as warriors, only as technicians performing a routine. Others are openly dismissive of our 'humanity', and reject as self-serving and naive the very idea that war can ever really be 'humane'.

Other societies are still interested in making history on their own terms and scorn humanitarianism, not because they are especially inhumane but because in the world of their imagination – the world of the 'saved' and the 'damned' – there is no room for the toleration of differences on which Rorty's rejection of cruelty is grounded. A Taliban soldier who believes that the parts of the soul and state should correspond is unlikely to find Rorty's rejection of cruelty anything more than dishonest moralising. A Somali warlord is still likely to find the differences of clan, religion and race more important than the similarities he shares with an American marine with respect to pain and humiliation. The moral universe of a child soldier in Sierra Leone is unlikely to be the same as that of a United Nations peacekeeper. In the case of all of them there is no place for liberal irony – their values are neither contingent nor absolute: they are whatever the bandit chief or clan leader or local mullah to whom they owe allegiance wants them to be.

In the end, we may pay a high price for continuing to find war 'ironic'. At the height of the Cold War the Polish poet Zbigniew Herbert was also concerned about the West's 'ironic' stance towards the struggle. Like many others he was alarmed that the West had begun to lose faith in universal truth. He especially deplored the contempt of many leading western thinkers for a perfect, rational, compassionate world; their challenge to the modern world's faith in technology and planning; their detached, self-mocking attitude towards culture and progress. He despaired of the ironic cast of the late twentieth-century mind. Even western Marxists, recognising similar if less pronounced symptoms in their own camp, were haunted by the secret fear that Nietzsche might eventually triumph over Marx.[37]

Herbert wrote a poem which expressed his fear about the death of God in the western imagination:

> First, there was the god of night and tempest, a black idol without eyes before whom they leaped, naked and smeared with blood. Later on, in the times of the republic, there were many gods with wives, children, creaking beds, and harmlessly exploding thunderbolts. At the end . . . superstitious neurotics carried in their pockets little statues of salt representing the god of irony. There was no greater god at that time. Then came the barbarians. They too valued highly the little god of irony. They would crush it under their heels and add it to their dishes.[38]

Herbert's fears may yet be realised even if his own country has now been absorbed into the western world. For if we worship any god at all it is surely the god of irony. That is why Herbert's poem is so telling.

The problem, of course, is not that the barbarians (whoever they may be in the future) will spill over the frontiers of the western world as they did in the past. The West remains more than powerful enough to fight its own corner. The problem is very different. Instead of intervening on behalf of others it may prefer to lock itself into its own world, to quarantine itself off from the infection of the outside world, like Caliban in his cell, unwilling to face Prospero's phantoms. The critics of humanitarian war claim that the West intervenes too often, the critics of humane warfare argue that its actions are less humane than it is willing to admit. But there is a quite different danger altogether: that we may abandon much of the world to the forces of barbarism. At the risk of taking issue with another twentieth-century poet, were this to happen the barbarians are unlikely to be seen as 'a solution'.

8 Conclusion

Cruelty, hatred, courage and risk – if not absent, all four are being reduced, or an attempt is being made to ensure they are no longer part of the character of war. Clausewitz tells us that every era fights its own wars, that their character changes. But he also tells us that the nature of war remains the same: it spans the centuries, and of the features he singled out, one was, for him, central. War is a *human* activity because it involves human emotions, and, as we have seen, two of the most important are hatred and courage. Eliminate them and you have transformed the nature of war; or in the words of David Ogg, its 'essence'.

We have seen the ways in which we are trying to make war more humane, but to humanise it we would have to do what Stephen Toulmin suggests we are doing in other walks of life: we would have to increase the *dignity* of human nature. One definition of the term is the capacity of the individual to remain the subject of a story, to retain human agency. For it is agency which confers responsibility. In becoming a responsible human being we affirm our humanity all the more. And it is in terms of dignity that we should see recent trends in the way the West now fights its wars.

Humanism and war

For the Greeks man was at the centre of war. The Gods were edged out. Human beings took responsibility for success or failure in battle. Providence, destiny and fate all played a reduced role. In the modern era, however, humanism was increasingly edged out too. Men were reduced to abstractions – the bourgeoisie versus the proletariat or the nation state locked in an internecine struggle with its neighbours, programmed to fight other races and peoples in the name of historical necessity. Today we tend to be more humanistic – to give more thought to individual human suffering, whether it is that of our own soldiers (hence the zero tolerance of casualties) or even that of our adversaries (our wish to avoid collateral damage).

In part, this is the product of the great disillusionment with the great utopian projects of the past. As our faith in universal narratives such as

Marxism has faded, we have come to value the individual much more. We recognise that we are doomed to struggle with an unintelligible chaotic world. If life has become less heroic it has become more demanding.

We are also less interested in changing human nature in the round and more interested in individual self-worth. In the great revolutionary era (1789–1989), the revolutionaries promised not just a change of political and economic system but a change of human nature. In the medieval world the transmutation of man had been the realm of religious experience. Not even the philosophers (the neo-Platonists excepted) attempted to intervene in a sphere which was considered exclusively God's. But the eighteenth century thought human nature could be improved. Social revolution involved an attempt to re-engineer man. If the nineteenth century had its great mechanical engineers, the twentieth century had its 'engineers of the human soul'.

The end of the Cold War which marks the end of the revolutionary era has re-centred the individual in the picture. And insofar as we still dream of re-engineering humanity, we do so in terms of the body not the soul. We are no longer interested in breeding true through eugenics, but marrying out human imperfections and congenital disorders through bio-engineering.

Humanity and war

We are also out of the city-busting business. As an American chief planner noted in his diary at the end of August 1990 in the build-up to the Gulf War, 'The American people [would] never stand for another Dresden.'[1] In terms of making war more humane we are, or so it would seem, trying to realise the goals of the great Enlightenment philosophers. We seem intent on realising the eighteenth-century hope that war could be waged state against state, not man against man. Writing in the mid-eighteenth century Montesquieu declared that the object of peace should be to do as much good to another state as possible; the object of war should be to do as little injury as possible. Rousseau went further in predicting that one day it would be possible to destroy a hostile state without killing any of its people.[2] Indeed, some of our weapons now allow us to move away from the age of mass destruction and serialised death which characterised the modern era.

In the age of the industrialised battlefield the weight of destructive capacity was the primary determinant of weapons development. In the contemporary era the reverse is true. Accuracy takes precedence over volume of fire-power and has become the most dynamic area of weapons innovation. 'Single-shot kill ratios' have been dramatically improved. As a result collateral damage has been reduced. The more accurate a weapon is, the more lethal; the more lethal, the less destructive.

We are also developing a new generation of non-lethal weapons. Their psychological objective is to demonstrate to the enemy the futility of opposition without killing so many enemy soldiers or non-combatants that an enemy's will to resist is enhanced rather than broken. This is what humane weapons hold out: the promise of eliminating the inhumanity of warfare.

Humanitarian wars

One of the most significant developments of recent years has also been an increasing use of western armies in humanitarian missions. We lack, it is true, any systematic evidence of changes in mass or elite attitudes to war, but we have public opinion polls and they show a substantial level of support for humanitarian missions. Indeed, one of the conditions of sending troops to a peacekeeping mission, or to discipline an undisciplined regime, is significant support at home. And although public opinion is volatile – it responds sometimes irrationally or capriciously to set-backs, defeats or disasters – and although public support is conditional, the evidence is that it is not conditional on knee-jerk reaction to casualties. Provided that casualty levels can be justified, or provided they know the purpose of a mission, public support can be assumed.

This is why the United States now numbers humanitarian missions as among its three principal 'national' missions. The language of national interest has largely disappeared from the discourse of war. Religion has been displaced too. We live in a post-Christian era – and although Christianity provides us with some of the ideals of Christian humanism, God has largely been displaced from the western imagination. In centring man in the picture we hold ourselves largely accountable not to God but to each other.

Humanism is itself a religion without God (and we should recognise that not all religions are theistic). Our ethical codes find faith in the ultimate rationale of human life: the avoidance of pain. Agnes Heller traces this back to Balzac's hero Rastignac who claimed that no one is responsible for a collective crime (he was talking specifically about capitalism). There is in this statement a recognition that *we* can commit a *collective* crime, an assumption that reflected the novel feature of modern culture: self-reflexivity. We can describe our deeds not as sins committed against God so much as crimes committed against each other, as well as ourselves. This recognition led the Nazis and Soviets to define those whom they offended as 'others' (not really human at all).[3]

Since the Holocaust we have been required to treat others as we would ourselves – that is why the Final Solution was the great watershed in western civilisation. We are responsible for the 'other' who looks at us, who faces us, who raises claims on us. We are responsible not for everyone but for everyone who is within our reach. This is especially important for western societies such as the United States and Europe which are both in the process of transforming themselves from multi-ethnic and multi-racial societies into genuine multi-cultural ones. Western culture is being redefined in contact with others of different creeds, races and cultures. If we do not recognise our humanity in others we will not recognise it in ourselves.

Whether the western world can continue to move in this direction is another matter. Two questions are raised. One I have addressed in Chapter 7. For as long as we are reluctant to sacrifice much of ourselves for others, humane war will continue to be suspect in the eyes of its critics. 'One of the foremost objectives in the development of new weaponry should be the reduction or total elimination of human risk.' So argue Alvin and Heidi Toffler whose book *War and Anti-War* has become a revered text in the US military since its publication in 1991. 'Put simply, weapons or equipment in harm's way should – to the extent possible – be unmanned.'[4] It is a telling word in its double meaning: that of making war no longer an exclusive activity of men, but more to the point taking courage or the need for it out of conflict. In making war more 'humane' for ourselves do we make it less 'human' for everyone else?

In the end the question is an ethical one. Traditionally our moral codes have told us how to deal with others. They have formed an integral part of human conduct and interaction, which as Aristotle tells us, is true of virtue too. Ethics is carefully crafted, in other words, not by abstract philosophy alone, but by practical action. In that sense, it is a uniquely human endeavour, and it has become more human still as we have begun to ground it not only in a privileged and exclusive relationship between ourselves and God (to whom traditionally we have held ourselves accountable) but an inclusive relationship with those we meet up with in everyday life.

Unfortunately, as war becomes more technological it is distancing public opinion and the warrior from its consequences. It is leading inevitably to what psychologists call 'dissociation'. An intimation of this came to the philosopher Theodor Adorno in 1944, when reading about the first of Hitler's missile attacks on London. As technology became more complex and sophisticated, so humanity would find itself cut out of the loop.

> Had Hegel's philosophy of history embraced this age Hitler's robot bombs would have found their place . . . as one of the selected empirical facts by which the state of the World Spirit manifests itself in symbols. . . . the robots career without a subject; . . . they combine utmost technical perfection with total blindness.
>
> . . . I have seen the World Spirit not on horseback but on wings and without a head and that refutes at the same stroke, Hegel's philosophy of history.[5]

Essentially, Adorno was making two important points.

The first was that although real war kills, and brutalises and numbs the mind, reality was becoming increasingly mediated. It is represented and in the course of representation desensitised. Even in the Gulf War, where cameras were mounted on the bombs themselves (imagine this on Hitler's VIs) the screens went blank at the point of impact. The moment of impact and its effects cannot be captured on film.

Second, the mediation of reality divorces society from war. It was Hegel who, on catching sight of Napoleon on his way to the battlefield of Jena (1806), formulated a philosophy of history in which war, as embodied in its world historical figures like Napoleon, became the expression of a national spirit, a community fighting for its beliefs. But modern technology – in this case Hitler's 'secret weapons', the V1 rockets (the first cruise) and the V2s (the first ballistic) missiles when targeted on London in the closing months of the war, had begun to hollow out war as a social experience. Adorno feared that in time societies would be able to target their enemies while immune from any threat or risk themselves. At that point war would cease to be an inter-subjective (and therefore ethical) experience.

And this is the danger of humane warfare. War becomes humane not only when it appears to take place on a television screen in one's home, but when it enlists societies in humane ways. With the end of conscription it no longer requires the actual participation of the citizen. Because of the bypassing of representative institutions it no longer requires democratic consent. And because wars are short and relatively cheap, governments do not even have to raise special taxes as Germany and Japan did in the Gulf War. These conditions, warns Michael Ignatieff, threaten to transform war into a spectator sport. Humane warfare offers the pleasure of a spectacle with the added thrill that it is real for someone but not the spectator – that, after all, constitutes its 'humanity'.

We have become so intoxicated by the idea of precise, risk-free warfare that we believe what we want to believe. Unfortunately, we may slip down the slope and find ourselves using violence with impunity, having lost our capacity for critical judgement. We may no longer be inclined to pay attention to the details of the ethical questions which all wars (even the most ethical) raise. As Ignatieff concludes:

> The fact that this new resort to military force is justified in humanitarian terms should give us pause, especially when the force can be exercised with lethal precision. For here we have an ancient spectre in modern form: violence which moralises itself as justice and which is unrestrained by consequences . . . if violence ceases to be fully real to the citizens in whose name it is exercised . . . why should it continue to be guided by restraint?[6]

The same is true of the military. Humane warfare heralds the military's increasingly ironic alienation from the battlefield and from battle itself. The wars of the future as envisaged by Pentagon war-games involve the abstraction of 'war's ugliness' by making it a digitalised phenomenon. The

West's wish to rationalise war is matched only by its will to still wage it. In its attempt to factor out fear and anxiety from the battlefield it may also attempt to spare soldiers the conflicting emotions and challenges which have made 'the soldier's tale' one of the defining subjects of literature. In removing human operators from their actions by mediating reality through technology, will we make our contact with reality increasingly 'unreal'? That is the ultimate challenge of humane warfare – does it render war unethical, and therefore more inhumane than ever before?

Notes

Introduction

1 J. Dower, *Embracing Defeat: Japan in the Aftermath of World War 2*, London, Penguin, 1999, p. 6.

2 See W. Mead, 'The Jacksonian tradition and American foreign policy', *The National Interest*, 1999/2000, No. 58, p. 5; and Charles Habbles Gray, *Post Modern War: The New Politics of Conflict* London, Routledge, 1997, pp. 136–7.

3 G. Schroeder, Government Policy Statement, Bundestag, Berlin, 19 April 1999 http://bundestagregierung.de/english/012/0102/03931/index.html

4 Suffering, of course, is in the eye of the beholder. The British Air Vice-Marshall Tony Mason described the air war against Iraq as 'the most humane method of expelling the Iraqis from Kuwait' (cited in M. Shaw, *Post Military Society: Militarism, Demilitarisation and War at the End of the Twentieth Century*, Cambridge, Polity Press, 1991, p. 202), but the sanctions imposed on Iraq for the next ten years after the war crippled the economy and increased the infant mortality rate significantly. With regard to Kosovo the casualties were also high for the Serbs themselves. According to the UN, the percentage of the Serbian population living in poverty doubled in the year after the war from 33 per cent to 63 per cent of the population. World Bank and International Monetary Fund reports show that 250,000 people lost their jobs as a direct result of the bombing of the civilian infrastructure. In Pancevo and Novi Sad, two towns that claimed the title 'the most bombed town in Serbia', the once thriving car factories which provided jobs for most of the towns' males were devastated. And of the 200,000 Serb refugees from Kosovo the children of most of them were denied schooling by the Milosevic regime because they were living proof of its defeat and humiliation. One of the problems with the way the West fights its wars is that 'humanity' requires that only enough is done to punish a regime, not remove it from the map. And because Milosovic remained in power the country was denied the kind of Marshall Aid Plans that rescued Japan and Germany after the Second World War. Indeed, to continue keeping the regime on the defensive the West insisted on a ban on reconstruction aid as well as the imposition of stringent new sanctions. And for the first time it put pressure on UNHCR and the International Committee of the Red Cross to reduce existing programmes in Serbia (see F. Fox, 'No place for pride', *The World Today*, 2000, No. 4, pp. 20–2).

5 Cited in N. Chomsky, *The New Military Humanism: Lessons from Kosovo*, London, Pluto Press, 1999, p. 4.

6 C. Guthrie, 'Why NATO cannot simply march in and crush Milosevic', *Evening Standard*, London, 1 April 1999.

7 M. Ignatieff, *The Warrior's Honour: Ethnic War and the Modern Conscience*, London, Chatto and Windus, 1998, p. 156.

8 Cited in R. Shacochis, 'Soldiers of the future: is America training warriors or humanitarians?', *Harpers*, December 1999, p. 45.

9 J.G. Ballard, *A User's Guide to the Millennium*, London, Flamingo, 1997, p. 75.
10 M. Atwood, *Cat's Eye*, London, Flamingo, 1996, p. 4.

1 Humanising war

1 See P. Paret, *Imagined Battles: Reflections on War in European Art*, Chapel Hill, The University of North Carolina Press, 1997, pp. 34–9.
2 D. Ogg, *Europe in the Seventeenth Century*, London, Adam and Charles Black, 1967, pp. 547–8. Ogg was writing a few years after the Balkans wars (1912–13) which saw atrocities to civilians on a scale not seen in western Europe in the Second World War. The Carnegie Commission concluded in its report in 1913 that war had 'suspended the restraints of civil life . . . and set in place the will to injure . . . both of which were "everywhere the *essence* of war"' (cited in M. Hall, *The Balkan Wars 1912–13*, London, Routledge, 2000, p. 138.
3 P. Vansittart, *In Memory of England*, London, John Murray, 1998, p. 111.
4 A. Danto, *An Analytical Philosophy of History*, Cambridge, Cambridge University Press, 1968, pp. 261–2.
5 J.R. Hale, *War and Society in Renaissance Europe 1450–1620*, London, Fontana, 1985, p. 39.
6 C.J. Esdaile, *The Wars of Napoleon*, London, Longman, 1995, pp. 300–1.
7 Cited in D. Maland, *Europe in the Seventeenth Century*, London, St Martin's Press, 1966, p. 19.
8 M. Frisch, *Sketchbook 1946–49*, New York, Harvest, 1983, p. 22.
9 J. Steinbeck, *A Russian Journal*, London, Minerva, 1994, pp. 120–1.
10 For the 'death event' see E. Wyschogrod, *Spirit in Ashes: Hegel, Heidegger and Man Made Mass Death*, New Haven, CT, Yale University Press, 1985, p. 52.
11 G. Myers, 'The Private Ryan Effect', *Armed Forces Journal International*, August 1999, p. 18.
12 Cited in S. Hynes, *The Soldier's War: Bearing Witness to Modern War*, London, Pimlico, 1998, p. 155. For the casualty figures see Terry Copp, 'If this war isn't over, and pretty damn soon, there'll be nobody left, in this old platoon; Ist Canadian Army February – March 1945', in P. Addison and A. Calder (eds),*Time to Kill: The Soldier's Experience of War in the West*, London, Pimlico, 1997, p. 149.
13 L. Garchik, 'War was healthy and so are sardines', *The San Francisco Chronicle*, 18 March 1991.
14 D. Shukman, *The Sorcerer's Apprentice: Fears and Hopes for the Weapons of the Next Millennium*, London, Coronet, 1995, p. 184.
15 K. O'Beirne, 'The war machine as child minder', in G. Frost (ed.), *Not Fit to Fight: The Cultural Subversion of the Armed Forces in Britain and America*, London, Social Affairs Unit, 1998, p. 37.
16 Cited in P.K. Lawrence, *Modernity and War: The Creed of Absolute Violence*, London, Macmillan, 1997, p. 169.
17 M. Ignatieff, 'A post modern war', *Time*, 12 April 1999, p. 78.
18 For the destruction of art treasures see J. Keegan, *War and Our World*, London, Hutchinson, 1998, p. 13. For Wilson see M. Green, *Children of the Sun*, London, Constable, 1977, pp. 468–9.
19 P. Fussell, *The Great War and Modern Memory*, Oxford, Oxford University Press, 1975, p. 7.
20 *Daily Telegraph*, 17 April 1999.
21 A. and H. Toffler, *War and Anti-War: Survival at the Dawn of the Twenty-first Century*, London, Warner Books, 1994, p. 141.
22 S. Toulmin, *Cosmopolis: The Hidden Agenda of Modernity*, Chicago, IL, University of Chicago Press, 1990. Offering a sociological definition of what it means to humanise modernity, Ronald Ingelhart calls 'post-modernisation' 'a move away from the emphasis on economic efficiency and bureaucratic authority and scientific rationality that characterised modernisation towards a more humane society with more room for individual autonomy, diversity and self-expression' (*Modernisation and Post Modernisation:*

Cultural, Economic and Political Change in 43 Societies, Princeton, NJ, Princeton University Press, 1997, p. 92).

23 C. Jencks, 'What is post modernism?', in W.T. Anderson (ed.), *The Fontana Post Modern Reader*, London, Fontana, 1995, p. 26.

24 P. Windsor, 'The twentieth century as self-conscious history', in N. Hagahara and A. Iriye (eds), *Experiencing the Twentieth Century*, Tokyo, University of Tokyo Press, 1985, p. 338.

25 M. Frayn, *Copenhagen*, London, Methuen, 1998, pp. 73–4.

26 'Round Table: the global order in the twenty-first century', *Prospect*, August/September 1999, pp. 50–8.

27 Ibid.

28 Ibid.

29 Cited in Maland, op. cit., p. 18.

30 Myers, 'The Private Ryan Effect', op. cit.

31 G. Orwell, *Collected Essays: The Journalism of George Orwell*, Vol. 2, ed. S. Orwell and I. Angus, London, Secker and Warburg, 1968, pp. 496–71.

32 T.G. Ash, *In Europe's Name: Germany and the Divided Continent*, London, Vintage, 1994, p. 22.

33 J. Ellis, *The Social History of the Machine Gun*, London, Pimlico, 1976, p. 20.

34 See D. Grossman, *On Killing: The Psychological Cost of Learning to Kill in War and Society*, Boston, MA, Little, Brown, 1996, pp. 270–1.

35 A. Ferguson, *An Essay on the History of Civil Society*, 4th edition, 1773, repr. Farnborough, n.p. 1969, p. 267.

36 See H. van Ginkel and E. Newman, 'Human Security', *Japanese Review of International Affairs*, spring 2000, pp. 59–83.

37 Speech by A. Blair, Economic Club of Chicago, 'The Doctrine of the International Community, 22 April 1999', http://www.usis.it/wireless/wf990423/99042319.html

38 C. Krauthammer, 'Humanitarian war', *The National Interest*, No. 57, fall 1999, p. 8.

2 War and the renunciation of cruelty

1 Cited in D. Ahern, *Nietzsche as Cultural Physician*, University Park, Penn., University of Pennsylvania Press, 1995, p. 42.

2 See F. Appel, *Nietzsche Contra Democracy*, Ithaca, NY, Cornell University Press, 1999, p. 152.

3 Ibid.

4 F. Nietzsche, *Twilight of the Idols*, London, Penguin, 1990, p. 103.

5 N. Mailer, *The Naked and the Dead*, New York, Rinehart & Co, 1948, p. 321.

6 J. Conrad, *Nostromo*, London, Penguin, 1990, pp. 94–5.

7 This is what John Lukacs writes of fascism and Hitler: 'He represented an enormous tide in the affairs of the world in the twentieth century. The force of this tide consisted of the energy, the discipline, the confidence and the obedience, and the vitality of the German people whom he succeeded in uniting beyond the accomplishments of any other leader in their history. ... Moreover – beyond Germany and in the minds of many people – Hitler's rule, his regime and his ideas, represented a new primary force beside the corroding alternatives of liberal democracy and "international" communism' (*Five Days in London May 1940*, New Haven, Conn, Yale University Press, 1999, pp. 6–7).

8 Mailer, op. cit., p. 326.

9 Cited in J. Patocka, *Heretical Essays in the Philosophy of History*, trans. E. Kohak, Chicago, Ill., Open Court, 1996, p. 125.

10 Cited in J. Lukacs, *The Last European War*, London, Routledge and Kegan Paul, 1976, p. 514.

11 Mailer, op. cit., p. 326.

12 Cited in A. Iriye, 'War as peace, peace as war', in A. Iriye and P. Windsor (eds), *Experiencing the Twentieth Century*, Tokyo, University of Tokyo Press, 1985, p. 36. Wilson's rallying cry captured the difference between the United States of 1776 – fighting

for its independence – and its declaration of war in 1917 – fighting for the self-determination of the rest of the world. In 1776 the Americans had valorised themselves as equals of the British. For Nietzsche this was the lowest degree of the will to power – to be seen as equal. 'One desires freedom so long as one does not possess power. Once one does possess it one desires to overpower' (cited in A. Renault, *The Era of the Individual: A Contribution to a History of Subjectivity*, Princeton, NJ, Princeton University Press, 1997, p. 137).

13 Cited in T. Smith, *America's Mission: The United States and the Worldwide Struggle for Democracy*, Princeton, NJ, Princeton University Press, 1995, p. 90.
14 See G. Bird and J.E. Smith, *The Spirit of American Philosophy*, New York, Oxford University Press, 1963. See also H. Putnam, 'William James' ideas', *Raritan*, 1989, Vol. 8, pp. 27–44.
15 Mailer, op. cit., p. 329.
16 Cited in Ahern, op. cit., p. 33. It was the cruelty of war that was of particular concern to the Japanese readers of Mailer's book. As the novelist Shiina Rinzo remarked, Mailer had made it clear that even Christians could not squarely confront the cruelty implicit in war and the will to power (John Dower, *Embracing Defeat: Japan in the Aftermath of World War 2*, London, Penguin, 1999, p. 504).
17 D. DeLillo, *Libra*, New York, Viking, 1988, p. 181.
18 P. Fussell, *The Bloody Game: An Anthology of Modern War*, New York, Scribners, 1991, p. 656.
19 E. Hemingway, *A Farewell to Arms*, New York, Scribner, 1957, p. 191.
20 Fussell, *The Great War and Modern Memory*, p. 202.
21 M. Herr, *Dispatches*, London, Picador, 1979, p. 206.
22 C.H. Gray, 'The cyborg soldier: the US military and the post modern warrior', in L. Levidow and K. Robins (eds), *Cyborg Worlds: Programming the Military Information Society*, New York, Columbia University Press, 1989, p. 26.
23 *The Times*, 21 December 1998.
24 *The Times*, 15 April, 1999.
25 U. Beck, *The Risk Society: Towards a New Modernity*, London, Sage, 1997, p. 87.
26 Cited in S. Hynes, *The Soldier's Tale*, London, Pimlico, 1998, pp. 202–3.
27 Ibid.
28 See Introduction by D. Bredshaw in A. Huxley, *Music at Night and other Essays*, London, Flamingo, 1994.
29 Herr, op. cit., p. 206.
30 Hynes, op. cit., p. 185.
31 Fussell, *The Bloody Game*, pp. 24–31
32 J. Heller, *Catch 22*, London, Vintage, 1994, pp. 62–3. (Copyright © Joseph Heller 1955) reproduced by permission of AM Heath & Co Ltd on behalf of Donadio & Olson Inc.
33 Hemingway, op. cit., p. 61.
34 J. Wenke, *Mailer's America*, Hanover, University Press of New England, 1987, p. 198.
35 See my discussion of Camus' philosophy in *War and the Twentieth Century: A Study of War and Modern Consciousness*, London, Brasseys, 1994, pp. 221–5.
36 DeLillo, op. cit., p. 58.
37 H. Read, *The Meaning of Art*, London, Faber & Faber, 1972, pp. 38–40.
38 K. Vonnegut, *Slaughterhouse 5*, London, Vintage, 1991, p. 2.
39 D. DeLillo, *End Zone*, London: Penguin, *1986* p. 68.
40 Vonnegut, op. cit., p. 44.
41 K. Vonnegut, *Mother Night*, London, Jonathan Cape, 1968, p. 40.
42 D. Smith, *Zygmunt Bauman: Prophet of Post Modernity*, Cambridge, Polity Press, 1999, pp. 163–5.
43 R. Rorty, *Contingency, Irony and Solidarity*, Cambridge, Cambridge University Press, 1989, p. 120.

44 J. Shklar, *Ordinary Vices*, Cambridge, Mass., Bellknap Press, 1984, p. 8.
45 S. Toulmin, *Cosmopolis: The Hidden Agenda of Modernity*, Chicago, Ill., University of Chicago Press, 1990, p. 160.
46 R. Tarnas, *The Passion of the Western Mind*, London, Pimlico, 1996, p. 401.

3　The redundancy of courage

1 P. Contamine, *War in the Middle Ages*, Oxford, Blackwell, 1984, p. 255.
2 F. Gilbert, 'Machiavelli: the Renaissance of the art of war', in E.M. Earle (ed.), *Makers of Modern Strategy: Military Thought from Machiavelli to Hitler*, Princeton, NJ, Princeton University Press, 1943, pp. 3–25.
3 J.R. Hale, *War and Society in Renaissance Europe 1450–1620*, London, Fontana, 1985, p. 71.
4 See N. Machiavelli, *The Art of War*, New York, De Capa, 1990, especially the Introduction by Neil Wood. See also M. Mallet, 'The theory and practice of warfare in Machiavelli's Republic', in G. Brock and Q. Skinner (eds), *Machiavellian Republicanism*, Cambridge, Cambridge University Press, 1990.
5 G. Hegel, *The Philosophy of Right*, trans. T.M. Knox, Oxford, Clarendon Press, 1967, pp. 210–11.
6 Ibid.
7 S. Houlgate, *Freedom, Truth and History: An Introduction to Hegel's Philosophy*, London, Routledge, 1991, pp. 251–2.
8 For an excellent discussion of the difference between a covenant and a contract see I. Torrance, *Ethics and the Military Community*, Occasional Paper 34, Camberley, Surrey, Strategic and Combat Studies Institute, July 1998.
9 Cited in W. Durant, *The Story of Philosophy from Plato to John Dewey*, New York, Pocket Library, 1960, p. 436.
10 F. Nietzsche, *Human, All Too Human*, trans. Marion Faber, Lincoln, University of Nebraska Press, 1984, pp. 232–3.
11 F. Nietzsche, 'Thus spake Zarathustra', in W. Kaufman (ed.) '*The Portable Nietzsche*, New York, Viking, 1968, p. 159. Even in Spain at the height of the Civil War the poet Stephen Spender saw the soldiers fighting for democracy (and the republic) as victims rather than heroes. They did not even hate their enemies. 'They cease to hate, for although hate/burst from the air and whips the earth with hail . . ./and although hundreds fall, who can connect/the inexhaustible anger of the guns/with the dumb patience of those tormented animals?' (cited in Fussell, *The Bloody Game*, p. 303).
12 D. MacGregor, *Hegel and Marx After the Fall of Communism*, Cardiff, University of Wales Press, 1998, p. 30.
13 Ibid., p. 30.
14 Ibid.
15 DeLillo, *End Zone*, p. 81.
16 A. Schopenhauer, 'On ethics', in *Essays and Aphorisms*, trans. R.G. Hollingdale, London, Penguin, 1988, p. 135.
17 P. Levi, *Other People's Trades*, London, Michael Joseph, 1989, pp. 93–4.
18 Beck, *The Risk Society*, p. 53.
19 *Human Development Report 1998*, Oxford, United Nations Development Programme, 1998, p. 78.
20 *Time*, 28 April 1994.
21 D. DeLillo, *White Noise*, New York, Penguin, 1984, p. 35.
22 Ibid., p. 116.
23 J. Chessneaux, *Brave Modern World: The Prospects for Survival*, London, Thames & Hudson, 1992, p. 165.
24 D. Lipton, *Risk*, London, Routledge, 1999, p. 94.
25 R. Cooper, *The Post Modern State and the World Order*, London, Demos, 1996, p. 44.
26 T.S. Eliot, *The Four Quartets*, London, Faber & Faber, 1986, p. 29.
27 G. Stix, 'Fighting future wars', *Scientific American*, December 1995, p. 74.

28 For an excellent discussion of these and other risks see K. Alibek, *Biohazard*, London, Hutchinson, 1999.

29 J. MacArthur, *Second Front: Censorship and Propaganda in the Gulf War*, New York, Hill & Wang, 1992, p. 90.

30 Cited in W. Grazer (ed.), *The Longman Literary Companion to Science*, London, Longman, 1989, p. 397.

31 Cited in L.A. Cole, *The Eleventh Plague: The Politics of Biological and Chemical Warfare*, New York, Freeman & Co, 1997, p. 100.

32 F. Furedi, *Culture of Fear: Risk-taking and the Morality of Low Expectations*, London, Cassell, 1998, p. 10.

33 E. Tenner, *Why Things Bite Back*, London, Fourth Estate, 1996, p. 36.

34 J. Bourke, *An Intimate History of Killing: Face to Face Killing in Twentieth Century Warfare*, London, Granta Books, 1999, p. 246.

35 R. Gabriel, *No More Heroes: Madness and Psychiatry in War*, New York, Hill & Wang, 1987, p. 77.

36 W. Holden, *Shellshock: The Psychological Impact of War*, London, Macmillan, 1998, p. 165.

4 War without hatred

1 *Catch 22* by Joseph Heller (Copyright © Joseph Heller 1955) reproduced by permission of AM Heath & Co Ltd on behalf of Donadio & Olson Inc.

2 G. Orwell, *Nineteen Eighty-Four*, London, Penguin, 1989, p. 13.

3 E. Hobsbawm, *The Age of Extremes: The Short Twentieth Century 1914–1991*, London, Michael Joseph, 1994, p. 4.

4 G. Orwell, *Collected Essays: Journalism and the Letters of George Orwell*, Vol. 3, ed. S. Orwell and I. Angus, London, Secker & Warburg, 1968, p. 144.

5 Cited in P. Gay, *The Bourgeois Experience from Victoria to Freud, Volume 3: Cultivation of Hatred*, New York, Norton & Co, 1993, p. 267.

6 R. Lowell, 'Memories of West St and Lepke', in C. Forché, (ed.) *Against Forgetting: Twentieth Century Poetry of Witness*, New York, Norton & Co, 1993, pp. 284–6.

7 U. Beck, *Democracy Without Enemies*, Cambridge, Polity Press, 1998.

8 B. Brecht, *Diaries, 1920–22* , ed. Herta Ramthun, London, Methuen, 1979, p. 27.

9 P. Laslett, *The World We Have Lost*, London, Methuen, 1971, p. 213.

10 Cited in J. Updike, *Hugging The Shore: Essays and Criticism*, London, Penguin, 1983, p. 814.

11 E. Montague, *Rough Justice*, London, 1926, p. 68.

12 Cited in J. Terraine, *The Smoke and the Fire: Myths and Anti-Myths of War 1861–1945*, London, Sidgwick & Jackson, 1980, p. 42.

13 V. Woolf, *Three Guineas*, ed. Morag Shiach, Oxford, Oxford University Press, 1992, pp. 207–8.

14 *Times Literary Supplement*, 26 March 1999, p. 33.

15 J. Winter, *Sites of Memory and Sites of Mourning: The Great War in European Cultural History*, Cambridge, Cambridge University Press, 1995, p. 46.

16 Laslett, op. cit., p. 235.

17 Cited in *UN Human Development Report 1998*, op. cit., p. 105.

18 R. Inglehart, *Modernisation and Post-Modernisation: Cultural, Economic and Political Change in Forty-Three Societies*, Princeton, NJ, Princeton University Press, 1997, pp. 42–5.

19 A. Munroe, 'Humanitarianism and conflict in the post-Cold War world', *RUSI Journal*, Jan/Feb 1999, p. 16.

20 For demythication see R. Bultmann and K. Jaspers, *Myth and Christianity: An Enquiry into the Possibility of Religion Without Myth*, New York, Noonday Press, 1958; and G. Vattimo, *Belief*, Cambridge, Polity Press, 1999.

21 B. Appleyard, *Understanding the Present: Science and the Soul of Modern Man*, London, Picador, 1992, p. 124.

22 Cited in J. Bordo, 'Ecological peril, modern technology and the post modern sublime', in P. Berry and A. Wernick, *Shadow of Spirit: Post Modernism and Religion*, London, Routledge, 1992, p. 168.
23 Ibid., p. 169.
24 *The Sunday Times*, 18 March 1999.
25 Inglehart, op. cit., p. 325.
26 For the concept of subpolitics see Beck, *Democracy Without Enemies*, pp. 36–8.
27 C. Moskos and D. Segal (eds), *The Post Modern Military: Armed Forces After the Cold War*, New York, Oxford University Press, 2000, p. 5.
28 Cited in C. Knorr and T. Read (eds), *Limited Strategic War*, New York, Praeger, 1962, p. 254.
29 M. Gordon and B. Trainor, *The Generals' War*, New York, Little and Brown, 1995, pp. 326–7.
30 G. Kolko, *Century of War: Politics, Conflicts and Society Since 1914*, New York, New Press, 1994, p. 432.
31 U. Eco, *Pensare la Guerra*, La Rivista dei Libri, 1 April 1991, pp. 9–11. This article was subsequently republished in U. Eco, *Cinque Scritti Morali*, Milano, Bompiani, 1997, p. 15.
32 J. Keane, *Reflections on Violence*, London, Verso, 1996, pp. 62–3.
33 Larry Woolf, *Postcards from the End of the World: An Investigation into the Mind of Fin de Siecle Vienna*, London, Collins, 1988, p. 240.
34 Keane, op. cit., pp. 120–2.
35 *The Times*, 16 March 1999.
36 Keane, op. cit., p. 120.
37 Beck, *The Risk Society*, p. 118. The fact that our children are expected to survive well into adulthood means that children form 'a great part of the family's emotional economy' (Inglehart, op. cit., p. 112).
38 *Human Development Report 1998*, op. cit., p. 35. The psychological effects of the war are likely to outlast this generation. As Nicole Janigro notes, already by 1993, 72 per cent of the children of Bosnia had witnessed the bombing of their homes; 51 per cent had witnessed murder; 39 per cent had lost someone close to them; and 19 per cent had even assisted in a massacre. The next generation has already lost its innocence. N. Janigro, *L'esplosione delle nazioi: Il caso jugoslavio*, Milan, Feltrinelli, 1993, pp. 51–2.
39 Cited in Gay, op. cit., p. 37.
40 Cited in F. Appel, *Nietzsche Contra Democracy*, Ithaca, NY, Cornell University Press, 1998, p. 101.
41 L. Woolf, *An Autobiography, Volume 2, 1911–1969*, Oxford, Oxford University Press, 1980, p. 114.
42 W. Lewis, *The Art of Being Ruled*, Santa Rosa, Calif., Black Sparrow Press, 1989, p. 193.
43 Cited in K. Theweleit, *Male Fantasies, Volume 1: Male Bodies: Psychoanalysing the White Terror*, Cambridge, Polity Press, 1988, p. 162. In fact even socialist revolutionaries were not happy to see women soldiers. In the Spanish Civil War George Orwell saw some in the Lenin barracks in Barcelona but by the time he arrived they no longer fought as they had in the early days side-by-side with men in the field. Instead, the women were laughed at and humiliated. 'A few months earlier no one would have seen anything comic in a woman handling a gun.' From *Homage to Catalonia* (1938) in Fussell, *The Bloody Game*, p. 264.
44 Cited in B. Moynahan, *The Russian Century: A History of the Last Hundred Years*, London: Pimlico, 1994, p. 126
45 A. Sullivan, 'America on the march for its lost manhood', *The Sunday Times*, 12 October 1997.
46 M. Dando, 'Non-lethal weapons', *Brasseys Yearbook 1996*, London, Brasseys, 1996, p. 394. See, for a full discussion of non-lethal violence, J. Alexander, *Future War: Non-lethal Weapons in Twenty-first Century Warfare*, New York, St Martin's Press, 1999.
47 See G. Foster, 'Non-lethality: arming the post-modern military', *RUSI Journal*, October 1997, p. 60.

48 J. Adams, *The Next World War: The Warriors and the Weapons of the New Battlefields in Cyberspace*, London, Hutchinson 1998, p. 144.
49 Cited in L. Freedman, 'The revolution in strategic affairs', *Adelphi Paper*, No. 318, London, International Institute for Strategic Studies, 1998, p. 16.
50 A. and H. Toffler, *War and Anti-War: Survival at the Dawn of the Twenty-first Century*, London, Warner Books, 1994, p. 134.
51 J. Anielmo, 'Satellite data plays key role in Bosnia Peace Treaty', *Aviation Week and Space Technology*, 11 December 1995.
52 N. Wise, 'Video games, new, 3D, gigabytes have – gotcha!', *Time Digital*, 10 March 1997, p. 39.

5 The humane warrior

1 Hale, *War and Society in Renaissance Europe*, p. 128.
2 *Ibid.*
3 S. Sarkesian and R.E. Connor, *The US Military Profession into the Ttwenty First Century*, London, Frank Cass, 1999, p. 19.
4 Ibid,, p. 21.
5 J. Keegan, *A History of War*, London, Hutchinson, 1993, p. 172.
6 A.J. Bacevich, 'Tradition abandoned: America's military in a new era', *The National Interest*, summer 1997, p. 23.
7 J. Lehman, 'An exchange of civil–military relations', *The National Interest*, summer 1994, p. 24. See also his article, 'Unmanning our service', *Daily Telegraph*, 12 October 1998; Tom Ricks, 'The widening gap between the military and society', *The Atlantic Monthly*, July 1997.
8 J.A. Williams, 'The post modern military re-considered', in C. Moskos, J.A. Williams and D.R. Segal (eds), *The Post Modern Military: armed forces after the Cold War*, Oxford, Oxford University Press, 2000, p. 274.
9 M. Shaw, *Post Military Society: Militarism, Demilitarisation and War at the End of the Twentieth Century*, Cambridge, Polity Press, 1991.
10 M. Silverman, *Facing Post Modernism: Contemporary French Thought on Culture and Society*, London, Routledge, 1999.
11 For medieval warfare see T.L. Allmand, *War, Literature and Politics in the Late Middle Ages*, Liverpool, Liverpool University Press, 1976.
12 C. Powell, 'US forces: challenges abroad', *Foreign Affairs*, Vol. 71, winter 1992–93, p. 32.
13 Sarkesian and Connor, op. cit., p. 59.
14 Cited in Armed Forces Press Service www.defenselink.mil/news/mar2000/no3152000–2003153
15 B. Boene and M. L. Martin, 'France: in the throes of epoch making change', in Moskos *et al.*, op. cit., p. 70.
16 B. Fleckenstein, 'Germany: forerunner of a post modern military', in Moskos *et al.*, op. cit., p. 95.
17 M. Ignatieff, *Virtual War*, London, Chatto and Windus, 2000, p. 190.
18 Inglehart, *Modernisation and Post Modernisation*, p. 92.
19 G. Frost (ed.), *Not Fit to Fight: The Cultural Subversion of the Armed Forces*, London, Social Affairs Unit, 1998, p. 7.
20 A. Giddens, 'Living in a post traditional society', in U. Beck, A. Giddens and S. Lash, *Reflexive Modernisation: Poltics, Tradition and Aesthetics in the Modern Social Order*, Cambridge, Polity Press, 1994, p. 63.
21 G. Conforio (ed.), *The European Cadet: Professional Socialisation in Military Academies*, Baden Baden, Nomos, 1998.
22 F. Baltistelli, 'Peacekeeping and the post modern soldier'. *Armed Forces and Society*, Vol. 23, spring 1997, pp. 467–84.
23 *The Times*, 3 April 2000.

24 N. Trustram, *Women of the Regiment: Marriage and the Victorian Army*, Cambridge, Cambridge University Press, 1984, pp. 43, 91. For the cult of masculinity see G.L. Mosse, *Fallen Soldiers: Reshaping the Meaning of the World Wars*, Oxford, Oxford University Press, 1990, pp. 59–62.

25 Frost, op. cit., p. 67.

26 Ibid., pp. 53–4.

27 Giddens, op. cit., p. 102.

28 Ibid., p. 103.

29 Shaw, op. cit., p. 74.

30 See E. Fredland and A. Kendry, 'The privatisation of military force', *Cambridge Review of International Affairs*, Vol. 12, winter 1999, pp. 114–30.

31 C. Moskos, 'Towards a post modern military: the United States', in Moskos *et al.*, op. cit., p. 16.

32 Giddens, op. cit., p. 83.

33 Fleckenstein, 'Germany', in Moskos, op. cit., p. 89.

34 N. Luhmann, *Writing Science: Observations on Modernity*, Stanford, Calif. Stanford University Press, 1998.

35 E. Offley, 'The military–media relationship in the digital age', in R. Bateman (ed.), *Digital War*, Novato, Calif., Presidio, 1999, pp. 284–5.

36 J. Hillen, 'The rise of the political general', in Frost, op. cit., p. 56.

37 For the abuse of women soldiers see E. Thomas and G. Vistica, 'At war in the ranks', *Newsweek*, 11 August 1997, pp. 32–3. For the report see *New York Times*, 11 September 1997. For an outspoken critique of the feminisation of the military see Brian Mitchell, *Women in the Military: Flirting with Disaster*, London, Brasseys, 1993.

38 E. Thomas and J. Barry, 'At war over women', *Newsweek*, 12 May 1997.

39 K. O'Beirne, 'The war machine as child minder', in Frost, op. cit., p. 36.

40 Ibid.

41 Thomas and Barry, op. cit.

42 T. Todorov, *Facing the Extreme: Moral Life in the Concentration Camps*, London, Phoenix, 1999, p. 295.

43 In the fifth century Greek society was unique in its exclusive, nervous maleness. The Greco–Persian wars were important in this respect. First, because the Greeks depicted the Persians as 'effeminate' (see E. Hall, 'Asia unmanned: images of victory in classical Athens', in J. Rich and G. Shipley (eds), *War and Society in the Greek World*, London, Routledge, 1993. Second, they handed on to the Romans the idea of a male-dominated society together with its corollary that political authority for women was a mark of barbarism. Thus it was only to be expected that the savage Icenii should choose Boudicca to lead their rebellion or that Gaulish women – 'with huge white arms', as the fourth-century historian Ammianus Marcellinus described them – should pitch in to save their husbands in a brawl.

44 Cited in H. McManners, *The Scars of War*, London, HarperCollins, 1994, p. 24.

45 *The Sunday Times*, 22 January 1991.

46 P. Boyer, 'Admiralty Board at war', *New Yorker*, 16 September 1996, p. 85.

47 I owe a great debt in this section to S. Drury, *Alexandre Kojeve: The Roots of Post Modern Politics*, London, Macmillan, 1994, pp. 185–6.

48 Cited in R. Shacochis, 'Soldiers of the future: is America training warriors or humanitarians?', *Harpers*, December 1999, p. 44.

49 Moskos, 'Towards a post modern military', in Moskos *et al.*, op. cit., p. 21.

50 *Guardian*, 14 March, 2000.

51 Shacochis, op. cit., p. 53.

52 F. Fukuyama, *The End of History and the Last Man*, New York, Free Press, 1992, p. 148. See also pp. 329–30.

53 R. Rorty, *Contingency, Irony and Solidarity*, Cambridge, Cambridge University Press, 1999.

54 F. Nietzsche, *Thus Spake Zarathustra*, London, Penguin, 1978, p. 159.

55 A. and H. Toffler, *War and Anti-War: Survival at the Dawn of the Twenty First Century*, London, Warner Books, 1994, p. 154.

6 Zoning the planet

1 H. McCallum, 'No more corpses on the road', *The Times Literary Supplement*, 15 August 1997, p. 26.

2 *New York Times*, 29 December 1992.

3 B. Smart, *Modern Conditions, Post-Modern Controversies*, London, Routledge, 1992, p. 115.

4 B. Breytenbach, 'Writing at the darkening mirror', in *The Memory of Birds in Time of Revolution*, London, Faber & Faber, 1996, p. 6. Breytenbach adds, 'Africa is in the paradoxical situation of being one of the oldest civilisations continuously having to invent itself. Could it be because the criteria of recognition are western and that Africa is always living below the horizon of historical perception and sinking fast?... History is a western way of digesting time; it is a white man's burden' p. 67). This view is shared by a number of other writers including the Nigerian author Achebe, who speaks of Africa as being outside history. The only African time is American time. Because of their servility to all things American the intellectuals have no time of their own; they have only an American future. Africa has been distanced from its traditions, from the masses and from its own language. It has no past, only a future lived on terms other than those devised by itself. See A.R. Gurnah, *Essays in African Writing*, London, Heinemann, 1993, p. 3.

5 R. Kaplan, 'The coming anarchy', *Atlantic Monthly*, February 1994, p. 72.

6 S. Strange and J. Stopford, *Rival States, Rival Firms: Competition for World Market Shares*, Cambridge, Cambridge University Press, 1991, p. 7.

7 J. Conrad, *Heart of Darkness*, London, Penguin, 1989, pp. 440–5.

8 S. Bellow, *The Dean's December*, London, Penguin, 1982, p. 205.

9 Cited in W. Naphy and P. Roberts (eds), *Fear in Early Modern Society*, Manchester, Manchester University Press, 1997, p. 191.

10 B. Zeman, *Pursued by a Bear: The Making of Eastern Europe*, London, Chatto & Windus, 1989, p. 21.

11 A. and H. Toffler, *War and Anti-War*, p. 104.

12 M. Ignatieff, *The Warrior's Honour*, p. 106.

13 Cited in J. Ellis, *The Social History of the Machine Gun*, London, Pimlico, 1993, pp. 101–2.

14 B. Enhreich, *Blood Rites: Origins and History of the Passions of War*, London, Vintage, 1997, p. 228.

15 H. Bloom, *The Western Canon*, London, Papermac, 1994, p. 349.

16 L.J. Borges, *Other Inquisitions: 1937–1952*, London, Condor, 1973, p. 167.

17 F. Nietzsche, *On the Genealogy of Morals*, trans. W. Kaufman and R.J. Hollingdale, New York, Vintage, 1967, p. 39.

18 E. Junger, *The Storm of Steel*, London, Constable, 1994, p. 154.

19 F. Hegel, *The Philosophy of History*, New York, Dover, 1956, p. 148.

20 Cited in D. Jablonsky, *Churchill and Hitler: Essays on the Political and Military Direction of Total War*, London, Frank Cass, 1994, p. 38.

21 Ibid., p. 47.

22 G. Kolko, *Century of War*, New York, New Press, 1994, p. 58.

23 F. Heissbourg, *The Future of Warfare*, London, Phoenix, 1997, p. 371.

24 A. Almend, *Discovering Islam: Making Sense of Moslem History and Society*, London, Routledge, 1988, pp. 133–7.

25 P. Mason, *A Matter of Honour*, London, Jonathan Cape, 1974, pp. 337–8.

26 J. Black, *European Warfare 1660–1815*, London, University College, 1994, p. 26.

27 B. Shacochis, 'Soldiers of the future', *Harpers*, December 1999, p. 117. Other societies have their own military ethos. For the Somalis see G. Hanley, *Warriors: Life and Death Among the Somalis*, London, Eland, 1993.

28 Cited in Y. Sadowski, *The Myth of Global Chaos*, New York, Brookings, 1999, p. 70.

29 Tofflers, op. cit., p. 54.

30 Cited in F. Furedi, *Mythical Past, Elusive Future: History and Society in our Anxious Age*, London, Pluto Press, 1992, p. 15.

31 Ignatieff, *The Warrior's Honour*, p. 117.

32 M. Keen, 'Chivalry, nobility and the man-at-arms', in C.T. Allmand (ed.), *War, Literature and Politics in the Late Middle Ages*, Liverpool, Liverpool University Press, 1976, p. 45.

33 D. Keen, 'The economic function of civil wars', *Adelphi Paper*, No. 320, London, International Institute for Strategic Studies, 1998, p. 18. D. Keen, 'War as a source of losses and gains', paper given at a Conference on the Third World after the Cold War, Queen Elizabeth House, Oxford, 5–8 July 1995, p. 6. As Keen adds, whatever side the respective parties are on, for the majority of those taking part including both government and rebel leaders the purpose of war seems to be 'not to win it, so much as to make money while it lasts and moreover, to ensure that it lasts long enough to make serious money' (D. Keen, 'When war itself is privatised', *The Times Literary Supplement*, 29 December 1995). Philippa Atkinson argues that in Liberia the belligerents have established trade links with parts of the population who are trying to protect their own livelihoods. 'It is this basic need to survive that makes it rational to become involved in trade with fighters.' Large parts of Liberian society had to some extent become dependent upon the war economy for survival. The dynamics of this particular dependency further feed into institutionalised corruption and organised anarchy as civil society is compelled to exploit every resource available to it. Atkinson concludes, 'political and economic ambitions at macro and micro levels are both better by the continuation of the war than by its end' (see 'The war economy of Liberia – a political analysis', unpublished paper for the International Institute for Strategic Studies, 1996, p. 18).

34 Jablonsky, op. cit., p. 215.

35 Ibid., pp. 210–11.

36 E. Boehmer, *Colonial and Post-Colonial Literature*, Oxford, Oxford University Press, 1995, pp. 42–3.

37 K. Tidrick, *Empire and the English National Character*, London, I. B. Tauris, 1990, pp. 11–12.

38 J. Patocka, *Heretical Essays in the Philosophy of History*, trans. Erazim Kohak, Chicago Ill., Open Court, 1996, p. 77. Heraclitus' quotation runs: 'One must understand that war (polemos) is shared and conflict (eris) is justice and that all things come to pass in accordance with conflict.' In her book *On Revolution* Hannah Arendt makes a similar observation. Both the classical and biblical accounts of the beginning of history (Cain's conflict with Abel, Romulus' with Remus) suggests there is no beginning without violence. As metaphors both are powerful because they tell us that 'whatever brotherhood human beings may be capable of has grown out of fratricide' (*On Revolution*, London, Penguin, 1990, p. 20).

39 See V. Havel and V. Kraus, 'Rival visions', *Journal of Democracy*, Vol. 7; No. 1, January 1996.

40 M. Ignatieff, 'To fight but not to die', *The World Today*, February 2000, p. 21.

41 Cited in L. Gardner, *A Covenant With Power: America and the World Order from Wilson to Reagan*, New York, Oxford University Press, 1986, p.11.

42 Cited in J.L. Borges, *The Total Library: Non Fiction 1922–1986*, London, Allen Lane, 2000, p. 208.

43 Z. Laidi, *A World Without Meaning: Crisis of Meaning in International Politics*, London: Routledge, 1998 p. 109. Laidi defines his terms in the following manner. Foundation is meant as the basic principle on which a collective project depends; unity means that 'world images' are collected into a coherent plan of the whole; an end or final

goal is meant to denote a projection towards an elsewhere that is deemed to be better.

44 D. Smith, *Zygmunt Bauman, Prophet of Postmodernity*, Cambridge, Polity Press, 1999, p. 212. For an attack on the 'purposelessness' of humanitarian aid see E. Luttwak, 'Give war a chance', *Harpers*, December 1999, pp. 21–4. Pity, of course, can be seen as a condition of world community. In pitying other people, writes Martha Nussbaum, for misfortunes that befall them through no fault of their own, we acknowledge the fact of our own vulnerability – the fact that we could just as easily be in their position. Pity, in other words, 'contains a thought experiment in which one puts oneself in the other person's place and indeed reasons that this place might in fact become one's own' (M. Nussbaum, 'Pity and mercy: Nietzsche's stoicism', in (ed.) R. Schacht *Nietzsche: Genealogy, Morality*, Berkeley, University of California Press, 1994, pp. 139–67. But I find Nietzsche's arguments against pity particularly valid in an era where the viewers who pity the deprived and dispossesed of the developing world tend to treat the world itself not as a global village, but as a theme park: famine, ethnic cleaning, genocide, all are visited by the television companies before they move on to the next encounter with misery.

45 Ignatieff, *The Warrior's Honour*, p. 98.

46 F. Nietzsche, *On The Genealogy of Morals*, trans. W. Kaufmann and R.J. Hollingdale, New York, Vintage Books, 1967, p. 44.

47 A. Wolfson, 'Humanitarian hawks? Why Kosovo but not Kuwait', *Policy Review*, December 1999, p. 41.

48 N. Chomsky, *The New Militant Humanism: Lessons from Kosovo*, Vancouver, New Star Books, 1999, p.5.

49 Laidi, op. cit., p. 14.

7 Humane war and the moral imagination

1 L. Yutang, *The Importance of Living*, London, Heinemann, 1949, pp. 6–9.

2 Ibid., p. 9.

3 Cited in M. Ignatieff, *Virtual War*, London, Chatto & Windus, 2000, p. 214.

4 R. Rorty, *Philosophy and Social Hope*, London, Penguin, 1999, p. 273.

5 M. van Creveld, *The Transformation of War*, New York, Free Press, 1991, pp. 159, 160.

6 G.W.F. Hegel, *The Philosophy of History*, Buffalo, NY, Prometheus Books, 1991. Although Hegel saw war as a way in which the world spirit manifested itself, Marx referred to war as the locomotive of history.

7 For the distinction between 'historic' and 'historical' see J.-L. Nancy, *The Birth to Presence*, Stanford, Calif., Stanford, University Press, 1993, p. 146.

8 Cited in R. Rosenbaum, *Explaining Hitler: The Search for the Origins of his Evil*, London, Macmillan, 1998, p. 317.

9 Cited in K. Cornish, *The Jew of Linz: Wittgenstein, Hitler and Their Secret Battle for the Mind*, London, Arrow 1999, pp.108–9.

10 Cited in P. Lawrence, *Modernity and War: The Creed of Absolute Violence*, London, Macmillan, 1999, pp. 11–12.

11 K. Whiteside, *Merleau-Ponty and the Foundation of an Existential Politics*, Princeton, NJ, Princeton University Press, 1998, p. 40.

12 Cited in P. Fussell, *The Bloody Game: Anthology of War*, New York, Scribners, 1991, p. 209.

13 J. Keegan, *The Face of Battle: A Study of Agincourt, Waterloo and the Somme*, London, Penguin, 1978, p. 57.

14 E. Creasey, *The Fifteen Decisive Battles of the World*, London, Dent, 1962, p. 27.

15 Writing in 1945 at the end of the Second World War Borges saw England's role in exactly the same light. Its historical destiny was to champion freedom, to fight again and again 'the cyclical battle of Waterloo' (J.L. Borges, *The Total Library: Non Fiction 1922–1986*, London, Allen Lane, 2000, p. 213).

16 F. Fanon, *Wretched of the Earth*, London, Penguin, 1977, p. 74.
17 J. Shklar, *Ordinary Vices*, Cambridge, Mass., Bellknap Press, 1984, p. 21.
18 T. Pynchon, *The Crying of Lot 49*, London, Vintage, 1996, p. 38.
19 Z. Laidi, *A World without Meaning*, p. 176.
20 See my *War and the Illiberal Conscience*, Boulder, Colo., Westview Press, 1998.
21 C. Lasch, *The Culture of Narcissism: American Life in an Age of Diminishing Expectations*, London, Abacus, 1980, p. 5.
22 A. Delbanco, *The Real American Dream: A Meditation on Hope*, Cambridge, Mass., Harvard University Press, 1999, p. 5.
23 Cited in S. Zizek, *The Fragile Absolute: Or Why is the Christian Legacy Worth Fighting For?*, London, Verso, 1999, p. 56.
24 See V. Havel, 'The hope for Europe', address in Aachen, 15 May 1996, repr. in *New York Review of Books*, 20 June 1996, p. 38.
25 R. Rorty, *Reason, Relativism and Truth*, Cambridge, Cambridge University Press, 1998, pp. 13, 271.
26 R. Rorty, *Contingency, Irony and Solidarity*, Cambridge, Cambridge University Press, 1999, p. xv.
27 A. Wolfson, 'Humanitarian hawks', p. 42.
28 R. Rorty, 'Human rights, rationality and sentimentality', in S. Shute and S. Hurley (eds), *On Human Rights*, New Haven, Conn., Yale University Press, 2000, p. 23.
29 Rorty, *Contingency*, p. 46.
30 Ibid., p. 189.
31 J.B. Elshtein, 'Don't be cruel: reflections on Rortyean Liberalism', in D. Conway and J. Seery (eds), *The Politics of Irony: Essays on Self Betrayal*, New York, St Martin's Press, 1992, p. 212.
32 Ibid., p. 211.
33 L. Mumford, *Faith for Living*, London, Secker & Warburg, 1941, p. 64.
34 N. Geras, *Solidarity in the Conversation of Humankind: The Ungroundable Liberalism of Richard Rorty*, London, Verso, 1995, p. 54.
35 C. Hill, *Puritanism and Revolution: Studies in Interpretation of the English Revolution of the Seventeenth Century*, London, Panther, 1969, p. 150.
36 Cited in C. Dunlop, 'The end of innocence: rethinking non combatancy in the post Kosovo era', *Strategic Review*, summer 2000, p. 10.
37 This was the view of the celebrated Marxist writer Georg Lukacs in his last book *The Destruction of Reason*. See C. Magris, *Danube: A Sentimental Journey from the Source to the Black Sea*, London, Harvill Collins, 1990, p. 188.
38 Z. Herbert, 'From mythology', in D. Weissbort (ed.), *The Poetry of Survival: Post War Poets of Central and Eastern Europe*, London, Anvill Press, 1991, p. 154.

8 Conclusion

1 Cited in W. Murray, 'Air war in the Gulf: the limits of our power', *Strategic Review*, Winter 1998, p. 34.
2 Cited in R. Hobbs, *The Myth of Victory: What is Victory in War?*, New York, Westview Press, 1979, pp. 3–4.
3 A. Heller, *A Theory of Modernity*, Oxford, Blackwell, 1999, p. 233.
4 Tofflers, *War and Anti-War*, p. 134.
5 T. Adorno, *Minima Moralia*, London, Verso, 1993, p. 55.
6 Ignatieff, *Virtual War*, p. 163.

Index